TEMPERATE FORESTS

Michael Allaby

Illustrations by
Richard Garratt

CHELSEA HOUSE
PUBLISHERS
An imprint of Infobase Publishing

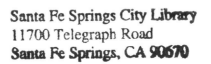

Temperate Forests

Chelsea House
An imprint of Infobase Publishing
132 West 31st Street
New York NY 10001

ISBN-13: 978-0-8160-5321-6
ISBN-10: 0-8160-5321-9

Library of Congress Cataloging-in-Publication Data
Allaby, Michael
    Temperate forests / Michael Allaby; illustrations by Richard Garratt.
        p. cm.—(Biomes of the Earth)
    Includes bibliographical references and index.
    ISBN 0-8160-5321-9
    1. Forest ecology—Juvenile literature. 2. Forests and forestry—Juvenile literature. I. Garratt, Richard, ill. II. Title. III. Series.
    QH541.5.F6A46 2006
    577.3—dc22   2005007659

Chelsea House books are available at special discounts when purchased in bulk quantities for businesses, associations, institutions, or sales promotions. Please call our Special Sales Department in New York at (212) 967-8800 or (800) 322-8755.

You can find Chelsea House on the World Wide Web at http://www.chelseahouse.com

Text design by David Strelecky
Cover design by Cathy Rincon
Illustrations by Richard Garratt
Photo research by Elizabeth H. Oakes
Composition by Erika K. Arroyo
Cover printed by Quad/Graphics, Dubuque, Ia.
Book printed and bound by Quad/Graphics, Dubuque, Ia.

Printed in the United States of America

This book is printed on acid-free paper.

From Richard Garratt:
To Chantal, who has lightened my darkness

CONTENTS

CHAPTER 4
HOW TREES WORK

CHAPTER 5
ECOLOGY OF TEMPERATE FORESTS

PREFACE

Earth is a remarkable planet. There is nowhere else in our solar system where life can survive in such a great diversity of forms. As far as we can currently tell, our planet is unique. Isolated in the barren emptiness of space, here on Earth we are surrounded by a remarkable range of living things, from the bacteria that inhabit the soil to the great whales that migrate through the oceans, from the giant redwood trees of the Pacific forests to the mosses that grow on urban sidewalks. In a desolate universe, Earth teems with life in a bewildering variety of forms.

One of the most exciting things about the Earth is the rich pattern of plant and animal communities that exists over its surface. The hot, wet conditions of the equatorial regions support dense rain forests with tall canopies occupied by a wealth of animals, some of which may never touch the ground. The cold, bleak conditions of the polar regions, on the other hand, sustain a much lower variety of species of plants and animals, but those that do survive under such harsh conditions have remarkable adaptations to their testing environment. Between these two extremes lie many other types of complex communities, each well suited to the particular conditions of climate prevailing in its region. Scientists call these communities *biomes*.

The different biomes of the world have much in common with one another. Each has a plant component, which is responsible for trapping the energy of the Sun and making it available to the other members of the community. Each has grazing animals, both large and small, that take advantage of the store of energy found within the bodies of plants. Then come the predators, ranging from tiny spiders that feed upon even smaller insects to tigers, eagles, and polar bears that survive by preying upon large animals. All of these living things form a complicated network of feeding interactions, and, at the base of the system, microbes in the soil are ready to consume the energy-rich plant litter or dead animal flesh that remains. The biome, then, is an integrated unit within which each species plays its particular role.

This set of books aims to outline the main features of each of the Earth's major biomes. The biomes covered include the tundra habitats of polar regions and high mountains, the taiga (boreal forest) and temperate forests of somewhat warmer lands, the grasslands of the prairies and the tropical savanna, the deserts of the world's most arid locations, and the tropical forests of the equatorial regions. The wetlands of the world, together with river and lake habitats, do not lie neatly in climatic zones over the surface of the Earth but are scattered over the land. And the oceans are an exception to every rule. Massive in their extent, they form an interconnecting body of water extending down into unexplored depths, gently moved by global currents.

Humans have had an immense impact on the environment of the Earth over the past 10,000 years since the last Ice Age. There is no biome that remains unaffected by the presence of the human species. Indeed, we have created our own biome in the form of agricultural and urban lands, where people dwell in greatest densities. The farms and cities of the Earth have their own distinctive climates and natural history, so they can be regarded as a kind of artificial biome that people have created, and they are considered as a separate biome in this set.

Each biome is the subject of a separate volume. Each richly illustrated book describes the global distribution, the climate, the rocks and soils, the plants and animals, the history, and the environmental problems found within each biome. Together, the set provides students with a sound basis for understanding the wealth of the Earth's biodiversity, the factors that influence it, and the future dangers that face the planet and our species.

Is there any practical value in studying the biomes of the Earth? Perhaps the most compelling reason to understand the way in which biomes function is to enable us to conserve their rich biological resources. The world's productivity is the basis of the human food supply. The world's biodiversity holds a wealth of unknown treasures, sources of drugs and medicines that will help to improve the quality of life. Above all, the world's biomes are a constant source of wonder, excitement, recreation, and inspiration that feed not only our bodies but also our minds and spirits. These books aim to provide the information about biomes that readers need in order to understand their function, draw upon their resources, and, most of all, enjoy their diversity.

ACKNOWLEDGMENTS

Richard Garratt drew all of the diagrams and maps that appear in this book. Richard and I have been working together for many years in a collaboration that succeeds because Richard has a genius for translating the weird electronic squiggles I send him into clear, simple artwork of the highest quality. As always, I am grateful to him for all his hard work. I also wish to thank Elizabeth Oakes for her fine work as a photo researcher.

I must thank Frank K. Darmstadt, Executive Editor, at Chelsea House. Frank shaped this series of books and guided them through all the stages of their development. His encouragement, patience, and good humor have been immensely valuable.

I am especially grateful to Dorothy Cummings, project editor. Her close attention to detail sharpened explanations that had been vague, corrected my mistakes and inconsistencies, and identified places where I repeated myself. And occasionally Dorothy was able to perform the most important service of all: She intervened in time to stop me making a fool of myself. No author could ask for more. This is a much better book than it would have been without her hard work and dedication.

Michael Allaby
Tighnabruaich
Argyll
Scotland
www.michaelallaby.com

INTRODUCTION

What is a temperate forest?

Long, long ago a sheet of ice thousands of feet thick covered North America from southern Alaska to a line running roughly from Seattle, Washington, to Boston, Massachusetts. Ice also covered most of northern Europe and the sea was frozen, so a person could have walked from America to Greenland and from there to Europe. To the south of the ice sheets, the land was covered in tough grasses, sedges, and small shrubs—tundra vegetation like that of northern Canada today. The weather was cold, dry, and windy, and the landscape was bleak.

Then, starting about 14,000 years ago in some places and 12,000 years ago in others, the air grew warmer and the ice began to melt. As it melted, the edges of the ice sheets retreated northward, leaving bare ground where no plant had grown for tens of thousands of years. Snow still blanketed the surface each winter, but in summer the dark-colored rocks absorbed the warmth of the sunshine and the warmth gradually penetrated deeper, to where the soil was still frozen. The frozen soil—called "permafrost"—slowly thawed.

Water from the melting ice filled rivers. In summer, when the snows of winter melted, water soaked into the ground. Tiny plant seeds and the spores of ferns, mosses, and fungi arrived, carried on the wind from lands far to the south. They had always arrived in this way, but in the past they had perished when they fell onto the barren ice. Now there was just enough warmth and moisture for some of them to germinate, and enough nourishment for some of the young plants to survive and grow. Here and there, patches of green appeared between the boulders and the sheets of bare rock that had been scraped smooth by the ice. Each summer the green returned, and each year it covered a bigger area.

At first it was the tundra that spread northward, following the edges of the retreating ice. Then, as the ground continued to grow warmer and the tundra plants helped to build the soil, other plants began to arrive. There were shrubs and then trees that stood tall and shaded the ground. Little by little, many of the tundra plants disappeared, unable to tolerate the shade or to compete successfully with the newcomers for moisture and nutrients. The landscape changed, as tundra gave way to forest. It was a gradual process that took several thousand years, but eventually it produced vast forests of birch, larch, spruce, fir, and pine trees.

A forest is an area of land where trees are the most conspicuous plants. The word also means a large number of trees that are growing so closely together that the leaves of one overlap those of its neighbors, and together the trees shade at least 60 percent of the surface. Coniferous trees, such as birch, larch, spruce, fir, and pine, have leaves that are reduced to needles or tiny scales. These contrast with the broad leaves of such trees as oak and maple.

The change was not permanent, however, for the climate continued to grow warmer and the ice maintained its retreat. Conditions suited other trees, such as oak, ash, and elm, and these began to predominate in the forest. The original forest still survives in the north. Today it extends as a belt across Alaska, Canada, Scandinavia, and Siberia. It is known as the boreal forest—"boreal" simply means northern—or by its Russian name, the *taiga*.

South of the taiga, the natural forest was quite different in character. Although the climate was now much warmer than it had been, the ground still froze in winter and when the ground is frozen, plant roots cannot find the moisture they need. The newly arrived trees coped with the dry soils of winter by shedding their leaves and effectively shutting down until spring. A tree or shrub that sheds all of its leaves at the same time is said to be deciduous.

Deciduous trees have delicate leaves that absorb sunlight efficiently all summer, but as the days begin to grow shorter, the trees withdraw some of their chemical contents and cease supplying others. The resulting chemical changes alter the color of the leaves. For a few weeks before the winds of the

late fall strip their branches and fill the air with flying, twisting, circling leaves, the trees are a riot of red, orange, yellow,
and brown.

A trail through a
temperate forest in late
summer, just as the
leaves are starting to
change color (Courtesy
of Fogstock)

Early spring is another colorful time. As the soil temperature starts to rise, there is a brief interlude before the leaf buds
open when the Sun shines directly onto the ground. During
this short interval, smaller plants of the forest floor seize
their opportunity to grow, flower, and produce seed. Then
the trees burst into bright green leaf and in a week or two the
forest floor is shaded from the sunlight.

The spring flowers, bright green young leaves, and spectacular fall colors are typical of the broad-leaved deciduous
forests of North America, Europe, and eastern Asia. Such
forests grow in regions where the weather is neither so hot as
it is closer to the equator nor so cold as it is closer to the

North or South Pole. The climate is temperate and these are temperate forests.

Farther from the equator, plants do not need to survive the winter cold, for the ground seldom freezes for more than a few days at a time, but the rainfall is intense in one part of the year and sparse during a dry season. The trees of these forests do not shed all of their leaves at the same time of year, but instead produce leaves that last longer. They are tough and leathery, with a waxy outer coat that makes them shine. Trees of this type—holly and live oak are typical examples— are broad-leaved, but evergreen. Evergreen trees do shed their leaves, but only when they are worn out, so the tree is never bare.

The ice sheets have now retreated from North America, Europe, and Asia, and temperate forest—mainly deciduous but evergreen in some places—is the natural vegetation over a large area. Any type of vegetation occupying a substantial part of the Earth's surface comprises a *biome*.

Although the temperate forest constitutes a biome, this does not mean it is everywhere the same. The tree types vary greatly. In some places all the trees are broad-leaved and deciduous. In others the deciduous trees are mixed with broad-leaved evergreen trees—where oak and holly grow side by side, for example. There are many forests in which broad-leaved deciduous trees grow alongside coniferous trees such as evergreen pines and deciduous larches, and some temperate rain forests are dominated by coniferous species.

A climate that suits a temperate forest is also suitable for farming. Much of the forest that once covered the eastern United States and western Europe was cleared long ago to provide farmland. It is only here and there that patches of the original forest can still be found. The forest will not disappear, however. Modern farms produce much more food than the farms of earlier times, so people may feed themselves from a smaller area of land. We can allow some of the less fertile farmland to return to forest. It will not be identical to the original primeval forest, but if it is planted with the original species, in time it will become very similar.

CHAPTER 1

GEOGRAPHY OF TEMPERATE FORESTS

Types of temperate forest

Broad-leaved deciduous trees dominate the most extensive type of temperate forest. Often called "summer deciduous forest," this is the forest that produces the dazzling colors of spring and fall. At one time it covered about 3 million square miles (7.8 million km^2) of eastern North America and Europe. It was the forest our ancestors encountered when first they migrated into these regions—and the forest they cleared away, either to hunt game more easily or to make way for their livestock and farm crops.

A different type of temperate forest grows along the western coasts of Chile and of South Island, New Zealand. These are regions with a maritime climate (see "Continental and maritime climates" on page 52). Winters are wet and mild, with temperatures seldom remaining below freezing for very long. Summers are warm and usually drier than the winters, and fog is very common. Temperatures seldom rise above 80°F (27°C). Although northern Chile is one of the driest places in the world, the region south of 37°S is one of the wettest, with an average annual rainfall ranging from about 102 inches (2,591 mm) on the coast to more than 200 inches (5,080 mm) in the mountains. South Island, New Zealand, has a generally moist climate, but the western coastal belt receives as much rain as southern Chile.

The forests here are rain forests that grow in a temperate climate: *temperate rain forests*. The most conspicuous trees in the Chilean forest are southern beeches (*Nothofagus* species), Patagonian cypress (*Fitzroya cupressoides*), and Chile pine or monkey puzzle (*Araucaria araucana*). Southern beeches are also common in the New Zealand forest (see "Related temperate-forest trees that occur in widely separated places" on page 23). In the north the beeches are mixed with kauri

1

pines (*Agathis australis*). There are also small areas of temperate rain forest in southern China and Japan, mostly dominated by evergreen oaks (*Quercus* species) and magnolias (*Magnolia* species), and in western Scotland, where the native trees are birch (*Betula* species), oak, hazel (*Corylus avellana*), and holly (*Ilex aquifolium*).

The most magnificent trees of any temperate rain forest are found in North America, however. An intermittent coastal belt that is nowhere more than about 125 miles (200 km) wide, extending from California to southern Alaska, is home to Douglas fir, western hemlock, western red cedar, Sitka spruce, giant sequoias, and coastal redwoods. These are some of the biggest trees in the world.

The North American forest differs from the temperate rain forests found in other parts of the world in being dominated by coniferous trees, rather than broad-leaved species. There are probably several reasons for this. In the first place, the summers are fairly dry. On average, less than three inches (76 mm) of rain falls in Vancouver, British Columbia, between the end of June and beginning of September. Seattle, Washington, is even drier, with only six inches (152 mm) of rain from the beginning of May until the end of September. The lack of rain in the middle of summer allows the ground to dry and this may impose an intolerable stress on broad-leaved trees. Evergreen coniferous trees, with needles rather than leaves, are better able to thrive in such conditions. The dry period has a second consequence: fire. The redwoods and other trees of these forests can survive fires.

Western hemlock (*Tsuga heterophylla*), western red cedar (*Thuja plicata*), and Sitka spruce (*Picea sitchensis*) grow to a height of 100–200 feet (30–60 m). Douglas fir (*Pseudotsuga menziesii,* also called Oregon fir and Oregon pine) and the giant redwood (*Sequoiadendron giganteum,* also called the Sierra redwood, big tree, and wellingtonia) can reach a height of 320 feet (98 m). These are tall trees, but the coast redwood (*Sequoia sempervirens*) can be as much as 390 feet (119 m) tall—the height of a 28-story apartment building. In many places the forest *canopy*—the topmost level of the tree crowns—is 200–230 feet (60–70 m) above ground level.

The General Sherman tree, a giant redwood growing in the Sequoia National Park, is believed to be the most massive tree in the world. It is 274.9 feet (83.8 m) tall and 27 feet (8 m) in diameter measured eight feet (2 m) above ground level. Its circumference at ground level is 102.6 feet (31.1 m) and its crown is an average 106.5 feet (32.5 m) across. Its trunk weighs an estimated 1,385 tons (1,258 tonnes). The General Sherman is thought to be 2,000–2,200 years old and it is still growing vigorously.

It is not true, however, that the General Sherman is the largest living organism in the world. The biggest single organism ever discovered is a honey fungus (*Armillaria ostoyae*) living in the soil and among the tree roots in the Malheur National Forest, in the Blue Mountains of eastern Oregon. It covers 2,200 acres (890 hectares) and is estimated to be at least 2,400 years old.

Why it rains more on mountainsides

When air rises, its temperature falls. Warm air can hold more water vapor than cold air can, so reducing the temperature of the air raises its relative humidity (RH), which is the amount of water vapor present in the air measured as a percentage of the amount needed to saturate the air at that temperature.

The *lifting condensation level* is an altitude at which the RH in rising air reaches 100 percent and the air becomes saturated. When air rises above the lifting condensation level, its water vapor starts condensing to form clouds. When the clouds are big enough, their droplets or ice crystals merge until they are heavy enough to fall as rain or snow.

Air is forced to rise as it approaches a mountain. The air is dry until it is lifted above the lifting condensation level; that is, all of the moisture it carries is present as water vapor (a gas) rather than liquid droplets, so the RH is less than 100 percent. Cloud starts to form at the lifting condensation level, and precipitation begins to fall on the mountainside. The air continues to rise, and more cloud forms at higher elevations. This intensifies the precipitation on the mountainside.

When the rising air reaches the top of the mountain it may continue to rise or it may subside down the opposite (lee) side of the mountain. If it continues rising, eventually it will lose enough water for precipitation to end, although cloud may extend some distance downwind. If the air subsides, it will sink below the lifting condensation level once more. Precipitation will then cease and the cloud will dissipate as its droplets evaporate.

The overall result is that mountainsides receive more precipitation than the low ground surrounding the mountain.

Temperate forests change in composition and appearance with increasing elevation. Temperature decreases with height, and mountains have a wetter climate than the surrounding low-lands (see the sidebar "Why it rains more on mountainsides" on page 3). On some mountainsides, although not everywhere, the lowland forest gives way to a forest of smaller, often stunted trees that are more widely spaced. The moist conditions favor mosses, ferns, and lichens and the trees are usually festooned with lichens, giving the forest an enchanted, magical appearance. It is called *krummholz*—a German word meaning "crooked wood."

Higher still, the trees become more widely scattered up to an elevation beyond which no tree can tolerate the climate. The *timberline* is the upper boundary of the forest. The height is determined by the temperature, so it varies with latitude—the lower the latitude, the higher the timberline. The timberline in the Sierra Nevada is at about 11,500 feet (3,500 m), in the Canadian Rockies it is at about 6,500 feet (1,980 m), and in the central Alps of Europe it is at about 6,800 feet (2,000 m). In contrast, the timberline in the mountains of New Guinea, which are much closer to the equator, is at about 12,600 feet (3,800 m).

Where do temperate forests grow?

The tropic of Cancer is a line of latitude located at 23.5°N. The tropic of Capricorn is at 23.5°S. The part of the world lying between these two lines is known nowadays simply as the Tropics. Two other lines of latitude, at 66.5°N and 66.5°S, mark the Arctic and Antarctic Circles. The regions between these latitudes and the North and South Poles are called the Arctic and the Antarctic.

These were not always their names, however. The Greek philosopher Aristotle (384–322 B.C.E) was the first person to divide the world into climatic regions. He called the Tropics the torrid zone and the regions to the north and south of the Arctic and Antarctic Circles the frigid zones. Aristotle called the part of the world lying between these two zones in each hemisphere the temperate zone. We no longer use the terms *torrid zone* and *frigid zone,* but we have kept the name *temperate zone.*

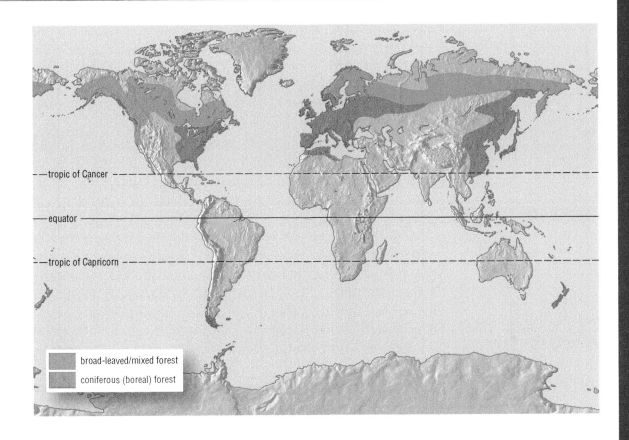

tropic of Cancer

equator

tropic of Capricorn

broad-leaved/mixed forest

coniferous (boreal) forest

Obviously, temperate forests are found within the temperate zone—they are forests that grow in a temperate climate. This is broadly true, but as the map shows, temperate forests occur only in certain parts of this zone.

There are few areas of temperate forest in the Southern Hemisphere, and they are quite small. Temperate forest occurs predominantly in the Northern Hemisphere. This is because there is much less land in the Southern Hemisphere than there is in the Northern Hemisphere, and much less of that land lies within the temperate zone. Cape Horn, the southernmost tip of South America, at 55.78°S, is as far from the equator as Copenhagen, Denmark, and Edinburgh, Scotland (at 55.68°N and 55.92°N, respectively). Large areas of land lie to the north of these cities. At 45.87°S, the city of Dunedin, in the south of South Island, New Zealand, is the same distance from the equator as Portland, Oregon, and Venice, Italy. Temperate forest occurs only in the southern-

Extent of the temperate forest biome. Temperate forest is the natural vegetation in the areas colored pale green, although large parts of these areas have been converted to farmland.

most part of South America and in New Zealand. In the Northern Hemisphere, in contrast, it covers most of the eastern half of the United States, Europe as far eastward as the Black Sea, eastern Russia and China, and Japan. To the north of the temperate forest there lies a wide belt of coniferous forest. This is the *boreal forest,* or *taiga.*

Although temperate forest covers a substantial area, it does not extend throughout the temperate zone, because temperate forest requires a mild, moist climate. Despite its name, the climate in many parts of the temperate zone is too extreme.

Most trees find it difficult to survive where hot, dry weather persists for more than about eight months of the year and the annual rainfall is less than about 16 inches (400 mm). Temperate forest grows in those areas where the climate is influenced by the ocean. Air moving inland from the ocean is moister than air over the interior of a continent, and it is cooler in summer and warmer in winter (see "Continental and maritime climates" on page 52). The central plains of the United States, the interior of Asia, and Australia are too dry.

Broad-leaved deciduous trees will not grow where there is an average of fewer than 120 days each year when the temperature is above 50°F (10°C). Coniferous trees can tolerate much colder conditions, so this temperature requirement defines the boundary between the temperate broad-leaved forest and the boreal forest. There are no large areas of comparable coniferous forest in the Southern Hemisphere, because none of the continents projects far enough to the south.

Many forests have sharply defined edges, but these are unnatural. Land that was once forested has been cleared of its trees and put to other uses—usually agriculture—producing a clear boundary between the forest and the deforested area. Natural forests merge gradually with the adjacent land. Moving away from the forest, the trees become increasingly scattered until the landscape is treeless. Where summers are long, hot, and dry, the forest gives way to scrub and finally to desert. Where summers are wet but the winters are dry, the forest gives way to grassland.

How temperate forests developed and how long they have existed

There are many species of broad-leaved deciduous trees to be found in temperate forests. They vary in size and shape and in their leaves, but all of them share certain features. The most important of these is that they produce flowers (see chapter 4). In common with many of the herbs that grow on the forest floor, the grasses and wildflowers that grow in the fields and by roadsides, and all of the crop plants that farmers grow, these forest trees are flowering plants. Botanists classify all of them in the subphylum called Angiospermae, thus separating them from nonflowering plants, such as the coniferous trees, ferns, and mosses.

Flowers first appeared about 130 million years ago, during the Cretaceous period, when dinosaurs walked the Earth.

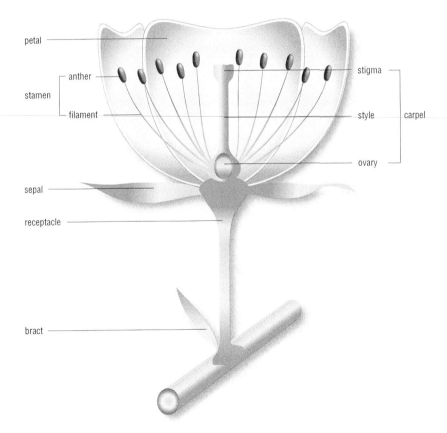

Structure of a flower. The anther and filament, together comprising the stamen, are the male parts of the flower; the female parts are the stigma, style, and ovary, together comprising the carpel.

Climates everywhere were warmer and wetter then than they are today, and the first flowering plants lived under conditions similar to those of the present-day Tropics. The very earliest of them were water lilies. These were soon joined by buttercups and the first flowering tree: a magnolia. The magnolia family (Magnoliaceae) also includes a number of other species, including the tulip tree or tulip poplar (*Liriodendron tulipifera*). Members of the Magnoliaceae occur naturally in North and South America and in Asia (see "Related temperate-forest trees that occur in widely separated places" on page 23).

Water lilies, buttercups, magnolias, the tulip tree, and all the other members of this group of plants produce very distinctive flowers (see the diagram). These are large, have many petals and sepals—called *tepals* because they are similar in shape and size—and also many carpels and stamens with the stamens arranged in a spiral. The flowers are symmetrical and bisexual—they contain both male and female organs (that is, the stamens and carpels). Scientists consider these features to be primitive, in the sense that in more advanced flowers, which evolved later, the features are modified and some of the flower parts are often missing.

Flowers are big and showy in order to attract pollinating insects. Nonflowering plants must rely on the wind or water to bring male sperm and female eggs together. Insect pollination is much more reliable and, not surprisingly, flowering plants spread rapidly and evolved into the many species that exist today. Until then forests had consisted of giant tree ferns, conifers, and other nonflowering plants. By the end of the Cretaceous period, 65 million years ago, flowering trees dominated most forests and flowering herbs grew on the forest floor beneath them.

Many of the most ancient species of flowering trees still exist, little changed. Both magnolias and tulip trees grow naturally in the forests of the southeastern United States, but although these plants are natives of America and Asia, they are just as familiar to Europeans and Australians. They have been planted all over the world. Their spectacular flowers make them popular ornamental plants, grown in gardens and parks, and tulip trees are also cultivated for their timber, known as yellow poplar or canary whitewood.

Forests change over long periods. New tree species arrive, old ones die out, and although the forest continues, its composition does not remain the same. If the climate becomes warmer or cooler, wetter or drier, some trees suffer and others thrive. Forests respond to changes in their environment.

Over the last few centuries, people have exerted an entirely new force for change: They have introduced new tree species. Magnolias and tulip trees are now grown all over the world, but they remain confined to gardens and parks. Other introduced species have escaped and become naturalized in their new surroundings. Some of them have then invaded the natural forest and altered it.

North American old-growth forests have proved resistant to invasion by introduced trees, but managed forests are more vulnerable. Perhaps the most invasive of all tree species, however, is the European sycamore or great maple (*Acer pseudoplatanus*)—a type of maple and quite unrelated to American sycamores, which are plane trees (*Platanus* species). The European sycamore was introduced into England sometime prior to 1500, but it was not planted widely until the 18th century. It is a handsome tree, highly valued during the period when large landscaped parks, designed to display individual trees and other features, were fashionable among wealthy British landowners. The tree also produces valuable timber. It escaped from the parks and plantations and European sycamore now produces seed more regularly and prolifically than do most native trees, and its seeds sprout very readily. Sycamore colonizes disturbed ground and invades neglected woodland, where there are openings in which it can grow. Most British forests now contain some sycamore and in many it is the most abundant tree.

There are other ways in which people can affect the composition of a forest. For instance, deer will eat the leaves from young saplings, killing them. Changes in hunting or culling policy, or the elimination of animals that hunt deer, can lead to a rapid increase in the deer population, resulting in changes in any forest to which they can gain access. Separately, imported timber can bring disease that escapes into the forests with devastating effect. Chestnut blight and

Dutch elm disease are modern examples (see "Diseases and parasites of trees" on page 132).

Forest expansion since the last ice age

No plants of any kind, much less forests, grow in the interiors of Greenland and Antarctica for the obvious reason that in these places the ground lies beneath ice that in some places is more than two miles (3.2 km) thick. If the climate were to grow warmer and these ice sheets were to melt, after a time plants would begin to appear. The first arrivals would be tiny and inconspicuous, surviving in crevices and hollows where they were sheltered from the freezing and drying wind. Then grasses would appear, and as water from the melting ice soaked the ground, sedges would establish themselves in the wetter places. Eventually, low-growing shrubs would arrive, along with trees that spread horizontally and were no more than about two feet (60 cm) tall. These would be followed by taller trees and finally by forests.

Neither Greenland nor Antarctica is likely to lose its ice sheet any time soon, but there was a time when the ice extended much farther than it does now. As the map shows, during the coldest part of the most recent ice age, the Laurentide ice sheet covered all of Canada and a large part of the United States.

There have been many ice ages. Scientists call them *glacials* and they are separated by periods of warmer conditions called *interglacials*. We are living in an interglacial at present. All glacials and interglacials have names. These are usually derived from the places where evidence for them has been found. Consequently, they have different names in different places.

The differing names also reflect the fact that the glacials and interglacials began and ended at slightly different times in different parts of the world. Our present interglacial breaks the rule by not being named after a place. It is called the Holocene, a name that means "entirely new" (from the Greek *holos*, "whole" or "entire," and *kainos*, "new"). The Holocene also marks the commencement of the Holocene epoch, a period of geologic time that follows the Pleistocene epoch,

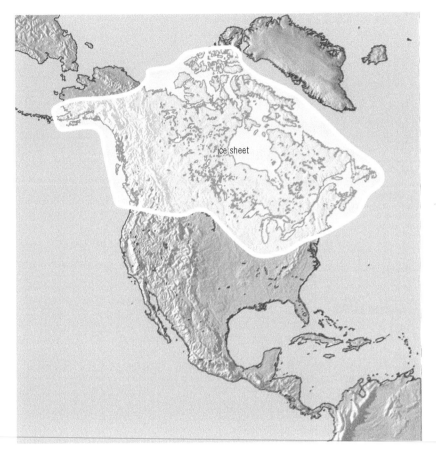

ice sheet

The Laurentide ice sheet. The map shows the area of North America covered by ice at the time of its greatest extent, about 20,000 years ago.

during which ice ages and interglacials followed one another for about 1.64 million years (see the appendix "Geologic time scale" on page 241). The sidebar "Holocene, Pleistocene, and late Pliocene glacials and interglacials, on page 13," gives the North American, British, and Northwest European names of the glacials and interglacials, together with their ages and durations.

During the Pleistocene ice ages, ice sheets spread to cover much of Europe and Asia as well as North America. Conditions were cold enough that they would have covered more of Asia, but the climate there was too dry for sufficient snow to accumulate. As the map shows, a tongue of ice extended deep into the interior of the continent from the Pacific coast.

At the start of an ice age, the trees die when the temperature falls below the minimum they can tolerate. Species by

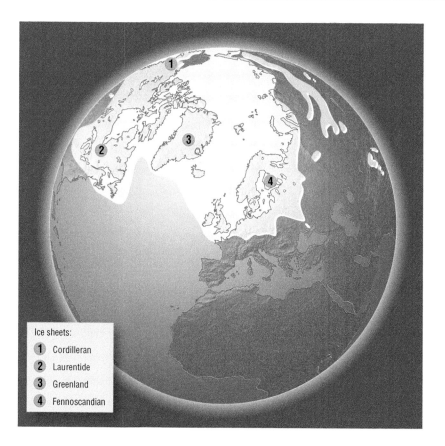

The world during an ice age. During the coldest part of the most recent ice age, ice sheets covered much of northwestern Europe and North America, and the sea was covered by ice.

Ice sheets:
1 Cordilleran
2 Laurentide
3 Greenland
4 Fennoscandian

species, the forests disappear. They survive away from the ice, where the climate is warmer. Thus as ice ages intensify and then give way to interglacials, the forests slowly move back and forth in response to the climatic changes. Remnants of the forest manage to survive in some places (see "Ancient forests that survive to this day" on page 14). During ice ages, these *refugia* contain the plants that supply seeds from which the forests regenerate when the ice age ends.

By about 14,000 years ago, the temperature was rising steadily in North America. The Laurentide ice sheet had started to retreat and by 12,000 years ago a belt of forest, comprising spruce (*Picea* species) and larch (*Larix* species), with some ash (*Fraxinus* species) and birch (*Betula* species), ran from the Atlantic coast along the southern margin of what are now the Great Lakes. Broad-leaved deciduous woodland was established in Florida. As the ice continued to retreat northward, the forest followed it. The coniferous forest advanced behind the retreating ice and the broad-leaved forest advanced behind the coniferous forest. The eastern part of the ice sheet was slow to move, however, with the result that the coniferous forest grew right up to the edge of the ice. Ice sheets do not melt at a steady rate. From time to time they halt and then advance before resuming their retreat. Two Creeks, Wisconsin, is one of a number of places where a temporary advance of the ice buried a forest about 11,800 years ago.

In eastern North America the spruce and larch forest gave way to forest dominated by spruce and pine (*Pinus* species),

Holocene, Pleistocene, and late Pliocene glacials and interglacials

Approximate date (1,000 years BP)	North America	Great Britain	Northwestern Europe
Holocene			
10–present	*Holocene*	*Holocene (Flandrian)*	*Holocene (Flandrian)*
Pleistocene			
75–10	Wisconsinian	Devensian	Weichselian
120–75	*Sangamonian*	*Ipswichian*	*Eeemian*
170–120	Illinoian	Wolstonian	Saalian
230–170	*Yarmouthian*	*Hoxnian*	*Holsteinian*
480–230	Kansan	Anglian	Elsterian
600–480	*Aftonian*	*Cromerian*	*Cromerian complex*
800–600	Nebraskan	Beestonian	*Bavel complex*
740–800		*Pastonian*	
900–800		Pre-Pastonian	Menapian
1,000–900		*Bramertonian*	*Waalian*
1,800–1,000		Baventian	Eburonian
Pliocene			
1,800		*Antian*	*Tiglian*
1,900		Thurnian	
2,000		*Ludhamian*	
2,300		Pre-Ludhamian	Pretiglian

BP means "before present" (present is taken to be 1950). Names in italic refer to interglacials. Other names refer to glacials (ice ages). Dates become increasingly uncertain for the older glacials and interglacials and the period before about 2 million years ago. Evidence for these episodes has not been found in North America; in the case of the Thurnian glacial and Ludhamian interglacial the only evidence is from a borehole at Ludham, in eastern England.

and from about 9,000 years ago by pine and birch forest with lesser amounts of alder (*Alnus* species) and spruce. In the Northwest, birch forest arrived about 11,000 years ago, mixed with poplar and aspen (both *Populus* species), willow (*Salix* species), juniper (*Juniperus* species), and spruce. This developed into alder-birch-spruce forest by about 5,500 years ago.

The Fennoscandian ice sheet began to retreat from Europe about 13,000 years ago, and sedges and grasses colonized the newly exposed ground. The first trees to arrive were juniper (*Juniperus communis*), arctic willow (*Salix herbacea*), and dwarf birch (*Betula nana*), low-growing plants that could survive the cold winds. Downy birch (*B. pubescens*), silver birch (*B. pendula*), and aspen (*Populus tremula*) were growing across northern Europe about 12,000 years ago. The landscape was fairly open in the north, like parkland, with patches of woodland separated by tundra. Farther south, the trees formed forests with downy birch the most abundant species.

About 11,000 years ago the advance was halted when the temperature fell once more and the ice age returned. A cold period that is shorter and milder than a full ice age is called a *stadial*. This one was the Younger Dryas (or Loch Lomond) stadial, named either for mountain avens (*Dryas octopetala*), an arctic and alpine plant typical of cold climates, or for the lake in western Scotland. Dryas pollen was discovered in soils, at levels that have been dated, in places that are now much too warm for the plant to occur naturally. When the stadial ended, about 10,000 years ago, the forest resumed its advance. Hazel (*Corylus avellana*) was widespread in northern Europe by 9,000 years ago and it was soon followed by birch and Scots pine (*Pinus sylvestris*).

The resulting birch-pine-hazel forest is still the natural vegetation over much of Europe immediately to the south of the taiga, although most of it has been cleared to provide land for farming or commercial forestry. Farther south the forests were mainly of elm (*Ulmus* species) and oak (*Quercus* species).

Ancient forests that survive to this day

Climate changes do not happen smoothly. They proceed faster in some places than in others and occasionally they reverse direction for a time. Ice that had been retreating advances or an advancing ice sheet retreats.

Plants take some time to colonize new areas. After the last ice age, birch and aspen advanced at about 0.5 mile (1 km) a year. Beech (*Fagus* species) and spruce followed them, but at less than 550 yards (500 m) a year. The time that it takes plants to respond to climate change can leave individual species and even some communities isolated when change happens too quickly for them. If the climate change is uneven over a large region, isolated species or communities may survive in places where the change has had least effect.

The four-toed salamander (*Hemidactylium scutatum*) may be one such species. This two- to four-inch (5–10-cm) amphibian occurs in eastern North America, mainly from Nova Scotia to New England and west to Minnesota, but also in several places in the southeastern United States. It lives in wet places in temperate forests. Scientists believe that as the ice sheets advanced during the last (Wisconsinian) ice age, four-toed salamanders along with other animals gradually moved south to where the climate was warmer. When the ice age ended, however, grasslands and other treeless areas developed between the forests in the south and those in the north. Larvae of fourtoed salamanders live in water, and these dry, treeless areas formed a barrier the salamanders were unable to cross. Consequently they remained isolated. The map on page 16 shows their approximate location.

Species that become isolated in this way are known as *relicts,* and the places where they survive are *refugia* (singular *refugium*). There are four areas in the United States, also shown on the map, where coniferous forests survived the ice age. They grew in two places that remained free of ice in Alaska, and above the ice in the Cascade, Rocky, and Appalachian Mountains. Visit these places today and you will see forests that have been there since before the last ice age began 75,000 years ago.

These are large, well-known refugia, but there are many smaller ones. As the forests advance they encounter places where trees cannot grow because it is too wet or the soil is unsuitable. The existing vegetation is not crowded out by the new arrivals and so it remains as small relict of earlier times.

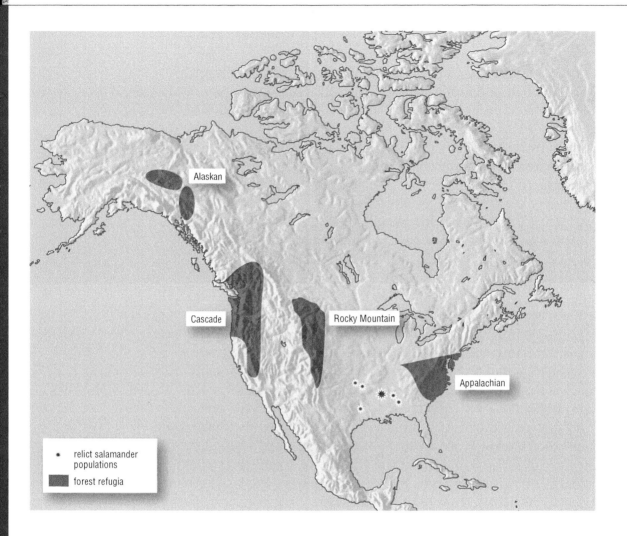

North American refugia

Rising temperatures may make plants in mountainous regions move to higher elevations. The new plant communities colonize the lower parts of the mountains, but the old communities survive in refugia above them.

Mountains themselves provide many different environments. There are sheltered hollows that are protected from the wind but also permanently shaded. While plants characteristic of warmer climates establish themselves on sunnier parts of the mountain, the change from glacial to interglacial conditions may allow ice-age plants that once covered a much larger area to survive in the sheltered hollows. These hollows are also refugia.

What trees can tell us about climates of the past

Ivy (*Hedera helix*) is an Old World plant that has been introduced into North America (poison ivy is a different species). Cultivated varieties are grown as ornamental plants, but wild ivy climbs across the faces of buildings, across the ground, and uses trees for support, eventually covering them completely. It is a woody climber that resembles the lianas of tropical forests.

This is no coincidence, for that is what ivy really is. It belongs to a plant family (Araliaceae) comprising several hundred species, most of which grow in the Tropics. They are especially common in Southeast Asia.

Ivy has broad, tough leaves with smooth surfaces, and it is evergreen. Broad-leaved evergreen plants are typical of the Tropics, and despite thriving so far from the equator, ivy has not lost all of its tropical characteristics. It cannot survive a long, hard winter, and it does not flower or produce seeds if the average temperature in the coldest month is lower than 35°F (1.6°C). It cannot tolerate drought and will survive, but not thrive, if the average temperature in summer is below about 55°F (13°C).

Its precise climatic requirements make ivy very useful to scientists called *paleoclimatologists,* who discover what climates were like in the distant past. Like all flowering plants, ivy produces pollen, which survives for a very long time in the soil (see "Using pollen and beetles to study the past" on page 157). When scientists find ivy pollen in a layer of soil of a known age, they can be certain that the climate at that time was mild and wet.

Holly (*Ilex aquifolium*) is another broad-leaved evergreen plant belonging to a mainly tropical family, the Aquifoliaceae. It also has precise requirements. Healthy holly trees mean that the climate is wet and the average temperature does not fall below about 31°F (–0.5°C) in winter and 55°F (13°C) in summer.

Holly and ivy are plants associated with Christmas because they are evergreen and symbolize eternal life—*holly* means "holy." Mistletoe (*Viscum album*) is another Christmas evergreen. Its presence indicates that the average summer temperature is higher than about 63°F (17°C), although it can tolerate winter temperatures as low as 19°F (–7°C).

English yew (*Taxus baccata*) is a handsome evergreen tree that lives for a very long time. It grows naturally in many parts of Europe, North Africa, and the Middle East, but not in the center of continents or in the far north. It requires a moist climate and it cannot tolerate hard winters.

These are just a few of many plants that have clear climatic preferences. Evidence that in the past they grew in a particular area provides scientists with an important clue to the climate at that time.

CHAPTER 2

GEOLOGY OF
TEMPERATE FORESTS

Plate tectonics

Antarctica is a barren, icy wilderness, yet there was a time when forests grew there. There were once tropical swamps in what is now Pennsylvania, and parts of England were once a hot desert, like the Sahara.

Plants are able to spread because their seeds are blown by the wind or carried by animals. They need not travel far. If seeds give rise to new plants just a short distance from their parent, the plant's descendants will travel far over hundreds of years. Seeds will sprout and grow only where conditions are suitable, however. Wind-borne tree seeds might land in Antarctica, but they would perish there, just as seeds from mangrove, a tropical tree, would perish in Pennsylvania. The fact that plants once grew in places where they could not survive today suggests that the climates of those places were once very different. The Pennsylvanian swamps, for example, existed during a time that geologists call the Carboniferous period (see the appendix "Geologic time scale" on page 241).

Climate change cannot explain how tropical swamps once existed in Alaska, however, or forests in Antarctica. Alaska is too close to the North Pole and Antarctica to the South Pole. Sunshine in these high latitudes is not warm enough for tropical plants, and the winters are too long and dark. No amount of climate change can compensate for their geographic position. Some other factor must be at work—and it is.

The continents are moving. At one time Alaska, Antarctica, and Pennsylvania lay in the Tropics. Tropical plants grew in lands that lay in the Tropics and that have since moved. About 400 million years ago, toward the end of the Devonian period, Antarctica lay in the temperate regions and temperate forests grew there. The illustration shows where the continents were 135 million years ago and 65 million years ago,

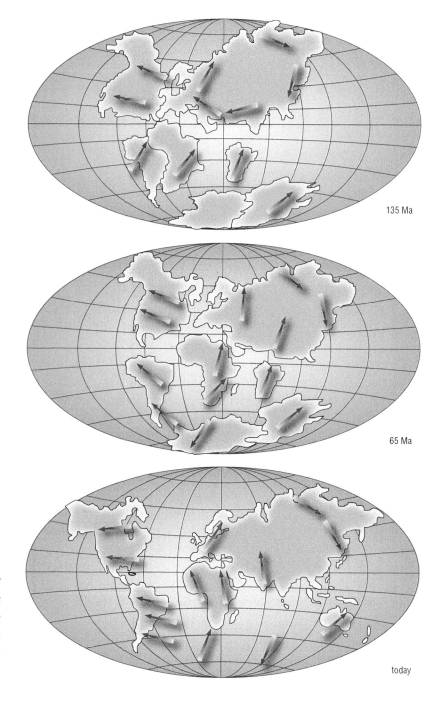

135 Ma

65 Ma

today

Continental drift. The maps show the arrangements of the continents 135 million years ago, 65 million years ago, and today.

compared with their positions today ("Ma" in the illustration means "millions of years ago"). The arrows indicate the direction they were and are moving.

Alfred Lothar Wegener and continental drift

Since the first realistic maps of the world were published in the 16th century, many geographers had puzzled over the fact that the continents on each side of the Atlantic Ocean looked as though they might fit together. Some thought it mere coincidence, but others suggested ways a single continent might have split into two parts that then moved apart.

The German meteorologist Alfred Lothar Wegener (1880–1930) went much further. Wegener compiled a mass of evidence to support what he called "continental displacement." This phenomenon came to be called *continental drift*. He studied the scientific literature for descriptions of rocks that were similar on each side of the Atlantic. He found plants with limited distribution that are separated by vast oceans and fossil organisms that are also distributed in this way.

Finally he proposed that about 280 million years ago, during the Upper Paleozoic subera, all the continents were joined, forming a single "supercontinent," which he called *Pangaea* (from the Greek *pan,* meaning all, and *ge,* meaning Earth), surrounded by an ocean called *Panthalassa* (*thalassa* means ocean). He theorized that Pangaea broke apart and the separate pieces drifted to their present locations; the continents are still drifting.

In 1912 Wegener published a short book outlining his theory, *Die Entstehung der Kontinente und Ozeane* (The Origin of the continents and oceans). He was drafted into the German army in 1914 at the start of World War I but was wounded almost at once. He developed his ideas further while recovering in a hospital, and in 1915 he published a much longer edition of his book (it was not translated into English until 1924).

His idea found little support. Geologists at the time believed the *mantle*—the material beneath the Earth's crust—to be solid, and they could not imagine any way that continents could move. They also found that some of Wegener's calculations of the rate of continental displacement were incorrect.

But support for Wegener's idea began to grow in the 1940s, when for the first time scientists were able to study the rocks on the ocean floor. These studies indicated that the oceans had grown wider by spreading outward from central ridges, where underwater volcanoes were erupting, laying down new rock. Wegener's theory was generally accepted by the late 1960s, but by then Alfred Wegener was dead. He had died in 1930 during his third expedition to study the climate over the Greenland ice sheet.

At present, the continued widening of the Atlantic Ocean is carrying North and South America westward at a rate of about 0.8 inch (20 mm) a year. India is moving northward into Eurasia, crumpling the rocks of the crust into the

Himalayan Mountains, which are still rising. As Africa and Europe move northward and eastward, the Red Sea is widening. Eventually it will grow into a wide ocean. The movement of the continents is called *continental drift,* and the theory explaining it was first suggested in 1912 by the German meteorologist Alfred Wegener (see the sidebar on page 21).

Evidence supporting Wegener's theory began to emerge in the 1940s from studies of the rocks on the ocean floor. Scientists found that some oceans are expanding. The American oceanographer Robert Sinclair Dietz (1914–95) called this process *seafloor spreading,* and in 1967 Dan McKenzie (born 1942) of Cambridge University brought together all that was known at the time and proposed a new theory: *plate tectonics.* A scientific theory is an explanation of a natural process, with solid evidence to back it.

The major crustal plates. The plates move very slowly, carrying the continents with them.

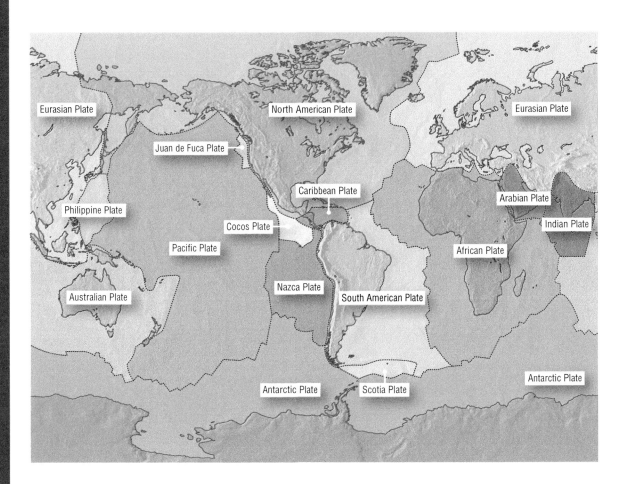

The theory of plate tectonics holds that the Earth's solid crust is composed of a number of blocks, or *plates*, that move in relation to each other. A tectonic process is one related to the deformation of the crust or to structures produced by such deformation. There are seven major plates: the African, Eurasian, Pacific, North American, South American, Antarctic, and Australian plates. There are also several lesser plates: the Cocos, Caribbean, Nazca, Arabian, Indian, Philippine, and Scotia plates. In addition, there are minor plates such as the Juan de Fuca plate, microplates, and fragments of former plates that have broken apart. The map shows the present location of the major and lesser plates.

The theory of plate tectonics explains many aspects of the Earth's geology, such as the reason why earthquakes and volcanic eruptions happen only in certain parts of the world. It also explains why some plants—and some temperate forests —are found in places thousands of miles apart, and nowhere else.

Related temperate-forest trees that occur in widely separated places

Alfred Wegener (see the sidebar "Alfred Lothar Wegener and continental drift" on page 21) was struck by the fact that certain plants occur naturally only in certain parts of the world and that those locations are separated by vast expanses of ocean. This type of scattered occurrence is called a *disjunct distribution*. There are a great many examples of disjunct distribution among plants and animals that are now extinct and known only as fossils. There are also many examples among living plants and animals. For example, marsupial mammals, the group that includes opossums and kangaroos, occur in Australia and New Guinea, and also in North and South America. Southern beeches (35 species of *Nothofagus*) are now grown in many parts of the world. They are handsome trees that produce valuable timber. They occur naturally, however, in New Guinea, southeastern Australia, Tasmania, and New Zealand, and also along the southwestern coast of South America. The monkey puzzle tree or Chile pine (*Araucaria araucana*) is a popular ornamental tree. As its name suggests, *(opposite page) Disjunct distribution. Members of certain plant families occur in widely scattered parts of the world. This is called disjunct distribution, and it suggests that the regions where the plants occur were once much closer together. The maps show the distribution of the Canellaceae (white cinnamon); Caricaceae (pawpaw); Magnoliaceae (magnolias and tulip tree); and Platanaceae (plane and buttonwood trees).*

it is native to South America, where it forms forests. It also grows naturally in New Guinea, northeastern Australia, and on islands in the South Pacific Ocean. These are individual species, but there are entire families of plants that have a disjunct distribution. The illustration shows four of these.

The Canellaceae is a small family of five genera and about 17 species of aromatic trees. Canella bark, obtained from *Canella winterana,* known as white cinnamon, is used as a tonic and flavoring, and in Puerto Rico it is used as a fish poison. The scented wood of *Cinnamosma fragrans* is used in religious ceremonies. *Warburgia* species produce a resin that is used to fasten handles to tools, leaves that are used in curries, and bark that is used as a purgative. As the map shows, this family occurs in Central America and the West Indies, where there are three genera, and in East Africa and Madagascar, where there are two genera.

The Caricaceae is a family of four genera and about 30 species of trees, one of which is *Carica papaya,* the papaya or pawpaw tree. Members of the family are most abundant in South America, with some in Central America, but one genus, *Cylicomorpha,* grows in tropical Africa.

About 200 species of trees and shrubs belong to the magnolia family, the Magnoliaceae. These include the tulip trees *Liriodendron tulipifera,* which is native to eastern North America, and *L. chinense,* which is native to central China. The Magnoliaceae occurs in North, Central, and South America and in Asia, but not in Europe or Africa.

Plane trees and buttonwood trees belong to the family Platanaceae. It is a small family, with only one genus (*Platanus*) and about seven species. Most species occur naturally in the United States, but *P. orientalis* is a native of the Balkan

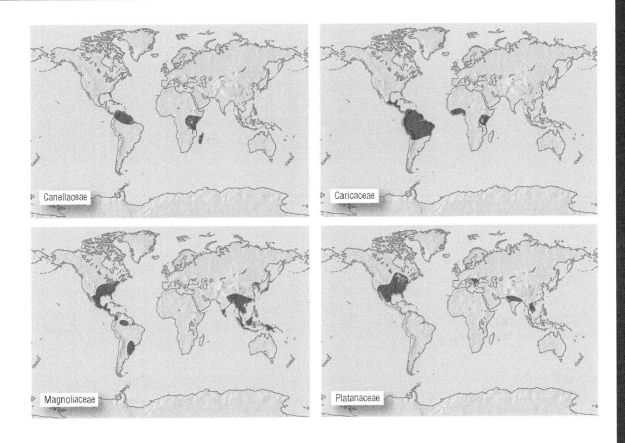

Peninsula of southeastern Europe and the Himalayas, and *P. kerrii* is native to Southeast Asia.

Disjunct distributions come about when a species or group of species—genus or family—evolves on a particular continent and the continent then splits into two or more parts, each carrying part of the population. As Wegener observed, continental drift is the only plausible explanation for the occurrence of closely related plants in widely separated parts of the world.

Soils of temperate forests

In a temperate forest, a layer of dead leaves covers the ground except on some well-trodden paths. Mixed with the leaves there are small twigs, remains of other plant material, and many small animals. Ants, beetles, snails, slugs, spiders, centipedes, and countless others, some of them too small to see except with a magnifying glass, live among this surface layer. Underneath the leaves, the bottom of the layer comprises plant matter that is damp, dark in color, and broken into fragments. This is plant material that has been almost completely decomposed by the activities of bacteria, fungi, and all the small animals. Beneath that layer is soil.

There are some places where more of the soil is visible. A deep layer is often exposed on the side of a steep bank and the rain may have washed away so much of the soil that the roots of a nearby tree stand out.

A vertical section of soil that is exposed in this way is called a *soil profile.* The side of a bank that has been exposed for a long time will be coated with soil that has washed down over it, so it will look all the same, but if you could find a freshly exposed profile you would notice that it comprises several distinct layers. These soil layers are known as *horizons.* Soil scientists, called *pedologists,* have divided an idealized soil into five levels, labeled O, A, B, C, and R, with a total of 10 horizons. The illustration shows all of these principal horizons, with their labels and descriptions. Pedologists often add much more detail than the illustration shows, to indicate important aspects of the chemical composition of the soil in each horizon. Soils vary widely in their physical and chemical composition, and many types of soil lack one or more of the full complement of horizons. Some soils possess no horizons at all.

It is obvious why soils must vary. They are made from mineral particles derived from the underlying rock. There are different types of rock and so there are types of mineral particle that differ in size, shape, and chemical composition. The leaves lying on a forest floor become incorporated into the soil, but forests do not grow everywhere. Grasses add a different kind of plant matter to the soil and grassland soils differ from forest soils. The floor of a coniferous forest is carpeted with needles. These decompose much more slowly than broad leaves. So the underlying rock and the type of vegetation determine the type of soil.

Forests require a fairly moist climate, grasslands a drier one, and rain hardly ever falls in a desert. Average temperatures also influence the type of vegetation growing in a par-

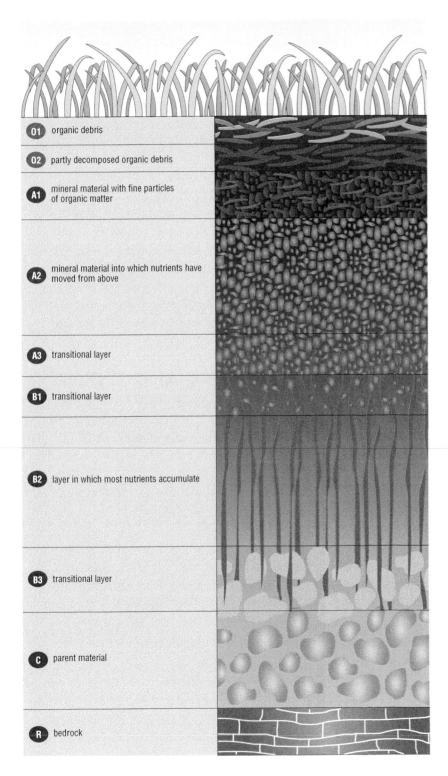

O1	organic debris
O2	partly decomposed organic debris
A1	mineral material with fine particles of organic matter
A2	mineral material into which nutrients have moved from above
A3	transitional layer
B1	transitional layer
B2	layer in which most nutrients accumulate
B3	transitional layer
C	parent material
R	bedrock

Soil profile. The diagram shows all the layers, called horizons, from the surface down to the underlying bedrock.

ticular area. Through its influence on the vegetation, climate indirectly influences the development of the soil. Climate also has a more direct effect because chemical reactions work

---

How soils are classified

Farmers have always known that soils vary. There are good soils and poor soils, heavy soils containing a large proportion of clay, sandy soils that dry out rapidly, and light, loamy soils that retain moisture and nutrients. Loam is a mixture of sand, silt, and clay—mineral particles of different sizes. In the latter part of the 19th century Russian scientists were the first to attempt to classify soils. They thought that the differences between soils were due to the nature of the parent material—the underlying rock—and the climate. They divided soils into three broad classes. *Zonal* soils were typical of the climate in which they occur, *intrazonal* soils were less dependent on climate for their characteristics, and *azonal* soils were not the result of climate. Azonal soils include windblown soils and those made from silt deposited by rivers on their floodplains. Individual soil types were placed in one or other of these broad groups. This system remained in use until the 1950s, and some of the Russian names for soils are still widely used, such as Chernozem, Rendzina, Solonchak, and Podzol.

American soil scientists were also working on the problem, and by the 1940s their work was more advanced than that of their Russian colleagues. By 1975 scientists at the United States Department of Agriculture had devised a classification they called "Soil Taxonomy." It divides soils into 10 main groups, called orders. The orders are divided into 47 suborders, and the suborders are divided into groups, subgroups, families, and soil series, with six "phases" in each series. The classification is based on the physical and chemical properties of the various levels, or *horizons,* that make up a vertical cross section, or *profile,* through a soil. These were called "diagnostic horizons."

National classifications are often very effective in describing the soils within their boundaries, but there was a need for an international classification. In 1961 representatives from the Food and Agriculture Organization (FAO) of the United Nations, the United Nations Educational, Scientific, and Cultural Organization (UNESCO), and the International Society of Soil Science (ISS) met to discuss preparing one. The project was completed in 1974 and is known as the FAO-UNESCO Classification. Like the Soil Taxonomy, it was based on diagnostic horizons. It divided soils into 26 major groups, subdivided into 106 soil units. The classification was updated in 1988 and has been amended several times since. It now comprises 30 reference soil groups and 170 possible subunits. The FAO has also produced a World Reference Base (WRB), which allows scientists to interpret the national classification schemes.

faster in warm, moist conditions than when it is cold or dry. Dead organic matter decomposes faster in warm climates than in cold ones.

Soils also change over time. When the ice age ended, the retreating ice sheets left behind a surface of bare rock, much of it shattered, with some finer particles filling crevices and hollows. Little by little this material became a soil. It was a young soil, newly formed. Temperate forests grow in mature soils that are deep enough for the roots of big trees. The nutrients that sustain the trees dissolve from the minerals into the water moving through the soil. They are recycled many times, but the water also carries them away, out of the forest, and so the soil gradually becomes less fertile. It grows older. The temperate forests have not yet existed long enough for their soils to become ancient, but one day they will be so. Many tropical soils are very deep, but they have lost most of their plant nutrients. The Tropics were not covered by ice during recent ice ages and so their soils have continued to age, and now they are very old.

Depending on their type and age, soils look different. Some are pale, some dark, and some gray. Some have a fine, almost powdery texture, some feel gritty, and some are so sticky you can shape them, like modeling clay. The characteristics of a soil affect its fertility—its capacity for growing farm crops. This makes the scientific study of soils, called *pedology,* important.

Since the 19th century, pedologists have made many attempts to simplify the study of soils by dividing them into clearly defined types. There are now several national schemes of soil classification and an international scheme that is used by the Food and Agriculture Organization (FAO) of the United Nations. Temperate forests often grow in soils classified as Inceptisols, Mollisols, and Spodosols in the U.S. Soil Taxonomy, or Chernozems, Kastanozems, and Podzols in the FAO system. The history of soil classification is summarized in the sidebar.

How water moves through a temperate forest

When it rains, puddles collect on the ground in some places, but in other places the water soaks into the ground and disappears at once. After a time, water may start to flow down gullies on hillsides that until then had been dry. A few hours later, provided there is no more rain, the ground once again looks and feels dry.

On city streets, the rainwater flows into storm drains that carry it away, and the puddles—in depressions so the water cannot flow to the drains—evaporate. This is not what happens in the forest. There, the rain is much gentler. The leaves shelter the forest floor so that the rain drips from them and falls slowly, and water also runs down the trunks of the trees. Some of the water evaporates before reaching the ground, so the rainfall is lighter inside a forest than it is outside. The raindrops are more likely to fall vertically—straight down—than they are in the open, beyond the forest edge, because the trees also slow the wind.

Once rainwater reaches the ground it continues to flow downward—to soak into the ground. It is able to move downward because soil is composed of solid particles derived from the underlying rock. The particles pack together closely, but there are small spaces, called *pores,* between them. Air fills the soil pores, but it can be displaced by water flowing through the soil. If water fills most of the pores, the soil is *waterlogged*. Walking across it will churn the soil into mud.

The total amount of pore space determines the amount of water a given volume of soil can hold. This is known as the *porosity* of the soil. Surprisingly perhaps, although soil particles vary greatly in size, their size does not affect the porosity. The diagram illustrates this. It shows three compartments of equal volume, containing one, eight, and many spherical particles. It looks as though there is more empty space in the compartment with just one particle—or perhaps in the one with eight particles. In fact, there is precisely the same amount of empty space in all three compartments. If the compartments held different soils, all three would be equally porous.

Equal porosity does not mean that water moves with equal ease through all three soils, however. Water passes more easily through a few large spaces than through many small spaces. The ease with which water passes is measured as the

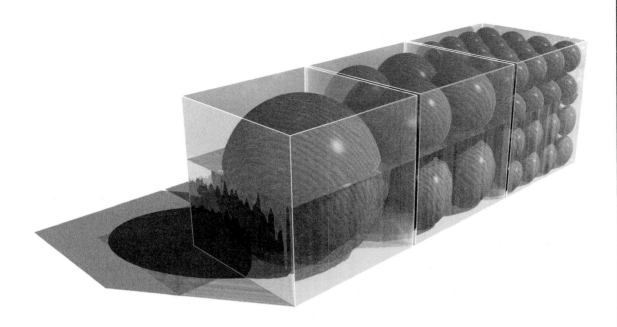

permeability of a soil, and it depends on the size of the pore spaces rather than their total volume. Two soils can be equally porous without being equally permeable. The more permeable the soil, the more quickly water passes through it, and the sooner it dries after rain.

Water draining downward through the soil eventually encounters a layer of impermeable material. This is usually the underlying *bedrock* or a layer of tightly compacted clay. Water cannot pass through it and so it accumulates above the layer, filling all the pore spaces and saturating the soil. The level below which the soil is completely saturated is called the *water table*.

Perhaps surprisingly, water in soil travels not only down but up. Water travels a short distance upward through the smallest pore spaces by a process called *capillarity*. Consequently, above the saturated layer there is a *capillary fringe* in which some of the pore spaces contain air and others contain water rising by capillarity. The capillary fringe is thicker in soils made from fine particles than it is in soils made from coarse particles, because water moves farther by capillarity through small spaces than it does through large spaces.

Porosity and permeability. Each box contains the same amount of air, so all three are equally porous. Water would pass more easily through those containing fewer particles, so they are not equally permeable.

mixed broad-leaved trees   mixed broad-leaved trees and conifers   meadow

well drained

excessive drainage

poorly drained

Effects of drainage on vegetation

Capillarity acts in all directions. Most of the water draining downward through the soil moves by capillarity rather than by gravity. It sinks by gravity only where the pore spaces are large—as they are in sand, for instance.

If water continues to drain downward, the water table will rise. If it rises all the way to the surface, the ground will be waterlogged and additional water will lie on the surface in pools. It may even cover a large area. The land is then flooded.

Some plants are more tolerant of wet soils than others, but very few can survive flooding because their roots need air for respiration. Consequently, the rate at which drainage removes surplus water from the soil affects the composition of a forest. As the diagram shows, a variety of broad-leaved trees grows on well-drained soil, different species mixed with coniferous trees grow on excessively or poorly drained soil, and only meadow, comprising sedges and grasses, will grow in soil that is sometimes flooded.

The underlying impermeable layer is unlikely to be horizontal, and if it is inclined, the water in the saturated layer will flow down the slope. The moving water is then known as *groundwater,* and the permeable soil through which it flows is an *aquifer.* In most soils, groundwater moves at speeds ranging from a few feet a day to a few feet a month. If the water reaches a place where the overlying soil is very thin and poorly drained, the water bubbles to the surface as a spring. If it reaches low-lying ground, it may also rise to the surface and continue its journey to the sea as a river.

CHAPTER 3

CLIMATE OF TEMPERATE FORESTS

Autumn, when the leaves change color and the forest blazes with patches of red and yellow. Soon the leaves will fall and the trees will be bare. (Courtesy of Fogstock)

Why there are seasons

Winters are cold. The ground freezes and in the forest the trees are bare. Sometimes the weight of ice and snow snaps a branch. Winter passes, and in spring the forest comes back to life. Summer is warm, and as it draws to a close the leaves change color and then fall.

These are the seasons. They are very familiar, but why do they happen? Why doesn't the weather remain the same all

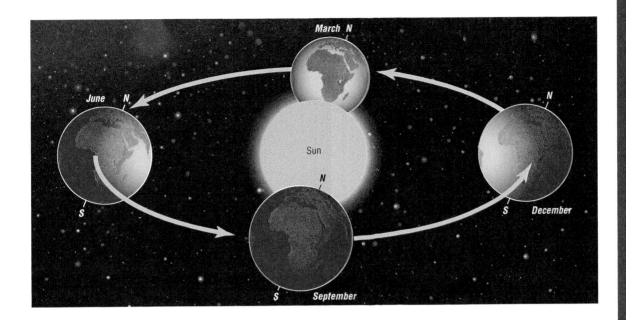

year round, as it does near the equator? And why do the seasons become more pronounced farther from the equator?

The answer is that the Earth is not upright. Earth turns on its own axis, making one complete turn every 24 hours. Earth also orbits the Sun, taking one year to complete each orbit. Imagine that the path of the Earth's orbit marks the edge of a flat disk, with the Sun at its center. This disk is known as the *plane of the ecliptic*. If the Earth's own axis were at right angles to the plane of the ecliptic, the Sun would always be directly overhead at the equator and it would shine equally onto both hemispheres. The axis is tilted about 23.5° with respect to the plane of the ecliptic, however, and the diagram shows the consequence of that tilt. As the Earth orbits the Sun, first the Northern Hemisphere and then the Southern Hemisphere is tilted to face the Sun.

The effect is most extreme at the *solstices*, on June 21–22 and December 22–23. At the June solstice the Sun is directly overhead at latitude 23.5°N. This latitude marks the tropic of Cancer. At latitude 66.5°N the Sun remains above the horizon for 24 hours. This latitude marks the Arctic Circle. At the December solstice the Sun is directly overhead at the tropic of Capricorn, at latitude 23.5°S, and remains above the horizon for 24 hours at the Antarctic Circle, at 66.5°S. The two solstices

How Earth's tilted axis produces the seasons. As Earth orbits the Sun, its tilted axis means that in June the Northern Hemisphere, and in December the Southern Hemisphere, is exposed to more sunlight.

are also known as midsummer's day and midwinter's day. The hours of daylight reach a maximum at midsummer's day and a minimum at midwinter's day, and the number of hours of daylight and darkness varies according to the latitude.

Midway between the solstices, the Sun is directly overhead at the equator. Consequently, on these days—March 20–21 and September 22–23–the Sun is above the horizon for 12 hours and below it for 12 hours everywhere in the world. These dates are called the *equinoxes*.

While the Sun is shining the surface of the Earth absorbs its radiation and grows warmer. At night, the surface loses the warmth it absorbed by day and grows cooler. Between the spring and autumn equinoxes there is more daylight than darkness and so the surface has more time to absorb heat than it does to lose it. The temperature rises, the plants respond to the warmth, and during the middle part of this period we enjoy summer. Between the autumn and spring equinoxes the opposite happens. There are more hours of darkness than there are of daylight and so the surface cools down and we have winter.

Although everyone experiences seasons, average temperatures in the Tropics are higher than temperatures in higher latitudes, and the coldest parts of the Earth are around the

Angle of sunlight. Latitude affects the intensity of sunlight. A. At the equator the Sun is almost directly overhead and its light is concentrated. B. In high latitudes the Sun is low in the sky and its light is spread over a larger surface area, making it less intense.

North and South Poles. The illustration shows why this is so. Sunshine falls more intensely in places where the Sun is approximately overhead (A in the picture) than it does where the Sun is low in the sky (B), because the Sun overhead illuminates a smaller area. Air over the Tropics is warmer than air over any other region of the Earth, and the contrast in air temperature sets up a worldwide movement of air called the *general circulation of the atmosphere*. This circulation, explained in the sidebar, transports heat from the equator into high latitudes and produces the world's climates.

How oceans affect climates

Air moves away from the North Pole as northeasterly winds and from the South Pole as southeasterly winds. Air moves toward the equator as the northeasterly trade winds in the Northern Hemisphere and southeasterly trade winds in the Southern Hemisphere. In temperate regions the winds are predominantly from the west.

Even the most constant winds do not blow all the time or always from the same direction, but these are the *prevailing winds*—the directions from which the wind blows more often than it does from any other directions. They are the winds produced by the general circulation of the atmosphere (see the sidebar "General circulation of the atmosphere" on page 38).

A person walking outdoors on a windy day can feel the wind pushing on him or her and can see the leaves, scraps of paper, and dust that it blows around. The wind exerts a pressure. The wind over the ocean exerts this pressure on the surface of the water. It pushes the water along the way it blows leaves and paper on land, but the wind blows more constantly at sea than it does over land, so its pressure is steadier. The water that it pushes along forms ocean currents, like rivers flowing through the sea.

On either side of the equator, the North and South Equatorial Currents flow from east to west. As they approach land they turn away from the equator and enter middle latitudes, where westerly winds carry them eastward. They continue to turn, however, until eventually they are flowing

General circulation of the atmosphere

The tropics of Cancer in the north and Capricorn in the south, mark the boundaries of the belt around the Earth where the Sun is directly overhead on at least one day in the year. The Arctic and Antarctic Circles mark the boundaries of regions in which the Sun does not rise above the horizon on at least one day of the year and does not sink below the horizon on at least one day in the year.

A beam of sunlight illuminates a much smaller area if the Sun is directly overhead than it does if the Sun is at a low angle in the sky. The amount of energy is the same in both cases, but the energy is spread over a smaller area directly beneath the Sun than it is when the Sun is lower. This is why the Tropics are heated more strongly than any other part of the Earth and the amount of heat falling on the surface decreases with increasing distance from the equator (increasing latitude).

The Sun shines more intensely at the equator than it does anywhere else, but air movements transport some of the warmth away from the equator. Near the equator, the warm surface of the Earth heats the air in contact with it. The warm air rises until it is close to the tropopause, which is the boundary between the lowest layer of the atmosphere (the troposphere) in which air temperature decreases with height, and the layer above (the stratosphere), where the temperature remains constant with increasing height. The height of the tropopause is around 10 miles (16 km), and at this height the air moves away from the equator, some heading north and some south. As it rises, the air cools, so the high-level air moving away from the equator is very cold—about –85°F (–65°C).

This equatorial air subsides around latitude 30°N and S, and as it sinks it warms again. By the time it reaches the surface it is hot and dry, so it warms this region, producing subtropical deserts. At the surface, the air divides. Sometimes called the horse latitudes, this is a region of light, variable winds or no winds at all. Most of the air flows back toward the equator and some flows away from the equator. The air from north and south of the equator meets at the Intertropical Convergence Zone (ITCZ), and this circulation forms a number of vertical cells called *Hadley cells,* after George Hadley (1685–1768), the English meteorologist who first proposed them in 1735.

Over the poles, the air is very cold. It subsides, and when it reaches the surface it flows away from the poles. At about latitude 50–60°N and S, air moving away from the poles meets air moving away from the equator at the polar front. The converging air rises to the tropopause, in these latitudes about seven miles (11 km) above the surface. Some flows back to the poles, forming polar cells, and some flows toward the equator, completing Ferrel cells, discovered in 1856 by the American climatologist William Ferrel (1817–91).

Warm air rises at the equator, sinks to the surface in the subtropics, flows at low level to around latitude 55°, then rises to continue its journey toward the poles. At the same time, cold air subsiding at the poles flows back to the equator. The diagram below shows how this circulation produces three sets of vertical cells in each hemisphere. It is called the "three-cell model" of the atmospheric circulation.

If it were not for this redistribution of heat, weather at the equator would be very much hotter than it is, and weather at the poles would be a great deal colder.

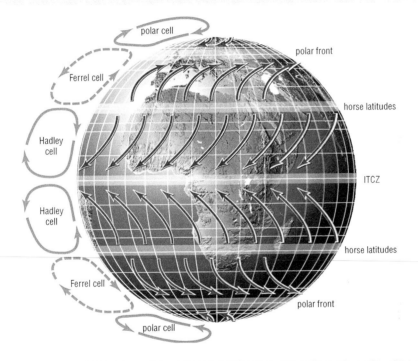

General circulation of the atmosphere. The movement of air transports heat away from the equator, forming three sets of circulation cells in each hemisphere. In the Hadley cells, warm air rises over the equator and subsides over the Tropics; some of the air flows away from the equator and some returns to the equator. Cold air subsides over the poles, flows toward the equator, and rises at the polar front; this forms the polar cells. The Hadley and polar cells drive the Ferrel cells, in which air rises at the polar front, flows toward the equator until it meets air in the Hadley cell, then subsides with the Hadley-cell air, producing the calm conditions of the horse latitudes.

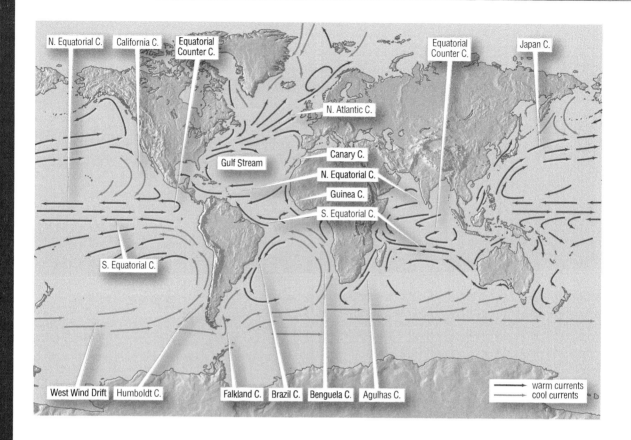

Ocean currents. In each of the oceans the currents flow approximately in circles, called "gyres," moving clockwise in the Northern Hemisphere and counterclockwise in the Southern Hemisphere.

back toward the equator. In each of the oceans the wind-driven currents follow approximately circular paths called *gyres.* Every current has a name. The map shows the principal currents.

Despite consisting of water moving through water, the ocean currents are perfectly real. In some cases they are even visible. *Kuroshio* means "black water" in Japanese, and it is the name of a current of dark-colored water that flows northward from the Philippines, past the Japanese coast, and then eastward into the North Pacific Ocean. The current is less than 50 miles (80 km) wide and moves at up to seven MPH (11 km/h).

The Kuroshio Current flows away from the equator, carrying warm water into higher latitudes. It crosses the North Pacific Ocean and turns southward as it approaches the North American coast, returning to the Tropics as the California Current carrying cold water.

All of the ocean gyres carry warm water away from the equator, past the east coasts of the continents. They are called *western boundary currents* because they are on the western sides of the oceans, and they are deep, narrow, and fast-moving. *Eastern boundary currents,* on the opposite sides of the oceans, are wide, shallow, slow-moving, and carry cold water toward the equator.

Air is warmed or cooled by contact with the surface beneath it. Consequently, the ocean gyres have a great influence on the air crossing oceans and on the climates of the lands bordering the oceans. Ocean gyres help to distribute the Sun's warmth more evenly, but the oceans have another influence on climate that is even more important. This occurs because water has a much higher *specific heat capacity* than dry land.

The specific heat capacity of a substance is the amount of heat it must absorb for its temperature to rise by one degree. Dry land is made from rocks of various types, and from soils made from rock particles. The specific heat capacity of water is about five times that of rock. This means that water absorbs five times as much heat as rock to make the same rise in temperature. Consequently, the oceans warm up much more slowly than the land in summer, which is why the sea or a lake feels cold even on a scorching summer's afternoon. Air crossing the ocean in summer is cooler than air crossing a continent. if there were no oceans, summer temperatures would be much higher than they are.

Water also cools much more slowly than land, for the same reason. In the middle of winter the sea is often warmer than the land—and the air over the land. If there were no oceans, winter temperatures would be much lower than they are.

The oceans therefore affect the climates of the world in two ways. They store heat, accumulating it slowly through the summer and releasing it slowly through the winter. In this way they moderate air temperatures, making summers cooler and winters warmer. They also transport heat directly. Ocean gyres carry warm water away from the equator and cold water back to the equator.

Air masses and fronts

As air moves slowly across a continent it acquires certain characteristics. It becomes drier, because each time it crosses high ground some of its moisture condenses to form clouds, and some of the clouds deliver rain, hail, or snow. There are few large expanses of water in midcontinent to replenish the air with water vapor.

The temperature of the ground surface determines the temperature of the air. Air absorbs very little of the solar radiation passing through it. Sunshine is absorbed by the land and sea surface. The surface grows warmer and the air above the surface is warmed by contact with it. Warm air rises and cooler air takes its place, to be warmed in its turn, so the warmth of the ground is spread throughout the air above it. In winter the ground is cold and so the air is also cold. Because it is cold, the air contracts—the way the air in a party balloon shrinks and makes the balloon shrivel if it is placed in a refrigerator for an hour or two. When air contracts, its molecules move closer together, making the air denser and therefore heavier. This increases the surface air pressure—the pressure the weight of the atmosphere exerts on the Earth's surface. Air pressure over continents is high in winter.

In summer, the ground becomes very warm. The air over the continent also becomes warm—although it remains dry. As it warms, so the air expands. Its molecules move farther apart, making the air less dense and less heavy. Surface pressure is low over continents in summer.

Eventually the air reaches the coast and moves over the ocean, and before long its characteristics start to change. Water evaporates into the dry air, making it moister. Contact with the sea surface warms very cold air in winter and cools very hot air in summer. As the temperature of the air rises or falls, its surface pressure also changes.

During World War I, a group of meteorologists at Bergen, Norway, led by Vilhelm Bjerknes, studied the physical aspects of the air. They concluded that the air over a large area was often at approximately the same temperature, pressure, and humidity everywhere, but that adjacent to it there would be air that was warmer or cooler, moister or drier. They gave the name *air masses* to these vast volumes of air (see the sidebar).

Adjacent air masses do not mix easily. This is because they are at different temperatures and therefore densities—cool air is denser than warm air. Where two air masses meet, either

Vilhelm Bjerknes and the Bergen School

Vilhelm Frimann Koren Bjerknes (1862–1951) was one of the founders of modern meteorology. He was born in Oslo, the son of a professor of mathematics, and held posts at several universities in Norway, Sweden, and Germany. In 1912 he was appointed professor of geophysics at the University of Leipzig, Germany, where he founded the Leipzig Geophysical Institute. While there he developed his ideas on weather forecasting, recruiting a team of assistants and colleagues who came to be known as the "Leipzig School."

Bjerknes returned to Norway in 1917 to found the Bergen Geophysical Institute and become its first director. It was there that he did his most important work.

As in Leipzig, Bjerknes surrounded himself with a team of colleagues, who became the "Bergen School." The team included Vilhelm's son Jakob Aall Bonnevie Bjerknes (1897–1975), who later became professor of meteorology at the University of California, Los Angeles, and Tor Harold Percival Bergeron (1891–1977), who later proposed a way raindrops might form in clouds containing large amounts of ice crystals.

The team established a network of weather stations throughout Norway, from which observers sent their observations and measurements to Bergen. Members of the Bergen School plotted these reports on maps, producing pictures of weather conditions over a large area at particular times.

Studying these pictures, they concluded that the characteristics of the air—its temperature, pressure, density, and humidity—remained constant over large areas, but that the air over one area was markedly different from the air over another. They gave the name *air mass* to these large bodies of air.

They also noticed that air masses did not readily mix with each other. Where two air masses met, there was a clearly defined boundary between them. At the time—it was during World War I—the newspapers were full of stories about opposing armies and the fronts separating them. It struck the Bergen meteorologists that air masses were a little like opposing armies, so they called the boundaries separating them *fronts*. They then developed a *frontal theory* to explain how fronts form, develop, and disappear, and how they produce the weather that is associated with them. This theory also explained how depressions form in air crossing the North Atlantic Ocean.

Modern meteorology and weather forecasting is largely based on the work of Bjerknes and his colleagues. Bjerknes was a popular teacher. He attracted talented scientists and made sure they received full recognition for their achievements. Bjerknes later joined the staff of the University of Oslo, where he remained until he retired in 1932. He died in Oslo.

Cross section through a frontal system. The system extends from the surface to the tropopause and does not affect air in the stratosphere. A mass of warm air is rising above the surrounding colder air, with fronts marking the boundaries between warm and cold air. The air behind the front defines the front: A warm front brings warm air and a cold front brings cold air.

cold, dense air pushes beneath warm, less dense air, or the warm air rides over the cool air.

There is some mixing at the boundary, or front, between the air masses. A front appears as a line on a weather map, but in fact it is a region called the *frontal zone,* 60–120 miles (100–200 km) wide. A front is named for the air behind it. It is a *warm front* if its passage means that warm air replaces cool air. If cool air replaces warm air it is a *cold front. Warm* and *cold* are relative terms. They mean only that the air is warmer or colder than the air adjacent to it.

Fronts slope upward from the surface and they move across the surface. Warm fronts slope at an angle of about 0.5°–1.0° and cold fronts at about 2°. The illustration shows the sequence of events when a warm front passes, followed by warm air, and then a cold front arrives heralding cooler air behind the front. An observer on the surface on the right of the diagram is in a cold air mass. As the warm front approaches, cloud associated with the front appears high overhead, and as the front draws closer the cloud base becomes lower and the type of cloud changes. When the front passes, the observer is in a mass of air that is warmer than the air ahead of

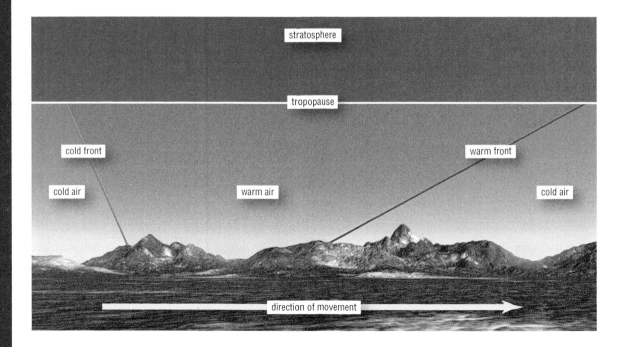

the warm front. In this warm sector, there are often sheets of dull, gray cloud and light but persistent rain or snow. Then the cold front arrives, heralding a mass of colder air. When it has passed the observer sees heaped clouds, sometimes bringing showers. As the cold front recedes the clouds associated with it appear progressively higher in the sky.

Warm fronts travel at an average speed of about 15 MPH (24 km/h) and cold fronts at about 22 MPH (35 km/h). Because cold fronts move faster than warm fronts, the cold air usually pushes beneath the warm air, progressively lifting it clear of the surface. Eventually all of the warm air has been lifted and the two fronts merge—they are said to be *occluded* or to form an *occlusion*. As the warm air rides up the cold front, its temperature decreases and its water vapor condenses to form clouds. These are of the heaped type that can produce showers or sometimes thunderstorms, and they develop in air that is rising rapidly. The cold front is steeper than the warm front and so air is forced to rise faster there than it does up the shallower slope of the warm front. At the warm front, condensation in the rising air produces sheets of smooth-looking cloud, often with drizzle or persistent rain or snow. Frontal systems are responsible for much of the changeable weather of temperate climates.

Jet streams and depressions

Air pressure is caused by the weight of the column of air above a particular place, all the way to the top of the atmosphere. It cannot be felt because it is always there, but it is as real as the pressure an elephant would exert if it sat on the hood of a car.

Warm air and cold air lie side by side, separated by a weather front. Warm air is less dense than cold air. This means that there is less air—there are fewer air molecules—in a column of warm air than there is in a similar column of cold air. Pressure is therefore higher at the base of the cold air column than it is at the base of the warm air column.

Air pressure decreases with height within both air columns because there is less air above to exert pressure. Since the densities of the warm and cold air are different, however, pressure decreases more rapidly in the denser cold air than it does in the less dense warm air. The difference in pressure between the two columns therefore increases with height, and it is greatest at the tops of the columns. These are located at the tropopause. This is the boundary between the lower atmosphere—called the *troposphere*—and the *stratosphere* above, and it is the level above which the temperature ceases to decrease with increasing height. Rising air stops when it reaches the tropopause, because it is then at the same temperature and therefore density as the air immediately above it.

Air tries to flow from a region of high pressure to a region of low pressure at a speed proportional to the difference in pressure, known as the *pressure gradient*. This is rather like the gradient of a hill. Imagine that the dense, high pressure air rises to form hills and the less dense, low pressure air forms valleys and hollows. Air then flows from high to low pressure, just as water flows down a hillside. Maps show the elevation of the land by means of contour lines—lines joining places that are all at the same height above sea level. If the contour lines are close together it means the ground rises steeply—a big increase in elevation for a short distance horizontally.

Instead of variations in the height of the surface above sea level, a weather map shows variations in atmospheric pressure. Weather stations measure the pressure and meteorologists then adjust these measurements to show the sea-level pressure. This is necessary because air pressure decreases with altitude and so the measurements from weather stations are affected by their elevations. Converting the pressures at all the stations to sea-level pressure makes it easy to recognize areas of high and low pressure and the rate at which pressure changes between them.

Places where the air pressure is the same are joined together by lines called *isobars*—from the Greek *isos* meaning "equal" and *baros* meaning "weight." If the isobars are close together it means the pressure changes rapidly over a short horizontal distance, and if they are widely spaced it means the pressure remains fairly constant over a large area. This is very similar to the way contour lines show hills, valleys, and plains, but isobars illustrate the changes across an invisible *pressure surface* rather than the solid ground surface. The closer together the isobars are, the steeper the pressure gradient, and because air flows down the pressure gradient like water down a hillside, the stronger the wind.

Because of the rotation of the Earth, however, the air does not move at right angles to the pressure gradient but parallel to it. On a weather map, the wind blows parallel to the isobars. In the Northern Hemisphere the air moves counterclockwise around a center of low pressure and clockwise around a center of high pressure. These directions are reversed in the Southern Hemisphere. When warm and cold air lie side by side, the pressure gradient becomes steeper with increasing height, because pressure decreases faster in the cold air than in the warm air. Maps of the pressure surface at different altitudes would show the isobars closing up. Therefore the wind speed increases. It is called a *thermal wind* because it is caused by a difference in temperature.

The biggest difference in temperature occurs where cold air moving away from the poles meets warm air moving toward the poles. Cold and warm air meet at several latitudes (see the sidebar "General circulation of the atmosphere" on page 38), but the sharpest and most continuous boundary occurs at about 30°–70°N and S, where tropical air meets polar air. At this boundary, wind speed increases with height and reaches a maximum between 30,000 feet and 50,000 feet (9,000–15,000 m). That is where a ribbon of wind, 60–300 miles (100–500 km) wide but only a mile or two thick, blows at speeds of 120–240 MPH (200–400 km/h) and sometimes faster in winter, when the temperature contrast is greatest. The ribbon of wind is called the *jet stream*. In fact there are several jet streams at different latitudes, but this is the most constant one.

Thermal winds blow with the cold air to the left in the Northern Hemisphere and to the right in the Southern Hemisphere. In both hemispheres, therefore, the jet streams blow from west to east (apart from an easterly jet stream that forms in summer over Asia).

Even the most reliable jet stream does not blow all the time or invariably from west to east. Jet streams twist and snake about, and this can have dramatic effects on the weather below (see "Blocking" on page 49). Waves in the jet stream produce *ridges* curving toward the pole and *troughs* curving toward the equator. Places on the surface below a ridge are in tropical air and those below a trough are in polar air. The illustration shows how ridges and troughs in the jet stream can affect the weather across the United States. Arrows in the diagram show the direction of the wind.

Air is drawn into the jet stream on the upstream side of ridges and flows out from it on the downstream side. Where air converges to enter the jet stream, air subsides, producing high pressure at the surface. Divergence draws air upward, producing low surface pressure. Fronts form between the areas of high and low pressure and the center of low pressure becomes a *depression*. As the waves in the jet stream move eastward, like waves in a rope that is secured at one end and shaken up and down at the other, they drag the frontal systems and depressions with them, as shown in the illustration.

Ridges and troughs in the jet stream across North America. The arrows show the wind direction and shading indicates the wind speeds in the jet stream.

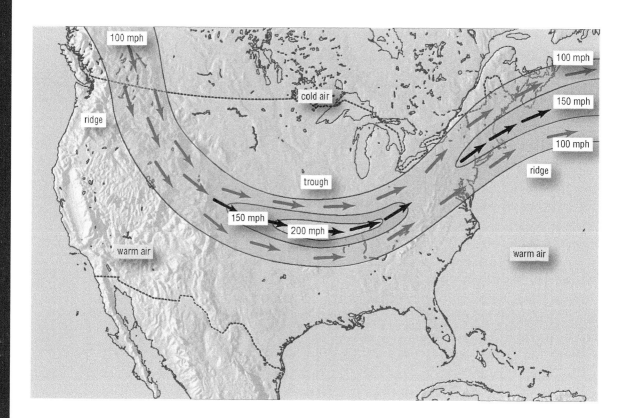

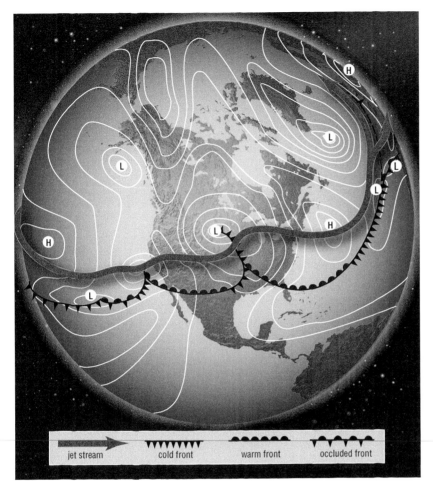

jet stream   cold front   warm front   occluded front

Jet stream and fronts. Frontal depressions develop beneath undulations in the jet stream, and as the undulations move from west to east they drag the frontal systems with them.

It is the front between tropical and polar air and the behavior of the jet stream this produces that make the weather in temperate latitudes so changeable and difficult to forecast.

Blocking

About 40,000 feet (12.2 km) above sea level, the jet stream blows from west to east, but high mountain ranges, such as the Rocky Mountains, slow the air passing over them and slightly alter its horizontal course. The resulting deviations affect the overlying air, all the way up to the jet stream, producing very long waves—the distance between one wave crest and the next is between about 2,500 miles (4,000 km) and 3,700 miles (6,000 km). The crests project to the north and the troughs to the south.

Atmospheric movement transfers heat away from the equator (see the sidebar "General circulation of the atmosphere" on page 38), but the efficiency of the process varies. When it is relatively inefficient, warm air accumulates in the

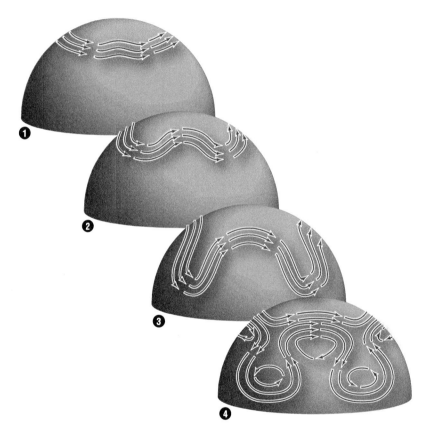

Blocking. These four diagrams show how waves in the jet stream develop over a period of a few weeks, over the course of the index cycle. 1. The jet stream flows west to east, with only slight undulations. 2. The undulations become more pronounced. 3. The undulations are now very pronounced; in some places the jet stream blows in a northerly and in other places southerly direction. 4. The flow has broken up and the jet stream circulates around cells of high pressure in the north and low pressure in the south; these cells remain stationary for some time, deflecting weather systems to the north or south. This is called "blocking."

south and air in the north becomes colder, increasing the contrast in temperature on either side of the front separating tropical and polar air. It is the temperature contrast that drives the jet stream, so when the contrast increases, the jet stream accelerates.

At this point the effect of the Earth's rotation becomes important. It is called the Coriolis effect, abbreviated as CorF (because it was once thought to be a force), and in the Northern Hemisphere it deflects moving air to the right. CorF is greatest at the poles, and at the equator its value is zero. Its magnitude is directly proportional to the speed of the moving air. As the jet stream accelerates, it temporarily overcomes the influence of the CorF and swings to the left. This carries it northward, where the CorF increases, swinging it to the right again. The result is a series of swings that make the waves bigger and closer together. The diagram shows the sequence of events.

By stage 3 in the sequence, the waves have become extreme. The troughs are bringing polar air far to the south. In winter this produces cold waves, with a sudden drop in temperature. Elsewhere, the ridges carry tropical air far to the north, producing unusually warm weather. The jet stream is blowing from the north in some places and from the south in others, and the two streams are fairly close together.

In stage 4, some of the air has taken a shortcut. The jet stream is once more blowing from west to east, but to its south there are sections of the jet stream that have been cut off from the main flow. They now form isolated pools of air, about 900 miles (1,450 km) across, with winds flowing around them. Those in the north, at about 55°N, consist of tropical air, and those in the south, at about 33°N, of polar air. Air circulates clockwise around the pools of tropical air and counterclockwise around the pools of polar air. In the Northern Hemisphere, air circulates counterclockwise around centers of low pressure and clockwise around centers of high pressure. The pools of tropical air are therefore *anticyclones* or *highs,* and the pools of polar air are *depressions* or *lows.* Anticyclones bring fine, settled weather. Depressions bring wet weather.

The sequence takes three to eight weeks to complete, but at the end, the isolated anticyclones and depressions remain, while the jet stream resumes its westerly flow to the north. The anticyclones and depressions are stationary, but weather systems continue moving from west to east, usually traveling at about 20 MPH (30 km/h) in summer and 30 MPH (50 km/h) in winter. When they reach the stationary highs and lows their way is blocked and so they divert around them. The process is called *blocking,* and the pools of air responsible for it are *blocking highs* and *blocking lows.*

Blocking highs and lows can persist for days or even weeks. They bring prolonged spells of unchanging weather. In the southern United States, at about the latitude of Dallas, Texas, this is most likely to be cool, overcast, wet weather. In Canada, at about the latitude of Edmonton, Alberta, it is usually fine weather that can contribute to the development of a drought. At the same time, frontal systems are diverted into regions to the north and south of the block that might otherwise have missed them.

Continental and maritime climates

Broad-leaved deciduous trees cannot tolerate prolonged drought. They need moisture. This requirement for water means that temperate forests do not grow deep inside continents, far from the ocean. They prefer a *maritime climate,* also called an *oceanic climate.*

As the name suggests, a maritime climate occurs near coasts and it is produced by *maritime air*—air masses that have formed over the ocean. As well as being moist, maritime air is relatively mild in winter and cool in summer, so the difference between summer and winter temperatures is much smaller than it is in the interior of a continent. At Belfast, Northern Ireland, for example, the average temperature in the warmest month is 58°F (14.5°C) and that of the coldest month 39°F (4°C). The difference between the two, or the *temperature range* for Belfast, is 19°F (10.5°C). Contrast this with Dodge City, Kansas, where the average temperature is 78°F (25.5°C) in the warmest month and 29°F (–1.5°C) in the coldest month, giving a temperature range of 49°F (27°C). Belfast has a maritime climate and Dodge City has a continental climate. The most extreme examples of maritime climate are found on oceanic islands. The Azores, a group of islands in the North Atlantic Ocean about 800 miles (1,287 km) to the west of Portugal, are in approximately the same latitude as Dodge City. The average temperature in the Azores ranges from 57°F (14°C) to 71°F (21.5°C) in the warmest month, a difference of 14°F (7.5°C).

Maritime climates are also wet. Moist air from the ocean is forced to rise as it crosses the coast. Some of its water vapor condenses to form clouds and it rains (see "Why clouds form" on page 56). The Azores receive an average 47 inches (1,186 mm) of rain a year and Belfast 33 inches (846 mm), but Dodge City receives only 20 inches (518 mm). Not every oceanic island has a wet climate, however. Seymour Island, for example, has a desert climate. One of the Galápagos Islands, about 650 miles (1,045 km) from the coast of Ecuador, it is low-lying and surrounded by the cold water of the Peru Current. Seymour Island receives only four inches (102 mm) of rain a year, and no rain at all from the end of April until the beginning of January.

These contrasts make it sound as though a line could be drawn between an area with a continental climate and an adjacent area with a maritime climate and a person could cross from one to the other. It would be like crossing the road—continental on one side and maritime on the other. It is not like that, however. With increasing distance toward or away from the coast, the climate changes quite gradually. The change is more abrupt where a range of mountains runs parallel to the coast and not very far inland. Approaching air loses a large proportion of its moisture as it crosses the mountains (see the sidebar "Why it rains more on mountainsides" on page 3) and the region on the lee side lies in a *rain shadow* and has an extremely continental climate.

The Coast Ranges in California demonstrate the effect. San Diego, California, has a temperature range of 14°F (8°C), and Phoenix, Arizona, on the inland side of the mountains, has a range of 39°F (21.5°C). There is less contrast in rainfall. Phoenix receives an average 7.5 inches (190 mm) of rain a year and San Diego receives 10 inches (264 mm). San Diego owes its relatively dry climate to the fact that air approaching from the Pacific Ocean has to cross the cold California

Current. Contact with the cool water reduces the temperature of the air, causing some of its water vapor to condense and thus partly drying the air shortly before it reaches the coast.

Scientists who study climates need a convenient way to describe the extent to which the climate in a particular place is continental or maritime. The most widely used method produces a number called the *Conrad index,* devised in 1946 by the American scientist V. Conrad. A Conrad index of 0 means a climate is fully maritime and 100 means it is fully continental. The table lists the Conrad index values for the places mentioned.

The table shows that the Azores, Belfast, and San Diego have maritime climates, and that Dodge City and Phoenix have climates of a more continental type.

Conrad index of continentality

Place	Index value
Azores	2.98
Belfast	5.75
Dodge City	48.03
Phoenix	39.13
San Diego	6.04

How climates are classified

Temperate forests prefer a maritime climate, but maritime climates are not all the same. In some, approximately the same amount of rain or snow falls in each month. Others have a dry season in which there is very little rain, and the dry season may be in the summer or the winter. There are climates with a hot summer and those with a warm or even cool summer. Describing a climate merely as maritime or continental provides some information, but it does not amount to a complete description, because it does not reveal what kind of maritime or continental climate it is. A system is needed for classifying climates, like the system for classifying plants and animals. Such a system will allow people to distinguish between the different types of maritime and continental climates, just as the system of biological classification allows people to distinguish between different kinds of mammals or birds. Then, when a climate type is named, everyone will know precisely what is meant.

In fact, there are many classification systems. The ancient Greeks devised the earliest ones, but those in use today have grown from systems that were developed in the 19th century. Botanists and plant geographers made up most of them. Plant geographers are scientists who define vegetation types and plot their geographic distributions, and the names they used to describe climates reflect this. They described "savanna climate," "tropical rainforest climate," and "tundra climate," for example. Some of these names are still used, but others, such as "penguin climate," have been dropped.

The only information available to scientists in the early days referred to average temperature and rainfall and to vegetation type. Much more detailed information is available nowadays, about both the climate itself and its effect on plants, animals, and people living in it. There are many more recording stations, satellites monitor the surface and atmosphere constantly, and computers make it possible to process large amounts of data. As a result, climate classifications have steadily grown more detailed and complicated.

The variety of classification systems is not due to disagreements among scientists or to the search for a perfect scheme. There can be no single classification that satisfies the needs of every user. Some schemes help geographers studying plant distribution. Others relate to crop requirements and are designed for agricultural use. There are also some that simply provide a list of descriptive names and there are highly technical classifications for the use of climate scientists.

Many of the most widely used schemes are based on one devised by the Russian-born German meteorologist and climatologist Wladimir Peter Köppen (1846–1940). The first version was published in 1900, and in 1936 Köppen issued a revised version of his classification.

The Köppen classification first divides climates into six general types, defined principally by temperature and designated by letters.

A Tropical rainy climates; the average temperature never falls below 64.4°F (18°C).

B Dry climates.

C Warm temperate rainy climates; temperatures in the warmest month are higher than 50°F (10°C) and in the coldest month are between 26.6°F (–3°C) and 64.4°F (18°C).

D Cold boreal forest climates; temperatures in the warmest month are higher than 50°F (10°C) and in the coldest month are lower than 26.6°F (–3°C).

E Tundra climate; temperatures in the warmest month are between 32°F (0°C) and 50°F (10°C).

F Perpetual frost climate; the average temperature never rises above 32°F (0°C).

These categories relate to plant growth. For example, trees will not grow where summer temperatures remain below 50°F (10°C), some plants will not grow where winter temperatures fall below 64.4°F (18°C), and an average temperature of 26.6°F (–3°C) means there will be frost and probably snow.

Köppen then divided each of these six categories into a number of further types based mainly on the amount and distribution of rain that they receive. This produced a total of 24 climate types. For example, a Cfb climate is a warm, temperate rainy climate that is mild in winter, warm in summer, and moist throughout the year. A Bwh climate is characteristic of a hot desert.

Finally, 24 additional letters are used to add more detailed information. Adding f, for example, means there is sufficient rain for plants to grow healthily in all seasons. Adding s means there is a dry season in summer, and adding n means that fog is frequent.

The Köppen classification is the one most widely used by geographers. When you see a map of the world showing climate types, it is most likely to be based on the Köppen scheme and it may use the Köppen letters in addition to colors.

Why clouds form

Water vapor is a gas consisting of separate water molecules, all moving rapidly in every direction. When two molecules collide they bounce off each other and fly apart. The more energy the molecules possess, the faster they travel and the harder they strike when they collide. If the molecules lose energy they slow down, and if they slow down sufficiently, molecules cling to one another when they collide, rather than bouncing apart. When the molecules begin to join together in small groups they cease to be a gas. They are then droplets of liquid water. The process by which water vapor turns into liquid water is called *condensation*. When it occurs in the air, the resulting mass of minute water droplets is visible as cloud or fog.

For cloud to form, the water vapor in the air must lose so much energy that its molecules join together. Air loses energy when it expands and gains energy when it is compressed. When you pump up a bike tire, the energy you expend in compressing the air entering the tire is transferred to the air molecules. They move faster and therefore they strike the sides of the pump harder. That makes the molecules in the pump casing vibrate faster, and you feel that increased vibration as a rise in temperature. In other words, when you compress air its temperature rises. If you then undo the tire valve and let out the air, the escaping air will feel cold. As the air expands, its molecules move farther apart and slow down, so the air temperature falls. When air expands, its temperature falls.

Water vapor loses energy if it expands, and it will expand if it moves into a region of the atmosphere where the surrounding air pressure is lower. Air pressure decreases with height, because the weight of overlying air decreases. The reduction in pressure allows the air to expand, expansion causes the temperature to fall, and therefore the temperature of the air decreases with height. Walkers preparing to climb high into the hills pack extra sweaters because they know it will be colder up there than it is down in the valley. The temperature falls by an average of 3.5°F every 1,000 feet (6.5°C/km). Air also expands and cools if it is forced to rise, for example by crossing a mountain, and sinking air is compressed and its temperature increases. These changes are said to be *adiabatic* (see the sidebar).

Air temperature decreases with height, and the amount of water vapor that air is able to hold varies with the temperature.

Adiabatic cooling and warming

Air is compressed by the weight of air above it. Imagine a balloon partly inflated with air and made from some weightless substance that totally insulates the air inside. No matter what the temperature outside the balloon, the temperature of the air inside remains the same.

Imagine the balloon is released into the atmosphere. The air inside is squeezed between the weight of air above it, all the way to the top of the atmosphere, and the denser air below it.

Suppose the air inside the balloon is less dense than the air above it. Denser air will push beneath it and the balloon will rise. As it rises, the distance to the top of the atmosphere becomes smaller, so there is less air above to weigh down on the air in the balloon. At the same time, as the balloon moves through air that is less dense, it experiences less pressure from below. This causes the air in the balloon to expand.

When air (or any other gas) expands, its molecules move farther apart. The amount of air remains the same, but it occupies a bigger volume. As they move apart, the molecules must "push" other molecules out of their way. This uses energy, so as the air expands its molecules lose energy. Because they have less energy they move more slowly.

When a moving molecule strikes something, some of its energy is transferred to what-ever it strikes, and part of that energy is converted into heat. This raises the temperature of the struck object by an amount related to the number of molecules striking it and their speed.

In expanding air, the molecules are moving farther apart, so a smaller number of them strike an object each second. They are also traveling more slowly, so they strike with less force. This means the temperature of the air decreases. As it expands, air cools.

If the air in the balloon is denser than air below, it will sink. As it sinks, the pressure on the air will increase, its volume will decrease, and its molecules will acquire more energy. Its temperature will increase.

This warming and cooling has nothing to do with the temperature of the air surround-ing the balloon. It is called *adiabatic* warming and cooling, from the Greek word *adia-batos,* meaning "impassable," suggesting that the air is enclosed by an imaginary bound-ary through which heat is unable to pass.

The warmer the air is, the more water vapor it can hold. At 80°F (27°C), for example, one pound of air at sea-level pres-sure can hold about 0.3 ounces of water vapor (20 g/kg), but at 32°F (0°C) it can hold only 0.06 ounces (3.5 g/kg). When the concentration of water vapor reaches the maximum the air can contain, the air is *saturated*. If more water vapor is then added, or if the temperature falls, some of the water vapor condenses into liquid droplets. The amount of moisture present in the air is called the *humidity*. There are several ways to measure this, explained in the sidebar.

Atmospheric water vapor will condense if the air temperature decreases. Since air temperature decreases with height, water vapor condenses when moist air rises.

There are three reasons why air may rise. It rises at weather fronts, where warm air rises up a cold front (see "Air masses and fronts" on page 41), and when a moving air mass crosses

Humidity

The amount of water vapor air can hold varies according to the temperature. Warm air can hold more than cold air. The amount of water vapor present in the air is called the *humidity* of the air. This is measured in several ways.

The *absolute humidity* is the mass of water vapor present in a unit of volume of air, measured in grams per cubic meter (1 gram per cubic meter = 0.046 ounces per cubic yard). Changes in the temperature and pressure alter the volume of air, however, and this changes the amount of water vapor in a unit volume without actually adding or removing any moisture. The concept of absolute humidity takes no account of this, so it is not very useful and is seldom used.

Mixing ratio is more useful. This is a measure of the amount of water vapor in a unit mass of dry air—air with all the water vapor removed. *Specific humidity* is similar to mixing ratio but measures the amount of water vapor in a unit mass of air including the moisture. Both are reported in grams per kilogram. Since the amount of water vapor is always very small, seldom accounting for more than 4 percent of the mass of the air, specific humidity and mixing ratio are almost the same thing.

The most familiar term is *relative humidity*. This is the measurement you read from hygrometers, either directly or after referring to tables—and it is the one you hear in weather forecasts. Relative humidity (RH) is the amount of water vapor in the air expressed as a percentage of the amount needed to saturate the air at that temperature. When the air is saturated the RH is 100 percent (the "percent" is often omitted).

high ground. Air also rises when, on warm, sunny days, the ground is heated. Air next to the ground is warmed by contact and rises by convection. Water vapor in air rising up a front condenses to form *frontal cloud*. Condensation in air rising over high ground forms *orographic cloud*. Moist air rising by convection forms *convective cloud*—often seen on fine summer afternoons as puffy, white, fair-weather cumulus.

There are different ways for clouds to form, and they form at varying heights because of variations in the amount of water vapor present in the air. Consequently, clouds vary

How clouds are classified

There is an internationally accepted scheme for classifying clouds on the basis of their height and appearance. Clouds are grouped into 10 distinctive types called *genera* (singular *genus*). The genera are subdivided into species and species into varieties. There are also accessory clouds (small clouds seen in association with a bigger cloud of a different type) and supplementary cloud features (extensions or protrusions from a cloud). Genera and species names have standard abbreviations. Stratocumulus (Sc), for example, may form in an almond or lens shape, producing the species lenticularis (len), abbreviated as Sc_{len}.

Cloud genera are described as low-level, medium-level, or high-level according to the height at which they most commonly form, although clouds can form at higher or lower levels. Large storm clouds, which have a low-level base but extend to a great height, are counted as low-level clouds, mainly for convenience. Most medium-level clouds have names beginning with the prefix *alto-* and the names of high-level clouds have the prefix *cirr-*.

CLOUD GENERA

Low-level clouds. Cloud base from sea level to 1.2 miles (2,000 m).

Stratus (St). An extensive sheet of featureless cloud that will produce drizzle or fine snow if it is thick enough.

Stratocumulus (Sc). Similar to St, but broken into separate, fluffy-looking masses. If thick enough, it also produces drizzle or fine snow.

Cumulus (Cu). Separate white, fluffy clouds, usually with flat bases. There may be many of them, all with bases at about the same height, and they may merge into a single cloud.

greatly in appearance. A way is needed to describe these different kinds of cloud clearly, so meteorologists use a system of cloud classification (see the sidebar) based on the height and appearance of the clouds.

Rain, snow, and hail

A cloud is made from water droplets, ice crystals, or a mixture of both. Cloud droplets are tiny—typically about 0.0004 inch (0.01 mm) across. There are usually about 283 droplets in

Cumulonimbus (Cb). Very large cumulus, often towering to a great height. Because they are so thick, Cb clouds are often dark at the base. If the tops are high enough they will consist of ice crystals and may be swept into an anvil shape (the supplementary feature incus).

Medium-level clouds. Cloud base from 1.2–2.5 miles (2,000–4,000 m) in polar regions, 4–5 miles (6,000–8,000 m) in temperate and tropical regions.

Altocumulus (Ac). Patches or rolls of cloud joined to make a sheet. Ac is sometimes called "wool-pack cloud."
Altostratus (As). Pale, watery, featureless cloud, forming a sheet through which the Sun may be visible as a white smudge.
Nimbostratus (Ns). A large sheet of featureless cloud, often with rain or snow, that is thick enough to obscure the Sun, Moon, and stars completely. It makes days dull and nights very dark.

High-level clouds. Cloud base from two to five miles (3,000–8,000 m) in polar regions, three to 11 miles (5,000–18,000 m) in temperate and tropical regions. All high-level clouds are made entirely from ice crystals.

Cirrus (Ci). Patches of white, fibrous cloud, sometimes swept into strands with curling tails ("mares' tails").
Cirrocumulus (Cc). Patches of thin cloud, sometimes forming ripples, fibrous in places, with no shading that would define their shape.
Cirrostratus (Cs). Thin, almost transparent cloud forming an extensive sheet and just thick enough to produce a halo around the Sun or Moon.

every cubic foot of air (100,000/L) and they fall very slowly. Droplets are constantly evaporating and water vapor is constantly condensing to produce new ones. A cloud looks very still and peaceful, but there is a great deal going on inside it.

Cloud droplets are too small to fall as rain, because droplets falling from the base of the cloud enter much drier air and evaporate long before they have time to reach the ground. Even raindrops can evaporate between the cloud and the ground. You sometimes see showers of them, looking like a gray veil, called *virga* or *fallstreaks,* hanging from the base of a cloud.

There are two ways for raindrops to form, depending on whether or not the cloud contains ice crystals. Most of the clouds in middle latitudes contain ice because they extend above the altitude at which the temperature reaches freezing.

If ice crystals are present, the cloud will also contain liquid droplets that are below freezing temperature but remain unfrozen because there are too few solid particles onto which ice crystals can grow. Instead of freezing, these *supercooled* droplets evaporate and the water vapor is then deposited onto the ice crystals. The ice crystals grow bigger and the supercooled droplets become fewer.

As they grow bigger, the ice crystals begin to collide with each other, forming snowflakes, and when the snowflakes are big and heavy enough they start to fall. As they fall, the snowflakes collide with more supercooled liquid droplets that freeze onto them, making the snowflakes still larger. Buffeting by air currents breaks some of the snowflakes apart, releasing tiny ice splinters that are carried aloft by rising air. These are solid particles onto which more ice crystals can form.

Other snowflakes continue falling, and growing larger as they do so. When they enter warmer air in the lower part of the cloud or between the base of the cloud and the ground, the snowflakes melt and become raindrops. Most of the rain that falls in temperate latitudes consists of melted snow, even in the middle of summer.

If the air temperature between the cloud base and the ground is lower than about 39°F (4°C), the snowflakes will not melt. They will fall as snow, and the colder the air, the smaller the snowflakes will be.

Some clouds contain no ice crystals. They do contain some much larger droplets, however. These fall faster than the small droplets and as they fall they gather up and merge with the smaller droplets they meet along the way. Whether it forms in this way or as a snowflake that melts, a raindrop consists of about 1 million cloud droplets.

Raindrops do not always fall from their clouds. If the cloud is a big cumulonimbus storm cloud, the currents of rising air inside it may be strong enough to sweep up raindrops from near the bottom of the cloud and raise them to the top, where they freeze into ice pellets. The pellets then fall again and are caught in rising air currents and carried back to the top of the cloud. As it moves through the cloud, a pellet collides with supercooled water droplets that freeze onto it. Large droplets spread over the surface of the pellet and freeze as a layer of clear ice. Small droplets freeze faster, forming white, opaque ice made from tiny crystals with pockets of air trapped between them. The pellet is then a hailstone. Eventually it will either enter a current of air moving downward that will throw it out of the base of the cloud, or it will grow so big that the rising air currents cannot support its weight and so it falls from the cloud.

Most hailstones are no bigger than a pea, but a severe storm can drop hailstones the size of golf balls and occasionally they can be even larger. Hailstones the size of softballs have been recorded, and on September 3, 1970, a hailstone 5.5 inches (14 cm) across, weighing 1.67 pounds (766 g), fell at Coffeyville, Kansas.

A hailstone grows by acquiring ice during its travels between the top and base of the cloud. The more of these circuits it makes, the bigger the hailstone will be. It falls from the cloud when it is too heavy to be carried upward, so the stronger the vertical air currents, the more circuits the hailstone can make and the bigger it can become. The size of the hailstones therefore indicates the size and energy of the cloud producing them.

Ice storms

Hailstorms can batter farm crops to destruction, but forest trees can withstand their blows. A tree is more likely to be damaged by a layer of clear ice that is heavy enough to snap its branches. Ice is surprisingly heavy. A layer of ice three inches (7.5 cm) thick on a branch one foot (30 cm) thick and 15 feet (4.6 m) long would weigh about 83 pounds (182 kg).

Clear ice can accumulate very quickly, with startling results: Roosting birds have been frozen onto tree branches, ground-nesting birds have had their wings coated with ice so they could not fly, and prowling cats have been frozen to the ground. When this happens it is called an *ice storm*. Ice forms on roads, airfield runways, railroad tracks, power and telephone lines, and radio and TV masts as well as on trees. An ice storm can bring transport to a standstill, cause power outages and telephone failures, and do structural damage to transmitter towers.

Ice storms usually happen ahead of an approaching warm front (see "Air masses and fronts" on page 41) when the air ahead of the front is below freezing temperature, the warm air behind the front is just above freezing, and there is a strong wind.

At the front, warm air is rising above the adjacent cold air, but at a very shallow angle of 0.5° to 1°. The shallowness of the angle means that the front overhangs a large surface area. When the base of the cloud overhead is about 6,500 feet (2 km) above the ground, the line where the warm front touches the surface may be up to 170 miles (275 km) away.

If the temperature of the air at ground level behind the front is well above freezing, the cloud along the lower part of the front will be warm enough to deliver rain rather than snow, but some of this rain will be barely above freezing temperature. The rain falls through the frontal zone and into the colder air ahead of the front—and in fact below it. This air is well below freezing temperature, and because the air is very cold, so are all the solid objects on the ground, including the trunks and branches of the trees. Rain that is barely above freezing temperature cools a little more as it falls through the cold air. When it strikes a solid surface it immediately starts to freeze.

Raindrops are too large to freeze instantaneously. The part of the drop that makes contact with the surface freezes at once. The remainder of the drop then spreads outward as a liquid coating that freezes on contact with the surface. Each raindrop freezes into a thin sheet of ice.

Freezing releases latent heat, however. This warms the surrounding air and will prevent more ice from forming unless the warm air is quickly removed. The strong wind achieves this, sweeping away the warmed air and replacing it with cold air.

As more and more raindrops strike the surface and freeze, together they rapidly build a thick coating of clear ice. Because of the wind, the rain falls at an angle and so the ice coats the sides of objects facing into the wind much more thickly than it does the opposite, sheltered sides.

Dew and frost

When a cool night with only the lightest of winds follows a warm day, water vapor often condenses onto surfaces, especially the leaves of plants growing close to the ground. This is dew. If the plants are covered with dew early in the morning it often means the coming day will be fine and sunny.

During the day, the ground and plant surfaces absorb the warm sunshine. As their temperature rises, the surfaces also radiate their own warmth into the sky, but they absorb heat faster than they lose it, so they grow steadily warmer. Air next to them is warmed by contact. Water enters the warm air by evaporation and transpiration (see "Evaporation and transpiration" on page 66).

After sunset the ground and plants cease to absorb heat, but they continue to radiate their own heat, so they cool down. Their temperature falls steadily until about an hour before dawn, when it reaches its lowest point. A shallow layer of cool air collects close to the ground. If there is more than the slightest breeze, this cold air will be swept away and replaced by warmer air from above, but if the air is fairly still the temperature in this surface layer remains low.

The relative humidity (RH) increases as the temperature falls (see the sidebar "Humidity" on page 59). If the RH exceeds 100 percent, water vapor will condense out of the air, provided there are surfaces onto which it can condense.

Leaves inside the layer of cool air and at the same temperature are ideal.

The air must not be completely still. If it is, condensation will quickly remove enough water vapor from the surface layer to reduce the RH to below 100 percent. Condensation will then cease and, although dew will form, the amount will be too small to be visible. A gentle movement of air will replenish the surface layer with a steady supply of moist air from above.

In winter it sometimes happens that the temperature drops to below freezing after dew has formed. When this happens the dewdrops freeze, coating surfaces with clear ice, often with round lumps due to the shape of the dewdrops.

Water vapor condenses to form dew at the *dew-point temperature*. If the air is fairly dry, the dew-point temperature may be below freezing. Dew will not form in summer under these conditions, but in winter the temperature in the surface layer may well fall to below freezing. Water vapor will then be deposited directly as ice crystals that cover surfaces with white *hoar frost*.

Frost protects plants against the cold. This is because ice conducts heat poorly, so it reduces the amount of warmth they radiate away. At the same time, the freezing of dewdrops and deposition of water vapor as ice crystals release latent heat that warms the underlying surface.

Plants suffer damage when the air is dry and the temperature falls low enough to freeze the liquid inside their tissues. This produces *black frost*. There is no surface coating of ice, but the frozen leaves die and turn black.

Weather forecasts often warn of *air frost* or *ground frost*. Air frost is the one that can harm plants. It happens when the air temperature falls below freezing. Ground frost occurs when the ground temperature falls below freezing, but the air temperature remains above freezing.

Evaporation and transpiration

A water molecule comprises two atoms of hydrogen (H) and one of oxygen (0), chemical formula H_2O. The molecule is arranged with both hydrogen atoms on the same side of the oxygen atom. This gives the molecule a negative electromagnetic charge on the oxygen side and a positive charge on the hydrogen side. The charges balance, so the molecule is neutral overall, but it carries a charge at each end.

When two water molecules are close together, an attachment called a *hydrogen bond* forms between a hydrogen atom of one molecule and the oxygen atom of the other. Molecules form small groups held together by hydrogen bonds. The groups are constantly breaking apart and forming again; they move around freely, sliding past one another, and they will fill every corner of a container. This is liquid water.

If a molecule absorbs enough energy, it will vibrate so violently that it breaks away from its group. It can then enter the air, where it is able to move freely. Free water molecules moving among the air molecules are water vapor. The transformation of liquid into vapor is *evaporation*. It is the opposite of condensation.

The energy the molecules absorb from their surroundings, which breaks the hydrogen bonds, does not alter the temperature of the water. It is *latent heat,* and when water vapor condenses precisely the same amount of latent heat is released.

Molecules are constantly escaping from every exposed water surface. When they leave the surface they enter a thin *boundary layer* of air, where they join other water molecules. Together these molecules exert a pressure that drives molecules back into the liquid. Consequently, water molecules are entering the liquid as well as leaving it.

If the water surface is at a higher temperature than the air beyond the boundary layer, water molecules will have enough energy to escape into the air. More molecules will leave the surface than enter it, and the water will evaporate.

Water will also evaporate if there is a wind. This is because the wind removes moist air from above the water surface and replaces it with dry air. Consequently, wind has a powerful drying effect—which is why people hang out laundry to dry in the wind. Where the wind blows mainly from a particular direction, it can dry the leaf buds and the growing tips of stems on the exposed side of a tree. This slows or even prevents growth on that side of the tree, while the sheltered side grows normally. The effect is to shape the tree in a way that makes it look as though it is bending before the wind.

Trees, shrubs, and the smaller plants that grow on the forest floor obtain water from the soil and use it to transport nutrients and sugars to all parts of the plant (see "How trees find food" on page 77). Water finally enters cells lying just below the surface of leaves. These are the cells from which the plant expels oxygen and absorbs carbon dioxide (see "Photosynthesis and respiration" on page 79) through small pores, called *stomata*. While its stomata are open, however, water molecules also escape through them. The water is replaced by water from the ground, and there is a steady flow of water from the ground, through the plant, and into the air. This release of water into the air is called *transpiration*.

Transpiration releases a substantial amount of water into the air. In summer, an oak tree transpires about 185 gallons (700 liters) of water a day. It is possible to measure the rate of transpiration under laboratory conditions, but in the open air it is extremely difficult to separate the water entering the air by transpiration from that evaporating from wet surfaces. Scientists measure the two together, calling them *evapotranspiration*.

Transpiration absorbs latent heat from the leaves, cooling them. This prevents them from overheating in hot weather. At the same time, evapotranspiration absorbs so much latent heat that it has a significant effect on the climate inside a forest. Depending on the tree species, the air inside a temperate forest can be up to 8°F (4°C) cooler than the air outside. The difference is due partly to the shade cast by the trees but partly to evapotranspiration.

The amount of water entering the air through evapotranspiration also makes the air inside a forest moister than air outside. The relative humidity (see the sidebar "Humidity" on page 59) varies with the seasons, but on average it is 4–9 percent higher inside a forest than it is in adjacent open country. Air above the forest is also moister than the surrounding air, so forests encourage cloud formation and rainfall.

Forests move water from the ground to the air. Forests on hillsides help to prevent soil erosion and flooding in the valley, and temperate forests everywhere have an important influence on the local climate.

Thunderstorms and gales

Evaporation absorbs latent heat, and the condensation of water vapor into liquid water releases precisely the same amount of latent heat. Just as evapotranspiration cools the air inside a forest, condensation inside a cloud warms the air, sometimes with dramatic results.

Warm air rises and, as it does so, it expands and its temperature falls adiabatically (see the sidebar on page 58). Air temperature decreases with increasing height, but the rate at which this happens is not necessarily the same in still and rising air. If the temperature of the rising air falls to that of the surrounding air, all the air will have the same density and the air will rise no farther. This air is said to be *stable*. While the rising air remains warmer than the surrounding air, it will continue rising. Air in this condition is *unstable*. It is also possible for stable air to become unstable while it is rising. This air is *conditionally unstable* (see the sidebar).

Water vapor continues condensing as unstable air rises, producing "heaped" clouds. If the air is sufficiently moist and sufficiently unstable it will produce cumulonimbus storm clouds (see the sidebar "How clouds are classified" on page 60).

Air is rising strongly inside a big cumulonimbus. Condensation and deposition produce ice crystals, snowflakes, hailstones, and raindrops (see "Rain, snow, and hail" on page 61). Snow, hail, and rain fall from high in the cloud and as they fall they drag cold air down with them, producing downdrafts. Eventually, the cold downdrafts chill the air in the updrafts, preventing air from rising. The cloud then dissipates, sometimes dropping all of its water in a brief cloudburst.

While the cloud remains active, particles carrying a positive electrical charge accumulate near the top of the cloud and particles with negative charge accumulate near the base. Scientists are uncertain of just why this happens, but after a time the upper part of the cloud carries a positive electrical charge and the lower part carries a negative charge. The negative charge at the base of the cloud then induces a positive charge on the ground surface below. When these charges have accumulated sufficiently to overcome the electrical resistance of the air, a spark travels between them.

Lapse rates and stability

Air temperature decreases (or lapses) with increasing height. The rate at which it does so is called the *lapse rate.* Although all air contains some water vapor, air that is not saturated with moisture—all of its moisture is present as vapor rather than liquid droplets or ice crystals—is said to be *dry.* When dry air cools adiabatically, it does so at 5.4°F for every 1,000 feet (9.8°C/km) that it rises. This is known as the *dry adiabatic lapse rate* (DALR).

When the temperature of the rising air has fallen sufficiently, its water vapor will start to condense into droplets. Condensation commences at the *dew-point temperature* and the height at which this temperature is reached is called the *lifting condensation level.* Condensation releases *latent heat,* which warms the air. Latent heat is the energy that allows water molecules to break free from each other when liquid water vaporizes or ice melts. It does not change the temperature of the water or ice, which is why it is called *latent,* meaning "hidden." The same amount of latent heat is released, warming the surroundings, when water vapor condenses and when liquid water freezes. Consequently, the rising air then cools at a slower rate, known as the *saturated adiabatic lapse rate* (SALR). The SALR varies, depending on the rate of condensation, but it averages 3°F per 1,000 feet (6°C/km).

The actual rate at which the temperature decreases with height in air that is not rising is called the *environmental lapse rate* (ELR). It is calculated by comparing the

The spark is lightning. It may travel between different parts of a cloud or between one cloud and another. These are seen as *sheet lightning.* It may also travel between the cloud and the ground, as *forked lightning.*

Lightning releases so much energy that it heats the air next to the spark by up to 54,000°F (30,000°C) in less than one second, making the air expand so violently that it explodes and then contracts again. The explosion is heard as thunder.

Lightning can instantly vaporize water inside the trunk and branches of a tree. The sudden expansion of the water makes the tree explode. The explosion may destroy the tree, but more commonly it strips away some of the bark.

When lightning strikes the forest floor, the electric current may not be sustained for long enough for the heat to ignite dry material. This is called *cold lightning. Hot lightning* sustains surface temperature, the temperature at the tropopause (it is about −85°F; −65°C at the equator), and the height of the tropopause (about 10 miles; 16 km over the equator).

If the ELR is less than both the DALR and SALR, rising air will cool faster than the surrounding air, so it will always be cooler and will tend to subside to a lower height. Such air is said to be *absolutely stable.*

If the ELR is greater than the SALR, air that is rising and cooling at the DALR and later at the SALR will always be warmer than the surrounding air. Consequently, it will continue to rise. The air is then *absolutely unstable.*

If the ELR is less than the DALR but greater than the SALR, rising air will cool faster than the surrounding air while it remains dry but more slowly once it rises above the lifting condensation level. At first it is stable, but above the lifting condensation level it becomes unstable. This air said to be *conditionally unstable.* It is stable unless a condition (rising above its lifting condensation level) is met, whereupon it becomes unstable.

Stable air brings settled weather. Unstable air produces heaped clouds of the *cumulus* type. The base of these clouds is at the lifting condensation level, and the cloud tops are at the altitude where the rising air has lost enough water vapor to make it dry once more, so it is cooling at the DALR. If the air is sufficiently unstable, however, the clouds can grow into towering *cumulonimbus* storm clouds. Equatorial air is usually unstable.

the current for just a little longer. Dry material catches fire, smolders below the surface until the storm has passed, then bursts into flame.

If wind fans the flames, the result may be a forest fire, although fires are much less common in broad-leaved deciduous forests than they are in coniferous forests. Wind can cause serious damage, even without fires.

Trees absorb the force of the wind and those around the edge of a forest shelter the interior. The wind speed 100 feet (30 m) inside a forest is less than 80 percent of that outside. Wind speed is reduced to 50 percent 200 feet (60 m) from the edge, and 400 feet (120 m) from the edge it is less than 10 percent of the speed outside.

Often it is the trees on the edge that suffer, but not always. Trees that stand taller than those around them are at risk, but there are few of those, because exposed trees suffer badly from the drying effect of the wind (see "Evaporation and transpiration" on page 66). It can also happen that the wind brings down trees deep inside the forest while those at the edge remain standing.

Wind is the movement of air around areas of low or high pressure. Its strength is proportional to the rate at which the pressure changes with distance from the center of the system (see "Jet streams and depressions" on page 45). Technically, a gale is defined as any wind with a speed greater than 32 MPH (51.4 km/h), but a gale strong enough to break or uproot trees blows at more than 55 MPH (88.4 km/h).

Forest fires

Lightning strikes are the most common cause of natural fires. Fires are rare in broad-leaved deciduous forests, however. These forests grow in moist climates, so the fuel they provide is usually too wet to ignite easily, and the living trees do not burn readily. Their leaves contain water that makes them difficult to ignite and their wood burns slowly. This is not to say that broad-leaved deciduous forests are immune to fire. They are not. A prolonged spell of hot weather with no rain will dry out the dead leaves and branches lying on the forest floor until any small spark may set them alight.

Fires are much more common in coniferous forests. Coniferous trees contain resins, which are highly flammable, and their needles contain much less water than broad leaves, so they catch fire more readily.

Forest fires look terrifying, but they are not necessarily harmful. Some forest trees depend on fire to allow their seeds to sprout (see "Fire, and trees that depend on it" on page 120).

The truly frightening fires blaze through the crowns of the trees, leaping from tree to tree. Most forest fires do not spread in this way. They start among the dry litter on the forest floor and spread rapidly along the floor and just below the surface as a *ground fire*. A ground fire produces smoke, but no flames, and most ground fires travel only a short distance.

A ground fire will kill herbs and shrubs, as well as tree seedlings and young saplings, but the larger trees suffer nothing more serious than some scorching of their bark. The fire is not very hot. The temperature is usually between about 194°F (90°C) and 248°F (120°C) in the surface litter, but decreases rapidly below the surface. Most of the organisms living a few inches below the surface remain unharmed as the fire passes above them.

If the fire should burst into flame, however, it can become more serious, because there is a chance that it may spread upward into the crowns. A *crown fire* blazes fiercely and is spread from tree to tree by burning cinders that are carried aloft in rising hot air and then blown forward by the wind before falling back into the canopy.

Once it starts, a crown fire generates its own wind. Hot air rises rapidly, producing very strong vertical air currents, and the removal of air produces low atmospheric pressure near ground level. Surrounding air rushes into the low-pressure area, to be heated in its turn.

As it approaches the center of low pressure, the converging air starts to turn. In the Northern Hemisphere it turns counterclockwise (it turns clockwise in the Southern Hemisphere), until instead of flowing directly into the low-pressure region, the air spirals into it. The spiral tightens toward the center. The air turns in ever-smaller circles and this makes it accelerate. It becomes a twisting wind, like a tornado, and it can blow with great force. The fire has then generated a *firestorm*.

The hotter the fire, the fiercer is the storm that it generates. Like a blacksmith's bellows, the wind feeds oxygen to the flames, making them burn faster and hotter—and therefore making the wind blow even harder. The wind will pick up any material lying loose on the ground. Most of this will be flammable plant material and the wind will feed it into the core of the fire. A firestorm will die down only when it exhausts its supply of fuel.

Dry weather and lightning combine to start forest fires and the wind helps them to spread. Weather causes the fire, but if it blazes out of control a forest fire produces weather of its own.

CHAPTER 4

HOW TREES WORK

How trees evolved

Life on Earth began in water, and plants are descended from green single-celled organisms called *algae* (singular *alga*) that drifted near the surface. Their descendants are still there, and thriving, as the algae that give some seawater its green color. Other algae developed further and became much bigger plants. These are seaweeds, and some species, known as *kelp,* grow like vast, dense forests on the seabed, their "leaves" waving gently as the currents move them like trees bending in the wind. Several seaweed species grow in this way.

Oaks (Quercus *sp.*) *are magnificent trees, and never more so than when silhouetted against a night sky lit by the rising full Moon. (Courtesy of Fogstock)*

Oarweed, also called tangle (*Laminaria digitata*), is up to 13 feet (4 m) tall, and furbelows (*Saccorhiza polyschides*) can reach 14.75 feet (4.5 m), but the biggest of all are some *Macrocystis* and *Nereocystis* species, known as giant kelps, which can grow to a height of 100 feet (30 m).

Kelp seaweeds are very treelike. They have stems resembling tree trunks topped by blades that look like leaves. The stems are not rigid, however. When the plants are exposed at low tide they lie limply on the shore and their rubbery stems bend easily. They have no need to be rigid because kelps float in water, with *holdfasts* anchoring their flexible stems securely to rocks on the seafloor.

When plants first moved onto land, about 450 million years ago, they had to adapt to very different conditions. The first arrivals were most likely algae, in which the cells are linked to make long filaments. You can still see algae like this, called blanket weed (usually *Cladophora* species), attached to stones in fairly narrow, slow-moving rivers, its dark green filaments gently waving in the current like long hair billowing in the wind. Algae like these grew on the edges of lakes and marshes.

Algae cannot survive for long out of water, because their cells dry out. Plants that grow on dry land, exposed to the air, have a waterproof *cuticle* that covers them completely, like a skin, with pores called *stomata* to allow gases to enter and leave the plant.

Cooksonia plants were among the first to have a protective cuticle and were growing around marshes by 428 million years ago. They were soon joined by species of *Rhynia* and *Zosterophyllum*. These small plants—the biggest was about 20 inches (50 cm) tall—incorporated another important innovation: They were the first *vascular* plants. That means they had a system of tubular cells through which water, nutrients, and the sugars produced by photosynthesis (see "Photosynthesis and respiration" on pages 79–85) could move through the plant. Plants that live in water do not need to transport substances, because everything they need is dissolved in the water around them and they can absorb nutrients directly into their cells. Land plants must take carbon dioxide from the air and water and a range of nutrients from the soil. This is possible only if different parts of the plant specialize and substances are transported to where they are needed.

The first vascular plants were at an early stage in specialization, and they did not have true roots. Instead they absorbed water and nutrients through hairlike structures called *rhizoids* that lay along the ground surface. This was not very efficient, which is why the plants were small.

Progress was rapid, however, and the ancestor of all *gymnosperms*—the firs, pines, spruces, hemlocks, larches, cedars, and related plants—was growing by 360 million years ago. Called *Archaeopteris,* this first tree was up to 33 feet (10 m) tall, with a trunk up to five feet (1.5 m) in diameter at the base and leaves resembling the fronds of a fern. Within a few million years there were forests of *Archaeopteris* and other early trees and tree ferns.

Trees have been spectacularly successful at overcoming gravity. Buoyancy, which keeps kelp upright, is of no help to land plants that seek to raise their leaves above their neighbors. Watertight plant cells become rigid, or *turgid,* when they are filled with water, and water pressure—the scientific term is *turgor pressure*—is sufficient to hold small plants upright. It is not able to support the weight of a large plant, however. Tall plants, such as shrubs and trees, have cells that produce a hard substance called *lignin.* When the cells die and collapse the lignin remains. The process is called *lignification* and its product is wood (see "How wood forms" on pages 94–97). Woody plants are able to grow tall—and they did. Those early forests contained *Lepidodendron,* with a straight trunk up to 6.5 feet (2 m) in diameter and up to 130 feet (40 m) tall, and *Calamites,* a giant ancestor of modern horsetails (*Equisetum* species) that grew to about 50 feet (15 m).

Trees are very distinctive. You may not know the names of many plants, but you can tell whether or not a plant is a tree. It is tall. When fully grown a tree is at least 33 feet (10 m) tall. Most trees—though there are many exceptions—have only one stem, or trunk. Branches emerge from the trunk, and the lowest branch usually joins the trunk at least four feet (1.2 m) above the ground. The trunk and branches are hard to the touch. If the plant is smaller than a tree and has several woody stems it is a shrub.

How trees find food

Animals move around in search of food. They find plants they can eat or, if they are meat eaters, other animals they can catch. Plants cannot move around—they are literally rooted to the spot, and it is their roots that feed them as well as anchoring them securely to the ground. A tree that towers majestically into the sky is a giant, its branches spreading wide so its millions of leaves are able to absorb the sunshine, but only part of the plant is visible. Below ground the tree has a system of roots that extends far beyond the crown above ground. The root system accounts for 20–25 percent of the total mass of the tree.

It is not easy to examine the roots of a full-grown tree. When a tree is blown down by the wind its roots are exposed, but individual roots break as the tree falls, and the part that remains—the *root plate*—is only a small fraction of the original root system. It is not practicable to dig out an entire tree and then carefully wash all the soil from the roots. Until recently scientists had no choice but to assume that the roots of a mature tree resembled those of a seedling—which they could see, measure, and scale up to an appropriate size.

Nowadays it is possible to use ground-penetrating radar, which identifies the roots and allows scientists to map their location and extent without damaging them. When this was first done the results came as a surprise: Tree roots are not at all how they had been pictured.

Rainwater dripping from leaves at the edges of the crown marks a *drip line* surrounding the tree. Botanists and foresters had supposed that a tree spread its roots sideways approximately as far as this line. The radar studies revealed that in fact the tree roots extend far beyond the drip line, in some cases as much as 10 times farther.

Scientists had also believed that most broad-leaved trees, such as oaks, had thick roots, called *taproots,* that descended vertically to a considerable depth. When a seed germinates, the *radicle,* which later becomes the root, grows vertically downward, and tree seedlings of these species do develop taproots. It was assumed that these continued to grow as the tree matured. In fact, the taproots do not develop. Almost all

Extent of the root system of a fully grown tree. Note that the roots extend a long way from the trunk but are quite shallow.

of the tree's roots are within the uppermost three feet (1 m) of the soil, and most of the fine roots through which the tree absorbs nutrients are within about eight inches (20 cm) of the ground surface. The illustration shows a complete tree, including the roots, as these have been revealed by modern studies.

Tree roots are woody, like the trunk and branches. They never bear leaves or flowers, but they produce many branches as they push their way through the soil. A *root cap,* made from a layer of tough tissue, protects the tip of each root. Abrasion with the soil strips away the root cap as the tip advances, but the tissue is constantly renewed and the cells of the active growing region never lose their protection.

On the surface of the root behind the tip, a layer of cells produce a fine "fur" of *root hairs,* each no more than about 0.2 inch (4 mm) long. These are the roots through which the tree absorbs most of its nutrients. The tree's root hairs would stretch for hundreds of miles if all of them were laid end to end. The root hairs are always located just behind the root tip. As the root grows longer, old hairs are shed and new ones appear. Nutrients enter the plant mainly near the root tips, although some enter along the entire length of the roots.

The roots seek moisture in the soil (see "How water moves through a temperate forest" on pages 29–33), and root hairs cling tightly to soil particles. Various minerals are dissolved in the water coating these particles, and as this water passes through the root hairs and into the main body of the root, the dissolved minerals go with it. Inside the root a complex filtering system allows some minerals to pass while excluding and excreting others. The root is very selective and is able to extract the important nutrient minerals from the dilute soil solution and concentrate them before passing them to the trunk, branches, buds, leaves, and flowers, where the nutrients are needed.

Trees—indeed, most plants—have help in acquiring nutrients. Their roots develop close relationships, called *mycorrhizae*, with soil fungi. The fungi obtain carbohydrates from the tree and supply minerals to the tree root, so both organisms benefit.

All plants require a range of mineral nutrients, known as *essential elements*. Those that are needed in relatively large amounts are known as *macronutrients* and include nitrogen, phosphorus, potassium, sulfur, magnesium, and calcium. A variety of minerals are needed in much smaller amounts, and not all of them by every species of plant. These are called *micronutrients* and include iron, copper, zinc, molybdenum, manganese, cobalt, and boron. The essential elements are constantly recycled, moving between the air, water, and living organisms. Plants also need carbon, hydrogen, and oxygen for the production of carbohydrates through the process of *photosynthesis*.

Photosynthesis and respiration

Throughout the cold, dark winter the forest lay dormant. Last year's leaves lay as a carpet across the ground and the trees were bare. The branches were bare, but there were buds on all the twigs, enclosing and protecting next year's leaves. Winter passed, and as the days grew longer and the sunshine warmer those buds swelled. Then, in the course of a few

The nitrogen cycle

Nitrogen is a colorless, odorless gas that composes 78 percent of the air. It is an ingredient of all proteins and consequently an essential macronutrient for all living organisms, but it is useless to most of them in its gaseous form. Before plants can absorb and utilize it, the nitrogen must be *fixed*—made to react with another element to form a compound.

Lightning makes nitrogen (N) react with oxygen (O), producing nitrogen oxides that dissolve in raindrops (H_2O) to form weak nitric acid (HNO_3). When nitric acid reaches the soil it is converted into nitrate (NO_3), a soluble form in which plant roots are able to absorb it. Certain soil bacteria are able to utilize nitrogen gas directly. In doing so, they convert the nitrogen to nitrate; this bacterial process is called *nitrification.*

Plants use the nitrogen they absorb to manufacture proteins. Animals obtain their proteins by eating plants. Plant and animal wastes and the remains of dead plants and animals decompose through the action of soil animals, fungi, and bacteria. The decomposers convert the proteins to ammonia (NH_3). Ammonia dissolves in water, and some of it is absorbed by plant roots and used to make more protein. Ammonia evaporates readily (it boils at $-29°F$; $-34°C$) and a small amount returns to the air. The remainder of the ammonia combines with carbon dioxide (CO_2) to form ammonium carbonate $((NH_4)CO_3)$. Nitrification by other bacteria converts ammonium carbonate to nitrous acid (NHO_2), with the release of energy: $(NH_4)CO_3 + 3O_2 \rightarrow 2NHO_2 + CO_2 + 2H_2O + energy$. (The arrow indicates the direction in which the chemical reaction moves; in this case ammonium carbonate reacts with oxygen to produce nitrous acid, carbon dioxide, and water with the release of energy.)

Nitrous acid reacts with magnesium (Mg) or calcium (Ca) to form magnesium or calcium nitrite ($Ca(NO_2)_2$ or $Mg(NO_2)_2$), which other bacteria nitrify to produce more nitrate: $2Ca(NO_2)_2$ (or $2Mg(NO_2)_2$) $+ 2O_2 \rightarrow 2Ca(NO_3)_2$ (or $2Mg(NO_3)_2$) $+ energy$.

Finally, another type of bacteria converts the nitrogen compounds to either nitrogen gas or ammonia; the process is called *denitrification.* Ammonia that evaporates into the air

weeks, all of them burst open and suddenly the forest was green. The trees were in leaf—and working.

Green leaves are factories that manufacture sugar, using carbon dioxide and water as the raw materials and sunlight as a source of energy. The leaves are green because they contain *chlorophyll,* a chemical substance that traps light energy.

is quickly oxidized to nitrate and returns to the soil, where it is absorbed by plants. Eventually, all the nitrogen that enters the soil returns to the air.

The diagram summarizes the cycle in which atmospheric nitrogen passes through living organisms and returns to the air.

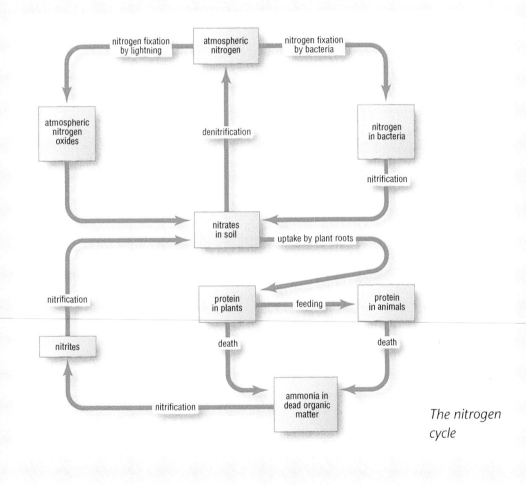

The nitrogen cycle

Chlorophyll is green. It is one of several *photosynthetic pigments*, each of which absorbs light at a slightly different wavelength. Two varieties of chlorophyll a are also known as P700 and P680. "P" is for "pigment" and the numbers refer to the wavelengths (in nanometers) of the red light they absorb. Chlorophyll a is blue-green. Chlorophyll b is very similar, but it is yellow-green. Xanthophylls and carotenoids are the most important of the other photosynthetic pigments. Xanthophylls are yellow and carotenoids are various shades of orange through red. Each pigment absorbs light at a slightly different wavelength, so the presence of several pigments widens the range of light the leaf cells can absorb. The two varieties of chlorophyll a are the most abundant and the most important.

All of the photosynthetic pigments reside on stacks of membranes, called *thylakoid membranes,* inside bodies called *chloroplasts.* Chloroplasts once lived independently and they

Photosynthesis

Green plants and some bacteria are able to use energy from sunlight (photo-) to assemble (synthesize) sugars. The process is called *photosynthesis* and it depends on a pigment called *chlorophyll.* Chlorophyll is green and it is what gives plants their green color.

Photosynthesis proceeds in two stages. The first stage depends on light, and it is called the *light-dependent* or *light* stage. The second stage does not use light energy, so it is called the *light-independent* or *dark* stage (although it also takes place in the light).

Light-dependent stage. When a photon (a unit of light) possessing precisely the right amount of energy strikes a chlorophyll molecule, the photon disappears and its energy is absorbed, allowing an electron (a particle carrying negative charge) in the molecule to break free. This leaves the chlorophyll molecule with a positive charge. The free electron immediately attaches to a neighboring molecule, thereby ejecting another electron that moves to a neighboring molecule. In this way electrons pass along an *electron-transport chain* of molecules. Each plant cell contains a number of chloroplasts and each chloroplast contains many molecules of chlorophyll, so while the plant is exposed to light there is a constant stream of photons being captured and electrons moving along the electron-transport chain.

Some of the transported energy is used to convert adenosine diphosphate (ADP) to adenosine triphosphate (ATP) by the addition of phosphate, after which the electron then returns to the chlorophyll. Converting ADP to ATP absorbs energy; converting ATP to ADP releases the energy. The ADP $\leftrightarrow$ ATP reaction (the double arrow indicates the reaction can move in either direction) is used by all living organisms to transport energy and release it where it is needed.

still have their own DNA allowing them to reproduce, but very early in the development of life on Earth they moved inside other cells. Today the chloroplasts live inside the *mesophyll cells* that form the inside of leaves. Each mesophyll cell contains 30–40 chloroplasts.

Chloroplasts are the "factories" in which the leaves take carbon dioxide (CO_2) from the air and water (H_2O) carried to them from the ground below as the raw materials for the production of sugars, such as glucose ($C_6H_{12}O_6$). The process by which light (*photo*) supplies the energy to assemble (*synthesize*) sugars is called *photosynthesis* (see the sidebar).

Energy that is not used to convert ADP to ATP is used to split a water molecule (H_2O) into a hydrogen ion, which bears a positive charge (H^+), and a hydroxyl ion, which has a negative charge (OH^-). (An *ion* is an atom that has gained or lost one or more electrons, so it bears a positive or negative charge.) The H^+ attaches to a molecule of nicotinamide adenine dinucleotide phosphate (NADP), converting it to reduced NADP (NADPH). The OH^- passes one electron to the chlorophyll molecule, restoring the neutrality of both chlorophyll and hydroxyl. Hydroxyls then combine to form water ($4OH \rightarrow 2H_2O + O_2\uparrow$). (The upward arrow in this chemical formula indicates that the oxygen is released into the air.) This completes the light-dependent stage.

Light-independent stage. Using ATP from the light-dependent stage as a source of energy, the first in a series of chemical reactions attaches molecules of carbon dioxide (CO_2) obtained from the air to molecules of ribulose biphosphate (RuBP), a substance present in the chloroplast. The enzyme RuBP carboxylase (the name is usually abbreviated to *rubisco*) catalyzes the reaction. In a cycle of reactions the carbon atoms, originally from the carbon dioxide, are combined with hydrogen obtained from NADPH; the NADP then returns to the light-dependent stage. The cycle ends with the synthesis of molecules of glucose and of RuBP. The RuBP is then available to commence the cycle again.

Glucose, a simple sugar, is the most common source of energy for living things; its energy is released by the process of *respiration*. Glucose is also used to synthesize complex sugars: starch and cellulose in plants and glycogen (also called animal starch) in animals. Plants use cellulose to build cell walls; starch and glycogen can be converted to glucose, releasing energy.

Photosynthesis is the process that assembles glucose. Glucose has a number of uses, one of which is as a fuel. Burning fuel such as coal, wood, oil, or gas creates the conditions in which carbon in the fuel can combine with oxygen in the air. This reaction releases energy—the heat of the fire. When the carbon in glucose combines with oxygen, the energy that is released is used to make muscles move, to drive chemical reactions, and to move molecules into and out of cells. The process by which it does so is called *respiration* and it is the opposite of photosynthesis. Respiration should not be confused with breathing. Breathing is the physical activity by which terrestrial vertebrates draw in air into the lungs so that oxygen from the air can enter the bloodstream. This supplies the oxygen needed for respiration, but breathing and respiration are not the same thing.

Photosynthesis takes place in chloroplasts, located in the leaves. Respiration takes place in *mitochondria,* bodies (*organelles*) that are found in every living cell. Like chloroplasts, mitochondria were once independent organisms, but they became incorporated into other cells.

In the overall reaction glucose ($C_6H_{12}O_6$) reacts with oxygen (O_2) to produce carbon dioxide (CO_2) and water (H_2O). It is easy to see how respiration is the precise opposite of photosynthesis when the two reactions are compared:

$$6CO_2 + 6H_2O + energy \rightarrow C_6H_{12}O_6 + 6O_2 \text{ (photosynthesis)}$$

$$C_6H_{12}O_6 + 6O_2 \rightarrow 6CO_2 + 6H_2O + energy \text{ (respiration)}$$

Respiration does not convert glucose to energy directly, but does so through a process called *phosphorylation,* in which phosphate groups are moved from one molecule to another. When ATP loses a phosphate group, that group is transferred to another molecule. Phosphorylation may cause a muscle cell to move, a molecule to enter or leave a cell, or a chemical reaction to take place. The phosphorylation that activates one molecule also converts ATP to ADP. Respiration releases the energy that is needed to phosphorylate ADP, changing it back into ATP and leaving it ready to do more useful work.

How trees reproduce

Trees spread their roots widely, and for some species this pro-vides an opportunity for new trees to grow. The roots are not far beneath the ground surface, and although roots do not produce leaves or flowers, shoots develop at intervals along the roots of some species. They are called *adventitious* shoots because they grow from an unusual position on the plant. The shoots grow into new trees, resulting in a group of trees all of the same species. In fact, they are all parts of the same tree, sharing the same root system. This type of reproduction is said to be *asexual* or *vegetative*. Not all species are able to reproduce in this way. Elms (*Ulmus* species), lindens and bass-woods (*Tilia* species), and aspens (*Populus* species) often do so. Aspens can produce a grove of thousands of trees, all from a single parent tree.

The ability to reproduce asexually makes a tree virtually immortal. Individual trees grow old and die, but there are always more growing from the original root system. Provided they do not succumb to a fatal disease or are unable to toler-ate a change in their environment—and provided no one cuts them down, of course—a tree can live in this way for thousands of years.

More important, perhaps, is the fact that asexual reproduc-tion allows trees to thrive in places where the climate is too cold for them to produce ripe seeds. All of the trees that reproduce asexually are capable of reproducing sexually, from seed, but to produce seeds they need more sunshine and warmth than northern regions can guarantee. They pro-duce healthy seeds only in warm years, and the amount of seeds is highly variable. Without an alternative means of reproduction they would be unable to compete with trees that are better suited to the climate.

Sexual reproduction involves the combining of *chromo-somes*—threadlike structures carrying genes that are present in the nucleus of all living plant cells—from a male and female parent. Most cells carry two copies of each chromo-some. Such cells are said to be *diploid*. When diploid cells divide in order to repair damaged tissue or to allow the plant to grow, they do so by a process called *mitosis*. Mitosis pro-duces two identical *daughter cells,* each of which is diploid.

The cells involved in reproduction—sperm and egg cells (called *ovules*)—are known as *gametes*. Gametes are *haploid,* which means they possess only one set of chromosomes. They are produced from diploid cells by a form of cell division called *meiosis,* in which the cell divides twice to produce four haploid cells.

Trees, like all other plants, have a life cycle that takes them through two distinct forms, one diploid and the other haploid. Each form gives rise to, or generates, the other. Thus the two forms are generations—each is both parent and offspring of the other—and the plant life cycle consists of an *alternation of generations.* The diploid generation is called a *sporophyte* and the haploid generation a *gametophyte.* One of these forms is much bigger and more prominent than the other. In bryophytes—mosses, liverworts, and hornworts—the plant one sees is the gametophyte. In all larger plants, including trees, the plant one sees is the sporophyte. Pollen grains, containing sperm, are the male gametophytes and egg cells are

Many trees produce edible fruits. These are English black walnuts (Juglans nigra). (Courtesy of Christ Jongman, Foto Natura, Minden Pictures)

the female gametophytes. The gametophyte generation is sheltered in the cones of coniferous (cone-bearing) trees and in the flowers of flowering trees (see "Differences between conifers and flowering plants" below).

When a pollen grain reaches the stigma of a flower or an ovule in the female cone of a conifer, a tube grows from the pollen grain and reaches the egg cell. Sperm then travel from the pollen grain along the tube and into the ovule, where the chromosomes from the two gametes unite. The fusion of gametes that produces the diploid cell that will become a new plant is called *fertilization*.

The resulting diploid cell is called a *zygote*. It divides by mitosis. As it does so, different cells begin to specialize and the zygote develops into an *embryo*. The embryo contains simple leaves, called *cotyledons* or *seed leaves*; a *plumule* that will grow into a shoot; and a *radicle* that will grow into a root. The embryo is surrounded by a store of nutrients that will sustain the young plant until it has grown large enough to feed itself, and the embryo and its food store are enclosed by a protective *seed coat*. The complete structure is then a *seed*, from which the next sporophyte generation may grow.

Differences between conifers and flowering plants

Two very distinct types of trees—conifers and broad-leaved species—grow in temperate forests. The two look so very different that it is easy to tell them apart. Conifers produce cones—*conifer* means "cone-bearing." No broad-leaved tree produces cones. Broad-leaved trees bear flowers. No conifer bears true flowers, although the male cones of some species look a little like flowers and are sometimes called flowers. Conifers and broad-leaved trees have very different leaves. Those of conifers are small and either very narrow and often sharp like needles, or flattened to form scales. As their name suggests, broad-leaved trees have broad leaves. Many conifers, although not all, have an overall conical shape, with a single straight trunk and straight branches that are shorter the higher they are. Broad-leaved trees have a more spreading, rounded shape.

These are obvious differences. There are other, more important differences in the way the two types of tree grow and reproduce. All conifers belong to a group of plants called *gymnosperms* that appeared on Earth about 400 million years ago. Broad-leaved trees belong to a group called angiosperms, and the first of them appeared about 130 million years ago. Garden flowers, grasses, farm crops, and shrubs as well as broad-leaved trees are angiosperms. The angiosperms proved so much more successful than the gymnosperms that there are now approximately 235,000 species of angiosperms, compared with only about 735 species of gymnosperms. About 550 of these are conifers. The others are cycads, sometimes called sago palms although they are not true palm trees; the ginkgo; and the gnetophytes, a group of tropical plants that includes trees, shrubs, lianas, and smaller plants.

Both gymnosperms and angiosperms are *vascular* plants. That is to say, water, dissolved nutrients, and sugars produced by photosynthesis are transported through the plants along channels. The channels that carry water and nutrients from the soil to every part of the plant are known as *xylem* tissue. Those that transport sugars from the leaves are called *phloem* tissue.

Xylem cells are dead. In gymnosperms the xylem tissue consists of long, tubular cells called *tracheids,* with tapered ends perforated by small openings called *pits*. Tracheids grow end to end with their tapered ends overlapping. Rings or spirals of a tough substance called *lignin* strengthen their walls. As well as conducting water, tracheids help to support the trunk and branches of the plant.

Angiosperm xylem consists of *vessel elements*, which are shorter and wider than tracheids. They conduct water more efficiently than tracheids but give little mechanical support. The plant relies on *fibers* for support. These are long, narrow cells rich in lignin.

Gymnosperms possess some fiber cells and angiosperms possess some tracheids, but vessel elements are found only in angiosperms. Botanists believe that vessel elements and fiber cells both evolved from tracheids.

Phloem cells are alive, although they possess no nucleus. In both gymnosperms and angiosperms, phloem consists of cells called *sieve elements*. These are cylindrical and have perforated ends called *sieve plates*. The cells are joined end to end to form *sieve tubes*. In angiosperms, each sieve element is linked to one or more *companion cells*. Companion cells have nuclei and are intensely active; they probably supply the sieve elements with energy and nutrients. Gymnosperm phloem lacks companion cells. Instead, *parenchyma* cells surround the sieve elements and may serve the same purpose. Parenchyma cells are unspecialized. They manufacture and store a range of substances.

Significant though they are, these are not the most important differences between the two groups of plants—the difference that gives them their names. That difference is the flower itself. At the base of the flower (see the sidebar on page 90) is the ovary, which contains and protects the ovules. Angiosperm means "seed vessel," from *angeion* ("vessel") and *sperma* ("seed").

Gymnosperms do not produce flowers. They have male cones that produce pollen and female cones that hold the ovules on their scales. The ovules are not contained in an ovary, and consequently the seeds that develop from the fertilized ovules are not protected by the ovary walls: They are naked. The Greek word *gymnos* means "naked," and so "gymnosperm" means "naked seed."

Lacking flowers to attract insects or other pollinators, gymnosperms rely on the wind for pollination, and their life cycle is more complicated than that of angiosperms. It takes three years for a gymnosperm to produce seeds from the time the cones first appear.

How seeds disperse

Once it has produced seeds a tree needs to disperse them. It could simply release them as soon as they were ready to germinate. This would be wasteful, however, because most of the seeds would fall to the ground around the base of their parent, where they would have to compete for light, water, and nutrients with their overwhelmingly bigger parent. Not all the seeds land beside their parent, of course. Some drift with the wind, landing farther away where conditions may be more favorable.

What is a flower?

A flower is the reproductive structure of a flowering plant, containing and protecting the gametophyte generation (the reproductive stage in the plant's life cycle). Flowers vary greatly in appearance. *Rafflesia arnoldii,* a plant that parasitizes the roots of tropical trees, has flowers up to 32 inches (80 cm) across that smell of rotting meat (to attract the flies that pollinate it). Scarlet pimpernel (*Anagallis arvensis*) flowers are 0.4–0.6 inches (10–15 mm) across. A sunflower (*Helianthus* species) is a composite of hundreds of tiny flowers, called *florets.* Some flowers are brightly colored and others, such as grass flowers, have no petals and are inconspicuous.

Despite the great variety of forms, however, all flowers can be related to a generalized description. A particular flower may not possess all of the parts of the general flower shown in the drawing, but those it does possess will be included in the description.

Small green leaves at the base of the flower where the flower stem, or *peduncle,* joins the main body of the plant are called *bracts.* Some plants have bracts that are shaped differently from the plant's other leaves.

The upper end of the peduncle is swollen to form the *receptacle.* The other parts of the flower are attached to the receptacle. *Nectaries* on the surface of the receptacle are glands that secrete nectar, a sweet-tasting liquid; as pollinating insects (and in some parts of the world birds and bats) probe flowers for nectar, pollen clings to their bodies.

Sepals are modified leaves attached to the receptacle below the main part of the flower. The sepals enclose the inner parts of the flower, forming the outer layer of the flower bud. They protect the flower until it is ready to open. Sepals are usually green, but in some species, such as *Poinsettia* and marsh marigold (*Caltha palustris*), they are colored. Together, the set of sepals composes the *calyx.*

Above the receptacle (and attached to it) there are the female and male reproductive organs. The female organ is called the *carpel* and the male organs are the *stamens.*

The carpel consists of the *stigma, style,* and *ovary.* The stigma has a sticky surface onto which pollen grains are deposited. The style links the stigma to the ovary, which contains the *ovules* (female gametes). Flowers evolved from modified leaves, and the carpel may have originated as a rolled-up leaf.

One solution to the difficulty is for fallen seeds to lie dormant in the ground until competing trees die. Most tree seeds need to germinate within 18 months or less, but some

The stamen consists of a *filament* at the top of which there is a club-shaped *anther,* where pollen grains are produced. Pollen grains mature into male gametophytes. The drawing shows only six, but a flower usually has many filaments and anthers.

If the ovary is attached to the receptacle above the level at which the filaments are attached (as in the drawing) it is said to be *superior.* If it is attached below the filaments it is *inferior.*

Petals are modified leaves that surround and partly enclose the male and female organs. The ring of petals is called the *corolla.* In some flowers the edges of the petals are partly joined and the petals form a *corolla tube.* Together, the outer calyx and inner corolla are known as the *perianth.*

A flower that possesses stamens, carpel, calyx, and corolla is said to be *complete.* Many flowers lack one or more of these parts and are therefore *incomplete.*

A flower that possesses both male and female organs is said to be *perfect.* A *staminate* flower has only stamens and a *carpellate* flower has only a carpel. Staminate and carpellate flowers are *imperfect.*

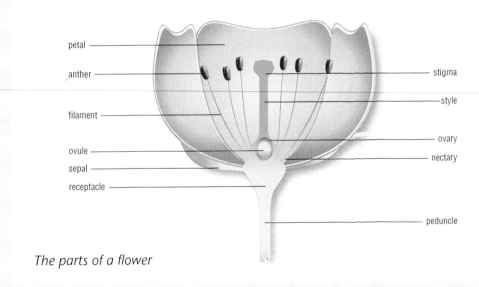

The parts of a flower

species produce seeds that remain viable for several years. These seeds remain in the ground, forming a *seed bank.* Paper birch (*Betula papyrifera*) and yellow birch (*B. alleghaniensis*) seeds are able to survive in this way. Certain coniferous trees, especially some pines (*Pinus* species), retain their seeds in their cones until conditions are suitable for them to germinate (see "Fire, and trees that depend on it" on pages 120–123).

A seed that germinates in a place overshadowed by full-grown trees will not produce a young tree that grows very large, but this may not matter. Walk through a forest and you will see many small tree seedlings. These look like young plants, but they may have remained at the same size for many years. They are waiting until a nearby tree falls. When it does they will grow rapidly to take its place. Not all tree species produce seedlings that can survive for long in this state of arrested development, but many common forest trees do, including hemlock (*Tsuga canadensis*), beech (*Fagus grandifolia*), sugar maple (*Acer saccharum*), and white oak (*Quercus alba*).

Other trees produce seeds that disperse passively, carried by the wind. Birches (*Betula* species), ashes (*Fraxinus* species), elms (*Ulmus* species), and maples (*Acer* species) are among the trees that produce winged seeds, or *keys*. The illustration shows the keys of maple and birch.

A winged seed—the botanical term is *samara*—spins as it falls. This slows its rate of fall. In still air the wings will have no other effect, because the seed falls vertically, but even the slightest breath of wind will carry the seed away from the parent tree.

Even with wings, seeds seldom travel far, and whether or not they germinate is very much a matter of luck. Most trees that rely on this type of dispersal produce vast quantities of seeds and the seeds themselves are usually small.

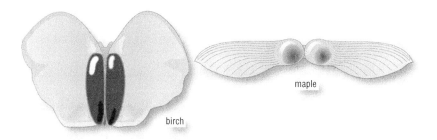

birch

maple

Winged seeds

There is another way to disperse seeds, however, and that is to recruit animals for the purpose. This is called *active dispersal*. Birds and mammals are free to move where they will, so they can carry seeds much farther than the wind can. Obviously, these seed carriers must be "paid," and the way to do that is to make the seeds edible. Squirrels are famous for their habit of gathering tree seeds, preferring those of hickory, beech, and oak. Some birds, such as the acorn woodpecker (*Melanerpes formicivorus*) and the Eurasian jay (*Garrulus glandarius*) also collect acorns from around oak trees.

They gather seeds in order to eat them, of course, so this may not seem to be the best way for a tree to reproduce. It works because the seed gatherers collect food when it is plentiful and store the surplus for the winter, when food is scarce. Squirrels bury their hoards, but they are notoriously inefficient at finding them again. They search for their stores by scent, but the seeds are odorless when the ground is dry. Consequently, the squirrels never recover all of their seeds and some, conveniently buried in fertile soil, are able to germinate. The jay, on the other hand, has a truly remarkable memory. It buries up to 4,000 acorns singly and remembers where it put every one of them, but a jay seldom eats all of them, and so some germinate. The acorn woodpecker does not help the trees at all, however. It drills holes in dead trees and fence posts and stores its acorns there, where they have no chance of germinating.

Flowering plants have developed a much better alternative to edible seeds: edible fruit. The fruit is rich in sugar and therefore a valuable source of energy. It is usually brightly colored, so the fruit eaters can find it easily, and it changes color as it ripens so consumers can tell when it is ready to eat—which is also when the seeds are ready to be dispersed.

The seeds are inside the fruit and have tough seed coats that make them indigestible. If the seeds are small, the animal will swallow them as it eats the fruit. They will then pass through its digestive system to be voided with the feces. By the time it defecates, the animal will be far away from the fruit tree and its feces will supply the seed with manure to help the seedling. If the seed is large, like that of a cherry or plum, the animal will eat the fruit from around it and leave the seed on the ground. Even then the seed may travel a long way, because the animal may have carried the fruit some distance to a place where it can eat without fear of being attacked or robbed.

How wood forms

At the tip of each twig there is a bud, made up of a dome-shaped mass of cells, known as *meristem* cells, that are able to divide to produce more tissue. Many trees also have meristem tissue in the *axils* where twigs join the main branch. Growth from these buds makes twigs longer and produces new twigs. This is *primary growth.* If it were the only type of growth, the tree would grow longer and longer twigs and a longer and longer trunk, but none of these would grow any thicker. The tree—if you could call it a tree—would sprawl across the ground as a spindly plant too weak to support its own weight.

It is *secondary growth* that makes the trunk and branches thicker—and that produces wood. Trees have trunks and branches made from wood, and wood is the most important material people obtain from trees.

Wood is a highly structured material. The grain, exposed when wood is cut, and the rings that are clearly visible in the cross section when a trunk or branch is severed reveal the structure.

Forming a ring around the trunk that extends into the branches, tracheids, vessel elements, fibers, and sieve elements (see "Differences between conifers and flowering plants" on pages 87–89) are packed together in *vascular bundles,* with the xylem and phloem lying side by side. Xylem is on the inside of the ring and phloem on the outside. *Pith rays* radiating from the center of the trunk or branch to the outer bark consist of stacks of *parenchyma* cells—all-purpose cells—most of which store starch, a source of energy for the plant.

Meristem cells are located among the vascular bundles and in the pith rays. Those in the pith rays divide to extend the rays as the trunk or branch grows thicker. The meristem cells in the vascular bundles form a layer, in most trees no more than one cell thick, of tissue called *vascular cambium.* A meristem cell is known as an *initial* and the cells it produces are called *derivatives*. In the vascular cambium each initial divides to produce two more cambium cells—initials. One of the initials then divides to produce a derivative—a different kind of cell. Initials nearest the center of the tree produce xylem cells and initials nearest the outside of the tree produce phloem cells.

Outside the phloem tissue there is a second cambium layer, called *cork cambium*. This cambium gives rise to the cells composing the "skin" of the tree. Cork cambium initials give rise to derivatives that lay down a coating of waxy material, called *suberin,* in their walls and then die. The dead cells form a layer of *cork* that makes the trunk or branch waterproof and protects it against attack by insects. Unlike the vascular cambium, the cork cambium is not permanent and does not surround the entire trunk or branch. It is produced where and when it is needed. After a few weeks its initials turn into cork cells and die, whereupon the cork cambium disappears. On the outside of the tree, the "skin" dries and splits as the tree grows, and more cork cambium is produced to fill the gaps.

As phloem cells die they turn into cork cells and add to the cork layer, while parenchyma cells among the phloem cells turn into meristem cells to produce new cork cambium. Together, the phloem, cork cambium, and cork layer make up the *bark* of the tree. The vascular cambium and xylem comprise the *sapwood.* If the sapwood is cut, liquid—sap— leaks from it. This is the living part of the trunk or branch. A tree will die if bark is removed completely in a ring all around the trunk. This is called *ringbarking,* and by severing the phloem it prevents sugars from the leaves reaching the roots. Unable to respire (see "Photosynthesis and respiration" on pages 79–85), the roots die, ending the supply of water and nutrients to the tree, and the entire tree dies.

Each year the vascular cambium produces more xylem and phloem cells. These are needed because, as the tree grows taller and its branches grow longer, its tissues need more water and its leaves produce more sugars, and more vascular tissue is needed to transport them. This gives rise to secondary growth, which happens because each new layer of xylem is laid around the outside of the preceding layer, making the trunk or branch grow thicker and, of course, necessitating the formation of more bark to cover it.

Meanwhile older xylem cells die. They are already strengthened with lignin and this tough substance remains, as does the lignin in the long fiber cells embedded in the vascular bundles. The old cells often fill with waste products, which alters their color. The cells are no longer capable of conducting water. Instead they form a dense mass of tough, fibrous material rich in lignin. This is *heartwood*, which forms a central column that adds greatly to the strength of the tree. The illustration shows a cross section through a tree trunk, with the layers labeled.

In temperate forests, growth does not continue throughout the year. It commences in spring, when the vascular cambium produces wide xylem cells with thin walls. These form a pale, fairly wide band around the previous year's xylem. Later in the summer the cambium produces smaller cells with darker, thicker walls that pack into a narrow, dark-

Cross section through a tree trunk, showing the dead heartwood, living sapwood (xylem tissue), vascular cambium, and the phloem, cork cambium, and cork, which together compose the bark.

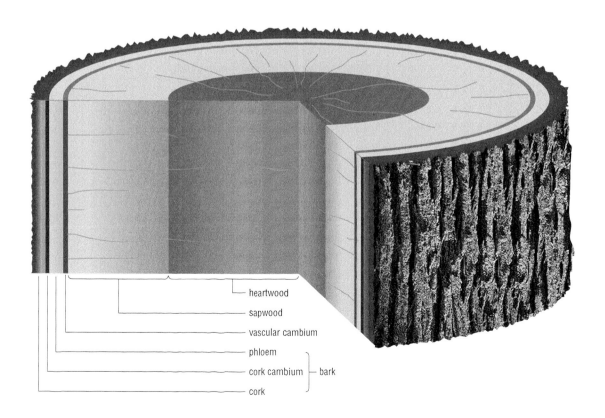

- heartwood
- sapwood
- vascular cambium
- phloem
- cork cambium ⎤
- cork ⎦ — bark

Peeling bark on paper birch (Betula papyrifera) (Courtesy of Jim Brandenburg, Minden Pictures)

colored band around the spring xylem. When growth ceases for the winter the secondary growth remains as two bands around the trunk or branch, one pale and the other dark. Each year another pair of these layers is added. That is how secondary growth produces the annual growth rings that are clearly visible when a tree is felled.

CHAPTER 5

ECOLOGY OF TEMPERATE FORESTS

How ecological ideas developed

One of the largest European temperate forests covers about 725 square miles (1,878 km^2) on the plain that straddles the border between Poland and Belarus. Its Polish name is the Białowieża Forest and in Belarus it is known as the Belovezhskaya Pushcha. It is a World Heritage Site.

The forest contains a variety of coniferous and broad-leaved tree species. There are Scots pine (*Pinus sylvestris*), Norway spruce (*Picea abies*), European common hornbeam (*Carpinus betulus*), small-leaved lime (*Tilia cordata,* sometimes called littleleaf linden), English oak (*Quercus robur*), Eurasian sycamore (*Acer pseudoplatanus*), maples (*Acer* species), ash (*Fraxinus excelsior*), two species of birch (*Betula*), aspen (*Populus tremula*), and European black alder (*Alnus glutinosa*). These are the principal species, but in addition there are more than 900 other species of vascular plants, as well as lichens, liverworts, and more than 1,500 species of fungi.

Obviously, a forest of this size harbors many animals. There are 55 species of mammals, including the European bison (*Bison bonasus*), gray wolf (*Canis lupus*), lynx (*Felis lynx*), and wild boar (*Sus scrofa*), as well as 212 species of birds, 11 of amphibians, and seven of reptiles. The forest has more than 8,500 species of insects.

Listing the species present in a forest, or any other area, gives the impression that the plants and animals are scattered evenly, as though you could take an area anywhere in the forest and find all the plants and most of the animals. It is not like that, however. There are plant *associations*. In some places linden (lime) and hornbeam grow side by side; in other places there are oak and hornbeam. In all, there are 12 of these associations in the Belarus forest and 20 on the Polish side of the border. The smaller plants form associations in the same way. Plant-eating animals prefer some plants to others and consequently the meat eaters that hunt them concentrate their searches in those same areas. Far from being an even spread of species, the forest is an immensely complex patchwork with a plant and animal composition that varies greatly from place to place.

The patchwork results partly from chance: Trees grow where their seeds fall, a matter over which the trees have no control. Beyond that, however, the complexity results from the fact that particular plant species prosper in some places

Parent birds must work hard to bring food to youngsters that may be as big as themselves. These are ravens (Corvus corax). (Courtesy of Michael Quinton, Minden Pictures)

and fail in others, and whether or not they succeed depends partly on the trees around them. In fact, all these species— trees, shrubs, herbs, and animals, not to mention the soil fungi and bacteria—shelter one another, feed on one another, and compete for food, water, light, and space. They form a community that is every bit as complicated as the human community found in a city.

Scientists were becoming aware of these communities during the 18th and 19th centuries. Charles Darwin (1809–82) was well aware of them, and the relationships within natural communities are central to his evolutionary theory. In *On the Origin of Species by Means of Natural Selection,* published in 1859, Darwin argues that inherited natural variations between individuals equip some better than others to thrive and reproduce under the conditions in which they find themselves living. Those conditions include the influences of other living organisms.

The German zoologist Ernst Heinrich Haeckel (1834–1919) was an enthusiastic supporter of Darwin who sought to work out all the implications of Darwin's theory. In 1866 Haeckel published a two-volume work called *Generelle Morphologie der Organismen* (General morphology of organisms)—"morphology" is the study of the form of organisms—in which he discussed a kind of large-scale economy of nature in which all species are engaged. Seeking a word to describe this idea he took the Greek *oikos,* meaning "household," and *logos,* meaning "discourse" or "study," to produce *Ökologie,* which was written in English as "oecologie." At the International Botanical Congress in 1893 the spelling was officially changed to "ecology."

Haeckel had given a name to the emerging science of natural communities. In 1923 one of the greatest of the early ecologists, Sir Arthur Tansley (1871–1955), published a book called *Practical Plant Ecology* in which he defined the new science:

> The word ECOLOGY, *as is well known, is derived, like the common word economy, from the Greek oikos,* house, abode, dwelling. *In its widest meaning ecology is the study of plants and animals* as they exist in their natural homes; *or better, perhaps, the study of*

their household affairs, which is actually a secondary meaning of the Greek word. [The italics are his.]

In 1935, in a paper in the journal *Ecology,* Tansley introduced another new term: *ecosystem.* He defined it fully in the second edition of *Practical Plant Ecology,* which was published in 1946 as *Introduction to Plant Ecology* and in which he also explained the term *biome.*

The most natural conception that has been suggested is that which regards the whole complex of organisms—both animals and plants—naturally living together as a sociological unit which has been called the biome, *whose life must be considered and studied as a whole.*

A wider conception still is to include with the biome all the physical and chemical factors of the biome's environment or habitat . . . as parts of one physical system, *which we may call an* ecosystem, *because it is based on the* oikos *or home of a particular biome.*

Most of the early ecologists had started out as botanists, and European ecologists devised ways of classifying communities of plants. They coined the name *phytosociology* for the study of plant communities. American ecologists developed the new science in a different direction, toward the concept of *climax* communities (see "Succession and climax" on pages 118–120).

Food chains, webs, and pyramids

Scurrying about the forest floor, a mouse is searching for berries that have fallen to the ground, seeds buried beneath dry leaves, tender young seedlings, and anything else that might make a tasty snack. Mice living in a temperate forest eat plant material.

The mouse forages at night, when it is dark. Even a full moon on a clear night is enough to keep it in its nest, where it is hidden and safe. It dares to venture forth only when it is dark. Darkness gives it some protection from its foes, but only from those that hunt by sight. It is no use against the owl that sits high on a branch, still, silent, and invisible from

Mice, such as this deer mouse (Peromyscus maniculatus), *feed on a variety of plant materials, but they also provide a tasty meal for owls and other hunters. Their large ears and sharp eyes allow them to remain alert at all times.* (Courtesy of Gerry Ellis, Minden Pictures)

the ground. The owl keeps watch with its ears. It can hear and locate the slight rustling a mouse makes as it pushes aside leaves and grass. An owl can find and catch a mouse in total darkness.

Plants provide the basic food for the entire forest community. This is because plants are the only members of the community with the ability to produce sugars, proteins, fats, and other nutrients out of air, water, and the mineral substances that are dissolved in the soil water (see "Photosynthesis and respiration" on pages 79–85). Food underlies all the relationships between species. Species compete with each other for food. Plants that compete for light are also competing for food, because they need light to manufacture sugars by photosynthesis. Some animal species eat plants, other animals eat only meat, and there are also animals, including humans, that eat both. The way food passes from organism to organism through the forest community is central to how the community functions.

Mice eat plant material and owls eat mice. The relation-ships between plants, mice, and owls look like this: plants → mice → owls. The arrow indicates that one group of organisms is consumed by another. A sequence of relationships, based on what each organism eats, is called a *food chain*. There is another forest food chain up in the trees, high above the forest floor. That one goes: leaves → caterpillars → small birds → hawks. This food chain is slightly longer; it has four links rather than three.

Insects and birds die, and uneaten leaves decay. Dead material provides food for earthworms, fungi, and a series of other organisms, all the way down to bacteria. The effect of decomposition is to release nutrient compounds that dissolve in the water moving through the soil and are then absorbed by plant roots (see the sidebar "The nitrogen cycle" on page 80). This produces a rather more complicated food chain, shown in the illustration.

Food chains are straightforward and provide a way of demonstrating clearly the relationships among the components of an ecosystem. A food chain diagram provides clues about what may happen if some component changes. If a disease *epizootic*—an epidemic that strikes nonhuman animals—kills large numbers of mice, for example, there will be less food for owls, and so many of their young will starve. Food chains have a major disadvantage, however, because life is not so simple as they suggest. As well as seeds and fruit, mice will eat insects. Many birds change their diet between seeds and insects, depending on what is available. In other words, the pattern of relationships among the members of the ecosystem is more like a web than a chain. It is a *food web*.

A food web diagram attempts to link all the food chains. In the web shown on page 105, for example, beetles, moths, butterflies, and bees all feed on flowers. Vireos eat beetles and butterflies and thrushes eat butterflies, moths, and bees. Mosquitoes feed on plant sap, but they also feed on the blood of mice and flycatchers. Flycatchers and mice eat mosquitoes. The diagram is complicated, but it is still only a very simplified version of the feeding patterns in a real ecosystem. Many relationships are omitted because including them would make the diagram so complicated as to be confusing.

There is an alternative way to represent ecological relation-ships based on feeding, and that is to divide the organisms according to the type of food they eat and then group togeth-er all the members of each type. The Greek word *trophe* means "nourishment," and relationships based on food are said to be *trophic*. Grouping organisms according to their diet therefore produces a trophic arrangement.

The first group is composed of plants. They produce food for all the other members of an ecosystem, so they are known as *producers*. Animals are *consumers*. These groups can be rep-resented graphically as bars of the same height but different widths and stacked by *trophic level* with the producers at the base. Above the producers are the herbivores—plant-eating animals. They feed directly on the plants, so they form the first consumer level; they are primary consumers. Carni-

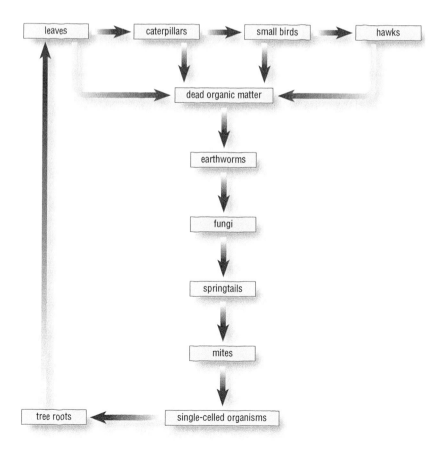

A food chain

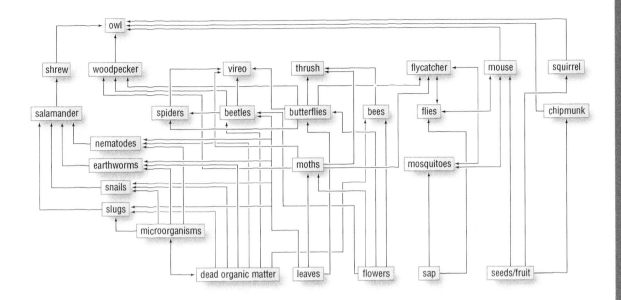

A food web

vores—meat-eating animals—feed on herbivores, so they form the next trophic level, as secondary consumers. Some carnivores feed on other carnivores. These animals are sometimes called *top predators,* and they form the highest trophic level, as tertiary consumers. The resulting diagram resembles a stepped pyramid. It is known as an *ecological pyramid* or as an *Eltonian pyramid* after Charles Sutherland Elton (1900–91), the British ecologist who first devised it. The illustration on page 106 shows a typical pyramid.

Pyramids count the organisms at each trophic level, but there is a problem: Exactly what are they measuring? If the pyramid shows the number of organisms at each level, it is a *pyramid of numbers.* It shows that there are many more plants than there are animals eating the plants, and many more herbivores than there are carnivores, which sounds sensible— but is it? If the plants are forest trees, each tree can support a large number of herbivorous animals, so the primary consumers may heavily outnumber the producers. This will be especially so if most of the primary consumers are insects. The pyramid will look very different if the producers are grass plants and the primary consumers are elephants. There will be many plants, very few elephants, and probably no secondary or tertiary consumers because no carnivores hunt adult

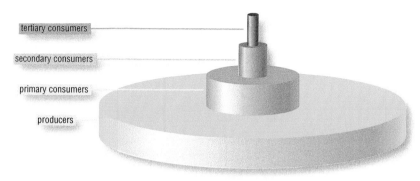

An ecological pyramid. The block representing each trophic layer should be approximately one-tenth the width of the block below it.

tertiary consumers

secondary consumers

primary consumers

producers

elephants. Complicating matters further, in most ecosystems there is a variety of organisms at each trophic level, making it unclear just what the pyramid means. Pyramids of numbers are seldom used for this reason.

It would be much better to group the organisms in trophic levels and then find the weight of all the organisms at each level. The weight, or more correctly the mass, of organisms is known as the *biomass,* and a pyramid that shows the biomass at each level is known as a *pyramid of biomass.* Biomass is measured as the dry weight of organisms, which is the weight after all the water is removed. This is important, because water accounts for most of the weight, and the amount varies greatly from species to species and from time to time. A pyramid of biomass usually has a similar general shape to the one shown in the illustration. This pyramid is much more useful, because it makes no distinction between insects, mice, and deer, or between wolves, bears, and owls, simply lumping all of them together based on trophic levels.

How energy flows through a forest

Sunshine provides the energy for every ecosystem, because the producers use sunlight as a source of energy for photosynthesis. The amount of food that plants produce represents the proportion of the sunlight falling on them that photosynthesis captures. Photosynthesis is not very efficient; plants capture no more than about one percent of the sunlight to which their leaves are exposed.

Plants use some of the captured energy to grow bigger and some to repair damaged tissues, but most of the energy is used for respiration (see "Photosynthesis and respiration" on pages 79–85). Respiration supplies cells with the energy they need to perform their ordinary functions. In other words, the captured sunlight is used for maintenance. No more than about 10–20 percent of the captured energy—10–20 percent

Winter in a temperate forest. It is too cold for plants to grow and although the pool remains unfrozen, the soil is dry because the water lies as snow above it, rather than below the surface, and water in the soil may be frozen. The trees have shed their leaves and will remain dormant until the spring. (Courtesy of Jim Brandenburg, Minden Pictures)

of that 1 percent, or 0.1–0.2 percent of the sunlight falling on the plants—is available as food for the primary consumers.

Consumers use most of the energy derived from the food they eat to maintain their own bodies. It is easy to see that this is so. Once they are full-grown adults, animals eating a healthy diet grow no larger. Their size and weight remains constant, yet they continue to eat regularly. The food they eat provides the energy to maintain their bodies, allowing them to move, digest their food, repair or replace damaged or worn tissue, heal wounds, and, most of all in the case of mammals and birds, to maintain a constant body temperature. Not surprisingly, therefore, only about 10–20 percent of the food that a primary consumer eats is converted into food for a secondary consumer. Similarly, only 10–20 percent of the food the secondary consumer eats is converted into food for a tertiary consumer. The energy represented by the remaining 80–90 percent is released by respiration and used to maintain the animal's body.

The fact that such a small proportion of captured solar energy passes from one trophic level to the next explains why pyramids of biomass rarely have more than four levels and why the width of the levels decreases so rapidly. Primary consumers need a certain geographical area within which to find sufficient plant food for their needs. Secondary consumers need a much bigger area in which to find enough animal food. A family of gray foxes (*Urocyon cinereoargenteus*) needs a range of about one square mile (2.59 km^2) in which to find enough food, and a pack of about 12 gray wolves needs 40–400 square miles (104–1,040 km^2). Gray wolves have largely disappeared from temperate forests because so much of the original forests were cleared that the remaining areas were simply not large enough to feed wolves. Carnivore-hunting carnivores need such a vast area that they must always have been rare.

It is possible to show the trophic levels in terms of the flow of energy from one to another in a pyramid similar to those already described. A pyramid of this kind is called a *pyramid of energy*. It is by far the most useful of the ecological pyramids, thanks mainly to the insight of Raymond Lindeman.

Raymond L. Lindeman (1915–42) was an American ecologist whose career was cut short by his untimely death at the age of only 27. In 1942 Lindeman published a scientific paper that opened up an entirely new area of ecological research. The paper was called "The trophic-dynamic aspect of ecology" and it appeared in the journal *Ecology*. In it Lindeman proposed a new way to study ecosystems, by measuring the amount of energy that passes from each trophic level to the next. This initiated the study of *ecological energetics*.

As with so many good ideas, the value of studying the flow of energy is obvious once someone else has thought of it. It is also fairly easy, because energy can be measured. Heat a sample of biological material in an oven to remove all the water, then burn the dry matter in an oven equipped with a calorimeter—an instrument that measures the amount of energy released. On average, one ounce of plant material releases 114–128 kilocalories of energy (16.7–18.8 kJ/g) and one ounce of animal material releases 142–156 kilocalories (20.9–23.0 kJ/g).

Armed with this information, it is possible to measure the efficiency with which energy is used. Ecological efficiency is the percentage of absorbed energy that is converted into biomass. Herbivorous mammals and birds have an efficiency of 0.3–1.5 percent, and carnivorous mammals and birds of 0.6–1.8 percent. Reptiles and amphibians are much more efficient, because they do not use their food to maintain a constant body temperature. Those that are herbivorous have an efficiency of 9–25 percent and the carnivores are 12–25 percent efficient.

Ecologists also measure energy to calculate the total amount of new biomass produced each year by the plants in particular ecosystems. This is called the gross primary productivity or production (GPP). Deducting the amount the plants use in respiration reduces the figure to the net primary productivity (NPP), and the remainder after account has been taken of the amount eaten by consumers is the net community productivity (NCP).

These calculations allow scientists to compare one ecosystem with another. In fact they are comparing the way different ecosystems use the energy available to them. Ecologists who study temperate forests use ecological energetics to compare broad-leaved forest ecosystems with coniferous forest and with mixed forest containing both broad-leaved trees and conifers. They also use this technique to compare natural forests with plantations, and plantations growing one group of tree species with plantations growing other species.

Decomposition and the cycling of nutrients

Down on the forest floor there is a layer of dead leaves and twigs. Scattered about there are fallen branches and occasionally fallen trees—old, almost dead trees brought down by a recent storm. A group of feathers is all that remains to show where an unwary bird fell victim to a predator. There may be a shed snake skin or droppings left by a passing animal, perhaps to mark the boundary of its territory, or even the dead body of a bird or mammal.

Material lying on the ground is called *detritus,* a Latin word that means "worn down." It is dead and discarded, but it is far from useless. The layer of this material never grows any thicker: It is being discarded all the time, but it does not accumulate because it provides food for an entire range of living organisms—the *decomposers.*

Among the detritus, especially in the damper, more shaded areas, live slugs, snails, wood lice, beetles, ants, millipedes, earwigs, insect larvae, and earthworms. These animals feed on dead plant material, so they are known as *detritivores.* They shred it into tiny pieces and drag the fragments below ground to eat them. This activity spreads the material through the upper soil, where smaller worms, mites, springtails, and similar tiny animals can reach it. The fragments they leave are food for microscopically small organisms, such as nematodes, rotifers, and protozoans.

It may look lifeless, but in fact the forest floor is densely populated. Beneath one square yard of surface area there may be more than eight million nematodes, 80,000 springtails, 80,000 mites, and 40,000 animals of other assorted species (10 million, 100,000, and 50,000 per square meter, respectively). In addition, there are fungi and bacteria. Altogether there are likely to be almost 850 species in every square yard

(1,000 per square meter). Not all of these organisms are feeding directly on the detritus. There are also small spiders, harvest spiders ("daddy longlegs"), centipedes, and other carnivores hunting the herbivores.

The soil community forms the unseen part of the ecosystem and, like the visible part of the ecosystem above ground, its members form a hierarchy that can be described by ecological pyramids. Because they live below ground, it is tempting to draw their pyramids upside down, but this would be incorrect. They are just like above-ground pyramids, with the detritus forming an equivalent to the producer level.

Detritus does not comprise growing plants, of course, and although all of it is consumed, the consumers are not eating whole leaves the way grazing mammals do, but particular ingredients that they select from the menu. Some of those ingredients are more easily digested than others, and the most digestible are taken first.

Fruit is rarely found lying on the forest floor. Rich in sugars and starches, fruits are highly nutritious and easily digested. Many mammals, birds, and invertebrate animals are attracted to them, and fungi and bacteria quickly colonize them. They soon disappear. Other items are consumed more slowly, but always in the same order, depending on their chemical ingredients. Sugars disappear first, followed by starches. Next the decomposers attack more complex sugars called *hemicelluloses* that are found in the cell walls of plants. Then pectins, carbohydrates, and proteins are consumed. This leaves the compounds that are much tougher to digest. Cellulose is the first of these to go. It is a complex sugar that provides most of the structure in the cell walls of plants; it is probably the most abundant of all the compounds found in living organisms. Cellulose is followed by lignins (see "How wood forms" on pages 94–97) and finally by suberins—the fatty compounds that make the cork in tree bark waterproof. The last plant compound to disappear is cutin, a mixture of big, very complex molecules that forms part of the waxy coat found on many leaves and the stems of nonwoody plants. Dead leaves that form an autumn carpet on the forest floor are among the last plant material to disappear, but in the end they, too, vanish to become part of the soil. The toughest leaves of all are the needles that fall from coniferous trees. Their thick, strong, outer coat makes them much more durable than the thin, more delicate leaves of broad-leaved plants that need to last for only one season.

At each stage in the process the organisms responsible leave wastes of their own. The overall effect is to break down the once-living tissues step by step until they are finally reduced to carbon dioxide, water, and a variety of simple chemical compounds that dissolve in the water passing through the soil. This is the water that plant roots absorb, taking up the dissolved nutrients at the same time. Decomposition is the process by which nutrients are recycled beneath the forest floor.

Habitats and niches

Living in a city has many advantages. Supermarkets supply food at all hours of day and night, houses and apartments provide shelter, medical services help people who are sick, and there are emergency services, mass transit and a wide range of entertainment and amenities. Provided a person is not too poor to enjoy its benefits, the city has much to offer. So far as people are concerned, the city is good *habitat*—a Latin word that means "inhabits."

People do not have the city entirely to themselves, of course. Many species of birds also find it a good place to live, as do the rats that live belowground, emerging at night to feed on the garbage people discard, the mice that sneak into homes, and the half-wild cats that hunt them. Spiders build webs to catch the innumerable flying insects, while cockroaches and beetles eat their way through the food stores and woodworms tunnel into old furniture. The city is good habitat to all of these and many more.

It is not good habitat for every species, however. Red foxes (*Vulpes vulpes*) have moved into many towns and thrive there, but the bobcat (*Felis rufus*) stays well away. What is good habitat for one species may be extremely inhospitable for another. People sometimes describe an attractive area as "good habitat," but strictly speaking the statement is meaningless unless it is qualified. The area may be good habitat for particular species or it may be good habitat for all the species typical of a certain ecosystem—temperate forest habitat, for example, or marshland habitat—but it cannot be good habitat for every species.

Habitats can change. If a habitat is stable, changing little over the years, the species occupying it will be adapted to a situation in which the resources on which they depend—of food, water, shelter, and nesting sites—are continually available. In this situation the species will tend to produce few offspring, but will care for them over a prolonged period so that the young are almost fully grown by the time they become independent. Ecologists call this reproductive strategy *K-selection*. In a stable habitat it gives the young the best possible chance of surviving. Humans reproduce in this way; ours is a *K-species*.

Unstable habitats are liable to change fairly suddenly and with little warning. The K-selection strategy would not work in such a situation, because the young would be subjected to the change before they were old enough to cope with it. In unstable habitats species are more likely to adopt an *r-selection* strategy. *R-species* produce many young that enter the world tiny and extremely vulnerable, but grow fast, eating the food around them before it disappears. By the time the habitat deteriorates, enough of them will be full grown to ensure that the population survives. Most of the young will perish, but this strategy gives them the best chance possible.

K-selection is always written with a capital K and r-selection with a lower case r because the terms were first used in an equation for calculating population size, called the *logistic equation*. The logistic equation was published in 1838 by the Belgian mathematician Pierre-François Verhulst (1804–49); it is:

$$N(t) = K/(1 + e^{c-rt})$$

where $N(t)$ is the population size at time t, K is the *carrying capacity* of the habitat, e (approximately 2.718) is the base of natural logarithms, c is a constant defining the value of N at time $t = 0$, and rt is the rate of increase (r) to time t. The carrying capacity is the number of individuals the habitat can support; if the population increases above this number it will later decrease again, and if it falls below this number it will later increase.

The most unstable of all habitats appears only occasionally and disappears rapidly. It is said to be *ephemeral*. A puddle of water that vanishes within a few hours and the body of a dead forest animal are examples of ephemeral habitats. They attract organisms—mainly bacteria and insects—that multiply rapidly, feed, grow, and then move away during the brief time the habitat remains.

The gray squirrel (*Sciurus carolinensis*) lives in the forest. It is a forest animal, so a temperate forest provides it with suitable habitat. Its habitat is the place it lives—that it inhabits. Knowing the habitat that suits a particular species tells us nothing about how the species lives, however. It tells us where it lives, but not what it does there. In fact, in spring and summer the squirrel spends most of its time high in the trees. The leaves are especially nutritious then, and the squirrel is eating them. It builds a big, untidy nest called a *drey* from leaves, far out along a branch or, if it can find one, in a hollow in the tree. It also builds flat feeding platforms on branches, where it can eat and rest in comfort. By fall the leaves are becoming less nutritious and the squirrel spends more time on the ground, looking for fallen nuts and the fruiting bodies of fungi. That is when it collects nuts and stashes them away for the winter. In winter it spends most of its time on the ground, eating the food in its stores. This is what the squirrel does, the way it lives; that is its *niche,* a word derived from the French *nicher,* meaning "to make a nest" or "to nestle."

A niche does not exist until a species occupies it. Leaves, nuts, fungi, trees and their branches are just those things until a squirrel comes along and finds a use for them. To the squirrel they represent an opportunity that it is equipped to seize, using them to construct its niche. The organism actually creates the niche that it then occupies, and every niche is unique. If the species should disappear, the niche it formerly occupied will be left vacant. Other members of the same species may return to occupy it, or another species may find it congenial and take it over. In this case the niche exists prior to being occupied, but only because a previous species had already created and defined it.

How trees are adapted to climate

Trees, like all other green plants, depend on photosynthesis to provide the sugars and energy they need to grow. Photosynthesis and its opposite, respiration (see "Photosynthesis and respiration" on pages 79–85), consist of sequences of chemical reactions. The speed of these reactions, and of all the other reactions that take place in a plant, varies according to the temperature. They cease altogether if the temperature falls below about 21°F (–6°C). When it is this cold, plants cannot grow at all and they become dormant. The reactions work best at temperatures higher than 41°F (5°C), and then their speed doubles with every 18°F (10°C) rise in temperature up to about 85°F (29°C), which is the temperature at which photosynthesis reaches its highest sustainable rate. The rate continues to rise with temperature up to about 95°F (35°C), but the acceleration is brief and the rate quickly falls back to its previous level. Photosynthesis starts slowing rapidly as the temperature rises past 105°F (40°C), and most plants die if the temperature remains higher than 113°F (45°C) for very long.

Prolonged high temperatures pose no threat to temperate forest plants, because the weather in temperate regions is never that hot for long enough to harm them. Winter temperatures usually fall below 41°F (5°C), however, and they often remain below 21°F (–6°C) for weeks at a time. There are times, therefore, when plant growth ceases.

A period of dormancy presents no problem for trees, provided it does not continue for too long. In order to reproduce, broad-leaved trees must produce flowers, fruits, and seeds, and this takes time, during which the temperature must remain higher than 41°F (5°C) and for part of which it must be considerably higher. Many tree species, including some maples (*Acer* species), lindens (*Tilia* species), and birches (*Betula* species), produce flowers very early in spring, before their leaves open, to take immediate advantage of the rising temperature. This gives them time to ripen their seeds by late summer or early fall.

Early flowering is an adaptation to the length of the growing season, but it is risky. Late frosts can postpone flowering or, if they occur after the flowers have opened, destroy the flowers. Cool summers slow the rate at which seeds ripen. If the flowers are destroyed the tree will produce no seed, and if its seeds form too late in the season they may not be fully ripe by the onset of winter.

Trees live for many years and an occasional failure to produce seeds is not serious, but a species that frequently fails to produce seeds is at risk of dying out. As old trees die, the shortage of seeds means there will be too few seedlings to replace them, and other species, better at producing seeds, will take their place.

Some species escape this trap by reproducing vegetatively (see "How trees reproduce" on pages 85–87). Trees that reproduce through *suckers*—shoots that arise from roots some distance from the main part of the plant—do so more in higher latitudes, where the climate is cooler, than in lower, warmer latitudes, where they rely more on producing seed.

During the coldest part of winter, when the ground is frozen, trees face a different problem. Their roots are unable to absorb ice, and they have no means of thawing the ground to release liquid water. Consequently, the winter is the equivalent of a drought—even if the landscape lies beneath a deep layer of snow. On sunny days the leaves may warm sufficiently for photosynthesis to start. They will open their stomata to allow carbon dioxide to enter and oxygen to leave, but when they do so water will evaporate (see "Evaporation and transpiration" on pages 66–69) and, with the roots embedded in frozen ground, there will be no rising water to replace it. It will not take many sunny winter days before the tree is seriously, even fatally, dehydrated.

Trees have adapted to this in two ways. Some produce thick leaves with a waxy outer covering that minimizes water loss. Holly (*Ilex aquifolium*) and ivy (*Hedera helix*) are well known examples. Others bear leaves only during that part of the year when leaves are useful. Trees that do this are said to be *deciduous*.

Deciduous trees produce thin, flimsy leaves. They are not very durable, but this does not matter, because they need to last for no more than five or six months. The leaves are disposable. This may sound wasteful, but in fact it is very efficient.

To grow flimsy leaves, the tree does not have to expend large amounts of materials, and it can grow them quickly. The leaves open early in spring and reach their full size in a matter of days. As summer draws to a close, the days grow shorter and the temperature begins to fall. When they detect these changes, the leaves reduce their production of *auxins*—substances that stimulate plant growth—and increase their production of *ethylene,* which inhibits cell growth. Tree growth slows and then ceases. The leaves cease producing chlorophyll, and many of the nutrients in the leaves flow back into the tree branch or trunk, where they are stored for the winter. This process exposes the remaining pigments, changing the color of leaves from green to yellow, orange, and red. Near the base of the leaf stalk, or *petiole,* there is a thin layer of parenchyma cells. This layer weakens until leaves begin to fall, and a few windy days strip the trees bare.

Enough light penetrates the forest from the side to allow plants to blanket the ground, but only where the sunlight reaches. Elsewhere the forest floor is in deep shade and few plants are able to grow. This forest is in Bavaria, Germany. (Courtesy of Konrad Wothe, Minden Pictures)

The tree has stored most of the useful chemical compounds from the leaves and the remainder are released as the leaves decompose (see "Decomposition and the cycling of nutrients" on pages 110–112).

Succession and climax

To an ecologist, demolition sites are interesting places. Once the old buildings have gone and the rubble has been carted away, all that remains is bare earth, rough, uneven, and compacted, where heavy machines have driven across it. Unless it is the middle of winter and bitterly cold, within a few days the first plants will have pushed above the surface. In the following few weeks, plants will spread until they cover the entire site. Then they will flower and produce copious amounts of seed—often the type of tiny seed that floats through the air on a "parachute" of fine hairs called a *pappus*. Ecologists are especially interested in what happens next.

Other plants have seeds that are slower to germinate. They take longer to appear, but when they do they grow strongly, shading out the first arrivals, called the *pioneers,* but feeding on nutrients released by their roots. Grasses appear, only to die away when the first woody shrubs rob them of the direct sunlight they need. Leave the site for long enough—though usually the builders start developing the area before this happens—and tree seedlings may begin to rise above the other plants. Eventually the site might turn into a tiny patch of forest.

This series of changes in the composition of the plant community is called a *sere* or *succession,* and each community that appears and is then replaced is called a *stage* or *seral stage.* The final community that becomes more or less permanently established is called the *climax.* Over much of the northeastern United States, the first Europeans to arrive in North America found forests dominated by various combinations of beech, birch, maple, and oak trees, together with the shrubs and herbs associated with them. These plant communities formed the climax vegetation. Oak and hazel dominated the primeval forest that once covered much of lowland Britain and therefore constituted the British climax.

Scientists began studying the way natural communities develop and change over time toward the end of the 19th century, and the idea of a sere producing a climax became very influential by the middle of the 20th century. Unfortunately, it can be misleading.

In the first place, one stage may or may not prepare the way for the next—for example, by releasing nutrients. Sometimes this is what happens, but there seems to be no way to predict it and it is far from inevitable. Nor is it possible to predict what the climax will be. If an area of forest is cleared and then left to regenerate, it will usually develop as forest once more, but not necessarily with the same trees in the same proportions. Which seeds germinate first and which trees manage to crowd out their rivals and become established is a matter of chance.

The idea of the climax suggests a community that remains unaltered for as long as it remains undisturbed. This seems to suggest a "balance of nature" in which every species has its place and function, but natural communities are not like that. There can be no "balance of nature" because communities are constantly changing, developing, and responding to disturbances that occur naturally and often.

Nowadays ecologists recognize that the relationships within plant communities, such as forests, are much more complicated than they were once thought to be. It is inaccurate to think of a regular series of stages through which bare ground is transformed into a type of vegetation that defines the area—as forest or grassland, for instance. Nevertheless, it is still true that plants will appear to colonize an area of bare ground. Pioneer plants that produce large quantities of rapidly germinating seed will emerge first. These will give way to a greater variety of stronger plants, and little by little the bare ground will be transformed. This will happen, but there is no way to predict the order in which species will appear or the community that will finally result, and there is no way of knowing when the process has reached a conclusion—if it ever does.

This realization has one major implication. In the days when people believed that a forest, essentially identical to the original natural forest, would develop on land from which forest had been cleared, it was enough to protect the site and allow the natural succession to proceed. Scientists know now that this will not guarantee the re-creation of the original forest or even of forest at all. The succession might terminate in impenetrable scrub, and if a forest did emerge, it would include species that have been introduced and become invasive. The only way to create a forest resembling the original forest is to plant it and then manage it carefully.

Fire, and trees that depend on it

A forest fire is a terrifying sight. The smoke is visible from miles away and the fire advances as a roaring wall of flame, leaping from treetop to treetop, devouring everything in its path. At least, that is the way the most sensational wildfires behave—the ones that approach the outskirts of cities, burning homes and forcing local residents to evacuate.

There have been many damaging wildfires in recent years, but they are not new. In 1902 a fire at Yacholt, Washington, burned about 250,000 acres (100,000 ha) of forest, and a similar area burned in 1933 at Tillamook, Oregon. The fires that struck southern California in October 2003 were much bigger. Driven by Santa Ana winds that blow from Arizona and Nevada toward the Pacific, accelerating as they are funneled through the Santa Ana Canyon, the fires burned about 740,000 acres (300,000 ha), killing two people in Mexico and 20 in California. More than 100,000 people were driven from their homes.

Not all wildfires are like that and, far from being harmful, most serve a useful purpose in rapidly converting dead plant matter into fertilizer. Some wildfires are started deliberately by arsonists, but lightning is responsible for igniting most. It is the litter that burns—the accumulation of dead leaves, twigs, and branches that have dried out during the summer—and the fire moves rapidly but remains close to the ground. It destroys shrubs and herbs and scorches tree trunks, and it will kill some tree seedlings and saplings, but otherwise it does no harm. The temperature among the burning litter is usually about 194–248°F (90–120°C). A few inches below ground the temperature is only slightly higher than normal. The fire spreads over a fairly small area and then dies down. Ground fires burn belowground, consuming fuel more slowly than surface fires and burning for longer. They consume root systems, producing no flames, but most ground fires die for lack of oxygen before they have traveled very far.

A surface fire becomes much more dangerous if it ignites the crowns of the trees. It is then a crown fire. Hot air rising from a burning tree crown lifts burning cinders high into the air. Carried by the wind, the cinders fall into the crowns of other trees, igniting them. In this way the fire can advance very rapidly. Really intense forest fires can generate firestorms (see "Forest fires" on pages 72–73).

Fires are rare in broad-leaved deciduous forest. Material lying on the ground is usually too wet to burn, and the trees are not very flammable. Their leaves contain a high proportion of water and their wood is also fairly moist. Coniferous trees have drier leaves and their wood contains resins, which are flammable, so fires are more common in coniferous forests growing in areas where summers are warm and dry. Fire is an entirely natural phenomenon in forests of this type and the forest trees are adapted to it. The fire clears away the dead leaves and wood that have collected on the forest floor, leaving behind a layer of ash, rich in plant nutrients.

Indeed, they do more. Some plants exude chemical substances that inhibit bacterial activity nearby. The fire burns some of these substances and produces charcoal, which absorbs others, allowing the bacteria to flourish—and the bacteria include species that "fix" atmospheric nitrogen (see the sidebar "The nitrogen cycle" on page 80). After the fire, the ground surface is blackened. A black surface is better than a pale surface at absorbing the warmth of the Sun, so the soil is warm. This stimulates microbial activity, seed germination, and the growth of young plants.

Attempts to prevent fires can result in uncontrollable wildfires. Extinguishing fires as soon as they are detected protects buildings in and close to the forest, but it also allows surface litter to accumulate. When eventually the litter ignites, the amount of fuel is so large that the fire quickly rages out of control. This is what happened in Yellowstone National Park in 1988 (see the sidebar on page 122).

Trees that grow in areas prone to fire have adapted in various ways. Some, such as quaking aspen (*Populus tremuloides*), balsam poplar (*P. balsamifera*), and paper birch (*Betula papyrifera*), produce copious quantities of seed that disperse widely. When fire has cleared and fertilized the ground, seeds of these trees germinate and the trees grow so rapidly they are able to produce a fresh crop of seeds before the bigger but slower conifers have had time to grow tall enough to shade them.

Despite being conifers, redwoods such as the coast redwood (*Sequoia sempervirens*) and Sierra redwood (*Sequoia-*

Yellowstone and coping with fire

In summer 1988 fire swept through Yellowstone National Park in the western United States. All attempts at control failed and the fires did not die down until the first substantial falls of winter snow extinguished them. By that time the fires had burned about 1 million acres (400,000 ha) of the park, amounting to about 45 percent of the total area. The fires damaged the vegetation, but in most places without killing all of it. Over about 20,000 acres (8,000 ha), however, the vegetation was almost totally destroyed.

When at last the smoke cleared, the landscape was one of utter devastation and it was difficult to believe that the park could recover. Yet in spring 1989 plants began to emerge from the ashes, and within a few years not only had the burned area recovered, its natural communities had been invigorated. Ninety percent of Yellowstone is forested and 90 percent of the trees are lodgepole pine (*Pinus contorta* var. *latifolia*). This is a species of trees that store their seeds in the canopy, often for years, until hot air rising from a fire stimulates their release. The forest is adapted to fire.

Fire occurs naturally in Yellowstone every few years, but for some years prior to the 1988 fire the policy had been to suppress fires as quickly as possible. This allowed dry, dead plant material to accumulate. When it was ignited, probably by lightning, the resulting fire was uncontrollable.

A new management scheme was adopted in 1992, dividing the park into three zones. In one zone, comprising about 10 large areas, fires are ordinarily suppressed, but controlled fires are started deliberately if too much flammable material accumulates. In another zone, covering most of the park, fires are allowed to burn but are controlled. In the third zone, comprising a strip 1.5 miles (2.4 km) wide just inside the park boundary, fires are permitted under even more strictly controlled conditions.

dendron giganteum) are difficult to burn. They have spongy bark that does not catch fire readily, and the bark is thick enough to protect the living tissue beneath from all but the hottest fires. Even then, if the fire is hot enough to burn the tree, new growth often sprouts from the stump. Other trees, including pitch pine (*Pinus rigida*), also recover by producing new growth from the trunk of a dead standing tree.

These are trees that can survive fire. Others actually depend on it. Longleaf pine (*P. palustris*), lodgepole pine (*P. contorta* var. *latifolia*), and jack pine (*P. banksiana*) are *serotinous*. This means that they delay releasing their seeds, keeping their cones tightly closed until they are warmed by hot air rising from a fire on the ground below. Then the cones open to release seeds that germinate in the warm ashes.

Most forest animals also survive fire. Birds and the larger mammals see or smell the fire long before it reaches them and simply move away. This can be a dangerous strategy for mammals, however, because just ahead of the fire there are predators looking out for escapees. Other animals shelter beneath logs or in burrows. During the 1988 Yellowstone fire about 250 elk (*Cervus elephas*) died from smoke inhalation, out of an elk population of about 31,000.

Forests where fire occurs fairly regularly at intervals of a few years come to be dominated by tree species that are either tolerant of fire or dependent on it. There are also species like aspen that are able to exploit the opportunity to grow rapidly and produce seed on the sites left temporarily empty by fire. Consequently, all of the trees in the regenerated forest tend to be the same age. Most fires affect only a limited area of the forest, however, so these forests often consist of a patchwork of areas, each patch containing trees that are all of the same age, but with the trees in one patch of a different age from those in another. This type of forest community is known as a *fire climax* or *pyroclimax* (from the Greek *pyr*, which means "fire").

Structure of a temperate forest

Trees expose their leaves to the sunlight, and in order to maximize that exposure their branches spread as widely as possible. Many coniferous trees bear their longest branches near the bottom and the branches are progressively shorter at higher levels. This produces a conical shape. In contrast, the leafy branches of broad-leaved trees are mainly near the top, where they form a *crown*. In a forest the crowns of adjacent broad-leaved trees or the longest branches of coniferous trees touch or overlap, producing a *closed canopy*. If the trees are more widely separated than this, so there is an *open canopy*, the area is known as *woodland*. A closed canopy shades all of the ground; the open canopy of woodland usually shades about 40 percent of the ground area.

Although a forest is defined as an area with a closed canopy, this is not literally true. There are gaps, even in conif-

Tall, slender aspen trees allow ample light to reach the ground, so the forest floor is densely carpeted with vegetation. (Courtesy of Fogstock)

erous forests where the trees retain their leaves throughout the year. Old trees die and fall, creating a gap in the canopy that remains open until a young tree grows up to close it again. In a broad-leaved deciduous forest the trees are bare in winter, so there is a time, from late fall until early spring, when there is no canopy.

Where the canopy is open, direct sunlight reaches the ground. This allows tall herbs, called *forbs,* to grow. These plants cannot survive in the deep shade of a closed canopy. The herbs in a deciduous forest take advantage of that brief interval between the time when the temperature is warm enough for photosynthesis and plant growth and the time when the leaf buds open on all the trees (see "How trees are adapted to climate" on pages 115–118). The herbs produce flowers, which are small, because there is not enough time to produce bigger ones and often brightly colored, to attract insects, then set seed and die down as the canopy closes and the light level falls. These herbs, such as primulas, snow-drops, narcissi, and crocuses, are the spring flowers that bring beauty to the forests, and they are widely grown in gardens. Coniferous forests shade the ground all the time and so they do not harbor spring flowers.

Among the herbs are also climbers, such as ivy, and shrubs and young trees at various stages of growth. The forest con-sists of mature trees, but it contains much more than tall trees, and its plants form distinct horizontal layers. These layers are sometimes called stories, like the stories of a tall building.

Mature, full-grown trees form the canopy. These trees are known as the *dominants.* Most of the dominants are of simi-lar height. Any that grow taller and protrude above the canopy are *emergents.* A tree that grows taller than its neigh-bors is able to capture more sunlight, but it is also more exposed to the drying effect of the wind above the canopy. The wind can kill leaf buds, so trees must pay a high price to win that extra light.

Among the dominants there are slightly smaller trees, known as *codominants,* and below those are still smaller trees, called *subdominants.* The dominants, codominants, and sub-dominants all belong to the same species. When a dominant

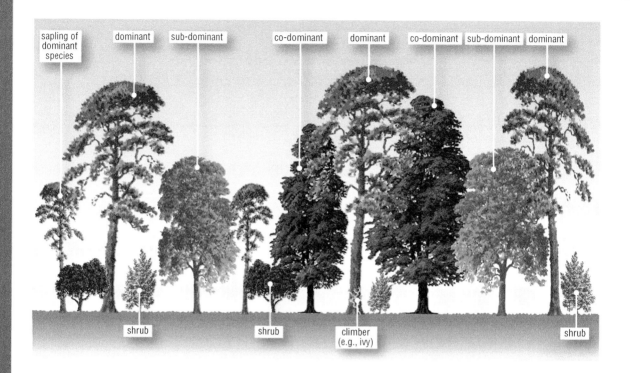

sapling of dominant species | dominant | sub-dominant | co-dominant | dominant | co-dominant | sub-dominant | dominant

shrub | shrub | climber (e.g., ivy) | shrub

Forest structure. The plants in a temperate forest form layers. The tallest trees (dominants and codominants) form the canopy. Saplings of these species form a lower layer, with shrubs below them and herbs growing close to the ground.

dies, the nearest codominant grows taller to take its place and a subdominant takes the place of the codominant. Together, the dominants, codominants, and subdominants compose the uppermost story, called the *canopy layer*.

Beneath the canopy layer there are smaller trees, still of the same species. The growth of these saplings is suppressed by the lack of light, but if the canopy should open they will grow up to join it. There are also smaller trees that, although they are their full size, are too short to reach the canopy. These saplings and small trees comprise the *understory*. The diagram shows a typical forest arrangement.

Shrubs that are between three feet (1 m) and 33 feet (10 m) tall make up the *shrub layer*. Woody plants such as gooseberry (*Ribes* species) and witch hazel (*Hamamelis virginiana*) that are less than three feet (1 m) tall form a *dwarf shrub layer*.

The tall herbs—nonwoody plants—form a story below the dwarf shrub layer known as the *tall herb layer* or *forb layer*. Forbs include such plants as the yellow trout lily (*Erythronium americanum*), large-flowered trillium (*Trillium grandiflorum*),

and lupins (*Lupinus* species). The smaller herbs, such as prim-
roses (*Primula* species), comprise the *herb layer* or *field layer.*
The lowest story of all is the *ground layer,* comprising mosses,
lichens, and other plants that grow close to the ground.

Not every temperate forest has all of these stories, and the
number of stories often varies from one part to another of
the same forest. Many forests lack an understory, for example, but most have a rich field layer.

Forest communities

Unless one keeps to well-marked paths it is easy to become
lost in a forest. The pattern of trees and shrubs looks the
same in every direction, giving the impression that the composition of the forest is the same everywhere, with its plant
species distributed uniformly.

It is true that except in clearings the structure of the forest
has the same principal components everywhere (see "Structure of a temperate forest" on pages 123–127), but the composition of an undisturbed forest varies greatly from place to
place. Trees compete with each other for light, water, and
nutrients, and they vary in their susceptibility to attack from
animals and disease. These factors produce changes in the
local composition of the forest, as particular species thrive in
some areas but are less healthy in others. Animals that feed
on the vegetation also vary from place to place because they
are drawn to their preferred food plants. Consequently the
predators of those animals also occur in some places but not
others.

Far from being a uniform expanse of plant and animal
species, a forest is more like a series of small compartments,
each a little different from those around it. The resulting pattern resembles a mosaic or an elaborately tiled floor.

Forest compartments are not quite like tiles, however,
because they lack sharp edges. Consequently, compartments
overlap each other, and where they overlap, adjacent compartments share certain species. The diagram on page 128
shows two adjacent compartments. For sake of simplicity,
each compartment contains only three species, colored blue,
yellow, and red. One compartment contains squares and the

other circles. Where the compartments overlap, there are blue, yellow, and red circles and squares. This combination of species produces different ecological conditions in which species can thrive that do not occur in either of the compartments. These are shown as blue, yellow, and red triangles. Consequently, while each compartment contains three species, the overlap area contains nine. This richness resulting from the overlap is known as the *edge effect*.

The diagram gives the impression that the edge effect is beneficial, and so it would be if species were distributed evenly throughout each forest compartment. But they are not. Some species need the protection of the species around them, so they grow only near the center of a compartment and fail to thrive near the edge. Dividing the forest into smaller and smaller compartments, for example, by driving roads through it or clearing areas, increases the overall length of forest edge, but it also confines the interior species into smaller and smaller areas until eventually they may disappear.

Edges tend to increase in length naturally. More light penetrates at the outer edge of a forest and the climate is warmer and drier there than it is deep inside. This favors plants that require light and warmth and suppresses those preferring cool shade. The edge climate is also windier, however, and

The edge effect. Where two ecosystems overlap, the overlap area supports species from both, plus species peculiar to the overlap.

Summer is a time of abundant food, when many birds and mammals raise their young. But sometimes there are accidents. This four-week-old great gray owl (Strix nebulosa) *has jumped out of its nest in an Idaho forest.* (Courtesy of Michael Quinton, Minden Pictures)

trees are more likely to be blown down, often bringing others down with them. Light penetrates and this extends the edge a little farther into the interior. It is possible for a large forest to be reduced to nothing but edge: Local clearances and roads divide the entire forest into patches so small that the interior species are no longer present. Edge forests are sometimes called by an English version of the Hindi word *jangal,* which describes the type of vegetation often seen beside roads: They are jungle.

Forests are often identified by their dominant species. The northern hardwood forest that once covered most of eastern Canada and the United States to the east of Minnesota consisted of white pine (*Pinus strobus*), sugar maple (*Acer saccharum*), beech (*Fagus grandifolia*), yellow birch (*Betula alleghaniensis*), and varying amounts of hemlock (*Tsuga canadensis*). Farther south in Illinois and Wisconsin the forest comprised sugar maple and basswood (*Tilia americana*), sometimes with red oak (*Quercus rubra*). From the southern edge of this forest as far as Texas the forest was mainly black oak (*Q. velutina*), white oak (*Q. alba*), pignut hickory (*Carya glabra*), and shagbark hickory (*C. ovata*), with an understory of flowering dogwood (*Cornus florida*). In the Gulf states the forest, extending to southern Massachusetts on its eastern side, was of white oak, loblolly pine (*P. taeda*), and shortleaf pine (*P. echinata*). To the east of that forest there was red oak, chestnut oak (*Q. prinus*), and tulip tree (*Liriodendron tulipifera*).

Most European forests contain beech (*Fagus sylvatica*) as the most widespread tree. This grows with sessile oak (*Q. petraea*) and pedunculate oak (*Q. robur*), field maple (*A. campestre*), ash (*Fraxinus excelsior*), and in some places small-leaved lime, also called littleleaf linden (*Tilia cordata*).

Animals that attack trees

White-tailed deer (*Odocoileus virginianus*) are highly adaptable animals that thrive everywhere from the edge of the North American tundra to northern Peru and Brazil, and they

Deer are woodland animals that feed on ground plants and the leaves of shrubs and low trees. (Courtesy of Fogstock)

have been introduced in Scandinavia and New Zealand. Their success is due to their ability to eat a wide variety of plants. Like all other deer, they are *browsers,* which means that they eat the leaves of trees and shrubs, a diet that attracts them to forests. Elk (*Cervus elephas*), known in Britain as red deer, and the European roe deer (*Capreolus capreolus*) also seek food inside forests.

Deer cannot reach very high, however, so they are able to feed only on low-growing plants and on leaves from the lower branches of trees. Their food is most plentiful around the edges of forests, and they seldom penetrate deep inside the forest, except when fresh young plant growth is abundant in an area cleared by forest fire (see "Fire, and trees that depend on it" on pages 120–123).

As well as feeding on leaves, stags (adult male deer) also rub their antlers against tree trunks to remove the fur-covered skin called velvet that covers them when they first appear and supplies them with blood while they are forming. This can strip away patches of bark. The loss of bark is not directly serious because it does not damage the vascular cambium, but exposure of the living tissue allows infection to enter and the injured tree may become diseased as a result.

Deer are not the only mammals to enjoy the regeneration that follows fires. Berries begin to appear about two years after a fire and they remain abundant for about 20 years. Black bears (*Ursus americanus*) enter the forest in search of the berries. Moose (*Alces alces*), known in Europe as elk, feed on sprouting trees and begin to arrive about three years after a fire. Snowshoe hares (*Lepus americanus*) feed in the forest five to 35 years after a fire, nibbling the emerging plants. Once the young trees are big enough to build dams and lodges, beavers (*Castor canadensis*) arrive in parts of the forest close to rivers. Many deer and moose shelter in forests even when they are not feeding in them.

Wolves (*Canis lupus*) do not eat leaves, but they hunt deer and follow them into the forest. A forest comprising open spaces and compartments of different ages following fires is likely to provide food for wolves.

American bison (*Bison bison*) do not enter woodland, but European bison (*Bison bonasus*) are forest animals. Bison eat forest plants, but they also trample and uproot plants they do not eat. If there were large herds, bison might cause serious damage, but these animals survive only in the Białowieża Forest (Belovezhskaya Pushcha), where there are too few of them to be harmful (see "How ecological ideas developed" on pages 98–101). Wild boar (*Sus scrofa*) are common in mainland Europe. They eat a variety of foods, but especially roots and tubers that they dig up from the forest floor. In doing so they also destroy seedlings and other plants.

Large mammals feed mainly in and around the edges of clearings. They have no effect on the interior of the forest, and ordinarily trees quickly recover from any damage the animals cause. There are circumstances, however, in which the damage can be excessive, and deer have caused considerable harm in some North American and European forests.

The problem arises when roads and isolated areas that have been clear-felled divide the forest into fragments, thereby extending the total length of forest edge (see "Forest communities" on pages 127–130). Opening up the edge allows deer and other large animals to penetrate more deeply into what was formerly the forest interior, and by increasing the area of suitable habitat it allows their populations to increase to a level where the damage they do becomes serious. The extended forest edge also attracts predators, such as foxes and domestic dogs and cats. They destroy the eggs of ground-nesting birds, kill fledglings, and even attack adult birds that once nested securely deep in the interior of the forest.

Diseases and parasites of trees

Like any other living organism, a tree can fall sick, and from time to time there are devastating outbreaks of disease that destroy countless millions of trees. Two of the most serious outbreaks in recent times occurred in North America and in Europe.

Chestnut trees (*Castanea dentata*) were once common throughout the forests of eastern North America. Then, in about 1904, a consignment of chestnut trees arrived at New York from China. These trees were infected with a fungus, *Endothia parasitica*. No one knew about the infection.

Probably they would have taken no action even if they had known, because in China *Endothia parasitica* produces only very mild symptoms. When the fungus infected chestnut trees on Long Island, New York, however, the effect was very different. It killed the American chestnut trees and also European sweet chestnut trees (*C. sativa*) that were being grown in orchards. The disease spread rapidly. There was no way to control it and attacks were invariably fatal. It was called *chestnut blight* and by about 1940 it had destroyed almost all the chestnut trees in North America.

The European outbreak was due to the resurgence of a disease first described in the 19th century. In 1838 John Claudius Loudon (1783–1843), an English gardening writer, reported a disease that was afflicting elm trees (*Ulmus* species). The disease broke out again in France in 1918, and in 1919 Dutch scientists identified the responsible fungus. Because the fungus was first identified in the Netherlands, the disease it causes came to be called, perhaps unfairly, *Dutch elm disease.*

Infection begins when tiny elm bark beetles (mainly *Scolytus scolytus* and *S. multistriatus*), no more than 0.1–0.2 inch (3–5 mm) long, burrow into the bark and carve out nuptial chambers where they mate and lay eggs. Their larvae feed on the wood and adults feed on sap. The beetles attack in vast numbers and are capable of killing a tree without help. They often have help, however, in the form of the fungus *Ophiostoma ulmi,* spores of which they carry into the tree. The fungus then grows in the vascular tissue (see "How wood forms" on pages 94–97) and blocks the xylem vessels. That is what kills the tree.

A serious outbreak of Dutch elm disease began in Europe in 1920 and spread to North America by 1930, to where the infection was carried by *S. multistriatus* but sustained by an American bark beetle, *Hylurgopinus rufipes.* By 1940 the disease had died down in Europe, but it continued for longer in North America. In the 1960s the disease returned to Europe, this time caused by *O. novo-ulmi,* a much more virulent strain of the fungus. The 1960s outbreak killed approximately 25 million of the 30 million elm trees then growing in Britain. Dutch elm disease has since spread over most of the temperate world. It is found wherever there are elm trees, although not all species of elms are affected equally severely.

Elm bark beetles are related to a group known as *ambrosia beetles*. These beetles cannot survive without *ambrosia fungi*, so called because in Greek mythology ambrosia was the food of the gods (their drink was nectar). Ambrosia was sweeter than honey and anyone eating it was thought to become immortal; it was also a medicine that was believed to heal any wound. There are several species of ambrosia fungi. Each beetle species has its own preferred species of fungus and every beetle has a small pocket on its front legs in which it carries the spores. When the beetle invades a tree, the fungus feeds on the wood and the beetle feeds on the fungus, tending it carefully and removing waste matter. Ambrosia beetles bore tunnels deep into the wood, and ambrosia fungi can cause serious damage to the tree.

Woolly aphids are tiny insects that also transmit a serious disease of trees. The insects feed on plant sap. There are many species, most of them specializing in one or a few species of trees. The felted beech coccus (*Cryptococcus fagisuga*) prefers American and European beech trees (*Fagus grandifolia* and *F. sylvatica,* respectively). The insect's name refers to the waxy, feltlike substance with which it coats large areas of the trunk. The "felt" contains spores of the fungus *Nectria coccinea,* which infects the tree with beech bark disease. The disease slows the growth of the tree and a severe attack can kill it.

Not all fungi require insects to carry them into a tree. Spores of tinder fungus (*Fomes fomentarius*), also called hoof fungus and touchwood, enter wounds in the bark of broad-leaved trees and the fungus grows inside the tree. It hollows out the trunk until this splits and the branches fall. The fungus produces fruiting bodies in the form of brackets that project from the sides of the trunk. These have a leathery texture. In the past dentists used the fungus to clean and dry tooth cavities prior to filling them, and since Roman times it has been used to cauterize wounds. After treatment, the material of the fruiting bodies becomes highly flammable and is easily ignited by a spark from a flint; it is the original tinder fungus. Artist's conk, also called artist's fungus, picture fungus, and false tinder fungus (*Ganoderma applanatum*) is similar. It is common in forests and sometimes kills beech trees. Its common name refers to the fact that a picture carved on its smooth surface will remain there permanently.

Honey fungus, also known as bootlace fungus (*Armillaria* species), is the most serious of all fungal parasites. It begins by infecting the stump of a fallen tree and spreads outward from there through the soil as black strands called *rhizomorphs* that resemble black bootlaces. These enter trees—usually young ones—through any tiny crack in a root or even by piercing the bark. The fungus then spreads throughout the tree, rotting and finally killing it.

Caterpillars—moth larvae—can also cause serious damage. They eat leaves, and an infestation of thousands of them can defoliate a tree, causing severe injury. Some of the moths responsible are named for the time of year when the adults emerge to lay eggs. The winter moth (*Operophthera brumata*), for example, emerges between October and February. Its caterpillars feed on several trees, including oak and spruce, and they are serious pests in fruit orchards. Caterpillars of the oak leaf roller moth (*Tortrix viridana*) live inside leaves that they roll up to make a compartment, and they often defoliate oak trees.

Differences between a natural forest and a plantation

A forest that has grown up naturally over the centuries contains a variety of tree species. These are not distributed evenly (see "Forest communities" on pages 127–130). Rather, there are patches of forest, each with its own collection of species, and each tree species forms part of its own smaller community of shrubs and herbs. When a tree falls it opens up the canopy. As the fallen tree slowly decomposes, providing food for a range of organisms and supplying nutrients to the living plants, a young tree, perhaps of a different species, grows up to take its place. Gradually the composition of the community changes, while the forest remains as a patchwork of communities.

Logging removes trees, thereby preventing them from dying naturally and decomposing. The nutrients they contain are no longer recycled, and although fertilizers can be applied to replace the nutrients that are lost, repeated logging of commercially valuable trees eventually alters the character of the forest.

Plantation forestry is the alternative to logging in natural forest. A plantation consists of trees that have been planted. It looks like a forest, but there are important differences.

A natural forest contains those species that arrived by chance and survived under the prevailing conditions. A plantation contains trees that will thrive on the chosen site and yield lumber for which there is a commercial market. It will exclude "valueless" trees that are naturally small or that fail to grow straight. Most plantations include large blocks of a single species. These are often coniferous trees, such as Sitka spruce (*Picea sitchensis*), Norway spruce (*P. abies*), Douglas or Oregon fir (*Pseudotsuga menziesii*), Japanese larch (*Larix kaempferi*), and lodgepole pine (*Pinus contorta*). All the trees in the block are planted at the same time and consequently all the trees are the same age. At one time this produced monotonous, straight-edged, unattractive forests. Nowadays other, usually native trees are planted around the edges of the stands, and the edges are less straight than they used to be in order to provide more visual interest.

When the trees reach marketable size they are felled. Again, a complete block is clear-felled, leaving the site bare. Shrubs and herbs thrive for a time, but then a new crop of seedlings is planted and the cycle continues. Plantation forestry is exactly like arable farming. Lumber is the crop. To produce it, trees are planted, thinned when they reach a certain age, grown to the required size, and then harvested. The only difference is that instead of taking one season to ripen, the tree crop takes about 50 years.

Obviously, there is a considerable difference between a natural forest and a plantation, but this difference should not be exaggerated. Plantations tend to support less wildlife than natural forests, but this may be due partly to the fact that they are often grown on land that was not formerly forested and is far from the nearest natural forest. It takes many years for forest species to arrive and forest communities to become established, but this will happen in time. A plantation consists of blocks of trees all the same age, but natural forest compartments are not very different, because they grow up after trees have fallen, opening the canopy, and a compartment often contains only one or two dominant species. Within a plantation there are several—often many—blocks of trees at different ages, resembling the compartments of a natural forest. Together the blocks of the planted forest provide a variety of habitats for forest plants and animals, and animals are able to move freely from one block to another. Plantations that have existed for several 50-year harvest cycles support a rich wildlife, but in many areas the plantations are not yet that old.

Most important, though, is the fact that plantations produce lumber as a crop, which means they are sustainable indefinitely, and in doing so they render logging in natural forest unnecessary.

CHAPTER 6

BIODIVERSITY AND TEMPERATE FORESTS

What does *biodiversity* mean?

On October 28, 1982, the General Assembly of the United Nations adopted the World Charter for Nature. The charter is not a law but a set of ideas and principles that are intended to guide governments as they formulate policies that affect living organisms, and governments are expected to enshrine these ideas and principles in relevant national legislation. The charter calls on governments not to waste natural resources, to avoid pollution, and to protect natural habitats. It begins with a statement of general principles, of which the first three are:

1. Nature shall be respected and its essential processes shall not be impaired.

2. The genetic viability on the earth shall not be compromised; the population levels of all life forms, wild and domesticated, must be at least sufficient for their survival, and to this end necessary habitats shall be safeguarded.

3. All areas of the earth, both land and sea, shall be subject to these principles of conservation; special protection shall be given to unique areas, to representative samples of all the different types of ecosystems and to the habitats of rare or endangered species.

The second of these principles refers to "genetic viability" and the need to protect habitats in order to maintain populations of plants and animals. That idea was developed in the years that followed, leading to the Convention on Biological Diversity. A convention is an agreement between governments to take certain kinds of action or to behave in certain ways. It is less formal than a treaty, although once it comes into force it becomes part of international law. "Biological diversity" is often shortened to "biodiversity" and the convention is often called the "Biodiversity Convention" (see the sidebar on page 143).

Not all governments have signed the Biodiversity Convention, but that is because they disagree with its approach rather than with its principles. Every government accepts that it is desirable to preserve as much biodiversity as possible, both globally and within its national borders. Before any government can take practical steps to implement the convention, however, it must decide just what it is trying to preserve. What does "biological diversity" mean?

The Biodiversity Convention defines biological diversity as "the variability among living organisms from all sources, including, inter alia, terrestrial, marine and other aquatic ecosystems and the ecological complexes of which they are part. This includes diversity within species, between species, and of ecosystems."

Diversity therefore exists at three levels. Diversity within species refers to genetic diversity—the naturally inherited variation between individuals of the same species. For example, some people have dark skin, some light skin, some have blue eyes and some have brown eyes, and there are several blood types or groups so that the composition of the blood varies from one person to another. These are examples of within-species diversity among people.

Conserving genetic diversity presents a difficulty. Since each individual is unique, the only way to preserve this amount of diversity is to prevent any individual from dying, which is clearly absurd. In practice it is taken to mean that genetic variations among populations of a species should be noted and, so far as possible, the populations preserved from extinction. Local populations of a species are sometimes classified as subspecies or varieties, but very often they are not given a distinguishing scientific name, although they may have a common one. For instance, the Florida panther is a local population of the puma (*Felis concolor*).

Species diversity refers to the differences between species and the overall number of species. The concept of a species provides the basis for the system of biological classification.

This system was devised in the 18th century by the Swedish botanist Carl Linnaeus (see the sidebar) and it assumes that species are quite distinct from one another. That is how it seemed until biologists began examining species at the genetic level. They discovered that different species share a substantial number of genes and that one species shades into another rather than being sharply distinct from it. Genetically, there may be more difference between two individuals of the same species than there is between the average genetic constitution of their species and that of a related species. As a result the concept of the species has grown

Carolus Linnaeus and the classifying of plants and animals

People have always needed some way to describe the plants and animals they saw, but without a formal system of classification this is more difficult than it might seem. Everyone knows what the name *wolf* means, but suppose that word did not exist because no one had ever seen a wolf, until one day someone encountered one. How might that person describe it? Perhaps they might call it "a big, lean, mainly gray dog." Plants were even more difficult. In 1623, a famous Swiss scientist called Caspar Bauhin (1550–1624) described a plant as: *Ranunculus alpinus humilis rotundifolius minore* ("low-growing, round-leaved, small-flowered, alpine buttercup"). This was accurate enough as a description, but it was difficult to remember, and anyone interested in botany had to master hundreds of descriptions like this one.

The first comprehensive system to classify plants and animals—and also minerals—using simple, memorable names appeared in 1735, in a book with the title *Systema Naturae,* written by Carolus Linnaeus (1707–78).

Carl Linnaeus—Carolus was the fashionably Latinized version of his name that he used in his publications—was born in Råshult, in southern Sweden, the son of a clergyman who was also an avid amateur botanist. Linnaeus studied medicine at the University of Uppsala. The university had a botanical garden where he spent much time; in those days medical schools maintained botanical gardens as a source of medicinal herbs. In 1730 Linnaeus became a lecturer in botany at Uppsala and he qualified in medicine in 1735, the year he published *Systema Naturae.* He was the first president of the Royal Swedish Academy of Sciences and physician to the Swedish Admiralty, and in 1742 he became professor of rather more vague. Nevertheless, it is convenient and useful to group similar organisms into species.

Distinguishing between ecosystems is less controversial, because an ecosystem is defined as a distinctive area with boundaries that can be identified (see "How ecological ideas developed" on pages 98–101). The convention does cover marine ecosystems, however, which are often more difficult to define. The level of protection is also drawn widely: It is not only the diversity among plants, animals, and fungi that is to be protected, but also that among microorganisms of all kinds, including bacteria.

botany at the University of Uppsala. He was made a nobleman in 1741, and changed his name to Carl von Linné. He died on January 10, 1778, following a stroke.

Systema Naturae contained detailed drawings of plants, animals, and minerals, grouping them according to their similarities. His classification of minerals was abandoned, but his system for classifying plants and animals formed the basis of the system used today. Linnaeus was a dedicated and very popular teacher, and devised his system partly to help his students.

In the case of plants, the similarities arose from the number of flower parts. Linnaeus believed this "sexual system" identified distinctive characteristics. Scientists now know that the number of flower parts can vary considerably among closely related species, so, despite its title, Linnaeus's system did not reflect natural relationships and was artificial. Despite this, the 10th edition of *Systema Naturae,* published in 1758, is the starting point for the modern classification of animals, nowadays regulated by the International Code of Zoological Nomenclature. Linnaeus's most important botanical work was *Species Plantarum,* published in 1753. This is the starting point for modern plant classification, regulated by the International Code of Botanical Nomenclature.

Linnaeus grouped similar organisms into *species,* similar species into *genera* (singular *genus*), genera into *classes,* and classes into *orders.* The French zoologist Georges Cuvier (1769–1832) later extended the hierarchy by grouping orders into *phyla* (singular *phylum*). Linnaeus found it possible to name any organism by using only two words. The first word, conventionally spelled with an initial capital letter, is the name of the genus and the second, or trivial, name is the name of the species. This is sometimes called the *binomial* system of classification. The buttercup that Bauhin described in five words is now known as *Ranunculus alpestris* L. The "L" is for Linnaeus, to identify the scientist who first named the plant. Human beings are named in the same way, as *Homo sapiens* L.

Why biodiversity matters

When a forest is cleared, the land that is exposed can be used for many purposes. Originally, forest was cleared to provide farmland, to raise livestock and grow food. This is obviously important. Or the land might provide space to build homes, schools, shops, hospitals, factories, and offices—places where people can live and work. People all need to live somewhere, they need schools, shops to buy things, and to work, and when people fall sick they need medical care. These, surely, are more important uses for the land than just leaving it to grow trees, aren't they? People cannot eat trees, and even if their homes are built from wood, some forest must be cleared away to make space to construct them.

There is no shortage of arguments to justify clearing forests and other natural areas. These arguments are usually very persuasive. Sites really are needed for perfectly sensible uses; greed is not the only reason people clear forests. So what arguments can conservationists advance to counter these?

They might point out that when the forest is cleared, it is not only the trees that will be removed. So will all the herbs, fungi, animals, insects, and other members of the forest community. They could mention, for example, that digitalis is an important heart drug that was first isolated from the foxglove (*Digitalis purpurea*), a plant that grows in forest clearings. Perhaps they could mention an area of 270 acres (109 ha) of forest that was scheduled to be sold in 1996. A graduate student from Cornell University discovered on that site a tiny mold fungus from which cyclosporin is obtained. This drug is used to suppress the immune system to help patients avoid rejecting grafted tissue. These are not isolated cases. More than 10 percent of the major drugs prescribed by physicians in the United States were derived from plants, and more than 25 percent of our most common medicines contain at least some ingredients originally isolated from plants. The National Cancer Institute has tested 35,000 species of vascular plants in its search for anticancer drugs and has found that many of them contain effective substances that have been extracted and analyzed. Plants may, and probably do, contain substances that have not yet been identified but that might be effective in treating a wide variety of serious illnesses. The

The Biodiversity Convention

In June 1972 the United Nations sponsored the largest international conference held until that date. Called the UN Conference on the Human Environment, it was held in Stockholm, Sweden, and was known informally as the Stockholm Conference. Delegates to the conference resolved to establish a new United Nations agency, to be called the UN Environment Program (UNEP). UNEP came into being in 1973. Its tasks are to collect and circulate information about the state of the global environment and to encourage and coordinate international efforts to reduce pollution and protect wildlife.

UNEP sponsored several major conferences over the years, and in 1992, 20 years after the Stockholm Conference, it organized the UN Conference on Environment and Development, also known as the Earth Summit and the Rio Summit because it took place in Rio de Janeiro, Brazil. It was the largest meeting of world leaders ever held. The aim of the 1992 conference was to relate environmental protection to economic development, and to this end the delegates agreed on the provisions that were set down in the Convention on Climate Change and the Convention on Biological Diversity—also known as the Biodiversity Convention.

A convention is a binding agreement between governments. Government representatives sign the convention, and when their own legislatures have accepted it, the governments ratify it by signing it again, confirming their willingness to abide by its terms. The lawmakers must then translate those terms into national law. When a majority of signatory governments have ratified the convention, it becomes part of international law and is known as a treaty. By the summer of 2005 157 countries had ratified the Biodiversity Convention.

The Biodiversity Convention reminds governments that natural resources are not infinite and promotes the principle of using resources in sustainable ways that ensure future generations will also be able to enjoy them. The convention requires governments to develop national strategies and plans of action to measure, conserve, and promote the sustainable use of natural resources. National plans for environmental protection and economic development should incorporate these strategies and plans, especially in respect of forestry, agriculture, fisheries, energy, transportation, and city planning. As well as protecting existing areas of high biodiversity, governments should restore degraded areas. The convention strongly emphasizes the need to involve local communities in its projects and to raise public awareness of the value of a diverse natural environment.

Many countries have now taken positive steps to implement the Biodiversity Convention.

plants have not yet been identified, but if we destroy the communities of which they are part we may lose them altogether. Forests may contain chemical compounds with the power to improve human lives and to save them.

These are selfish reasons, however. There are other reasons for retaining areas of natural forest, reasons that have nothing directly to do with curing diseases and improving life for human beings, their farm livestock, or their household pets. Wild plants contain genetic material that one day may be of value to other plants. Genetic engineering makes it possible to transfer genes that confer desirable qualities from one plant to another. The loss of wild plant populations implies the loss not only of the source of those genes but also the natural genetic pattern against which scientists can measure the changes they introduce.

Scientists and conservationists recognized long ago the importance of preserving natural communities of plants and animals as far as possible in a state where they remained undisturbed by human activities. The variety of species such communities contain, and the genetic variety this represents, came to be known as "biological diversity" and abbreviated to "biodiversity." As evidence emerged of the rate at which biological diversity was being lost, concern over the situation increased until governments felt compelled to take action.

When the heads of the governments of 178 nations gathered at the United Nations Conference on Environment and Development held in Rio de Janeiro, Brazil, in June 1992, preserving biological diversity was high on their agenda. That conference—nicknamed the Earth Summit—was the largest summit meeting of world leaders ever held, and one of its major achievements was the Convention on Biological Diversity—the Biodiversity Convention (see the sidebar).

Typical trees of temperate forests

Temperate forests occur naturally over such a vast area that it is not surprising they contain a wide variety of tree species. Botanists group related species into genera and related genera into families (see the sidebar "Carolus Linnaeus and the classifying of plants and animals" on pages 140–141), and many of the most widespread trees of temperate forests belong to just two families: Fagaceae and Betulaceae. The Fagaceae, or beech family, includes the oaks, beeches, southern beeches, and sweet chestnuts. These trees grow naturally throughout the temperate and tropical regions and are the dominant species in many temperate forests. The Betulaceae, or birch family, comprises the birches, alders, hornbeams, and hazels, which grow throughout the temperate regions of the Northern Hemisphere as far north as southern Greenland, and at higher elevations in the Andes of South America.

Oaks (*Quercus* species) are probably the most common trees of all, but this is partly due to the fact that there are approximately 600 species. North America, with 85 native species, has a greater variety of oaks than any other continent. Many oaks produce valuable timber. White oak (*Q. alba*), found on the eastern side of the continent, is the most commercially important North American oak. It is a huge tree, growing up to 160 feet (49 m) tall and with a trunk that is up to five feet (1.5 m) across. Its timber was once used for shipbuilding and to make railroad ties. It is still used to make furniture and barrels. The most durable oak timber comes not from white oak, however, but from live oak (*Q. virginiana*), native to the southern states and Mexico.

Pedunculate oak (*Q. robur*), also known as common oak and English oak, is the most famous of the European species. It grows in the same areas as sessile oak (*Q. petraea*), also called durmast oak, and the two trees look similar. The species can be distinguished by the way their acorns grow. Pedunculate oak bears its acorns attached by long stalks, or *peduncles,* while those of sessile oak sit directly on the twig.

Most oak trees are deciduous, shedding their leaves in the fall, but those growing in warmer climates are evergreen. Evergreen oaks are known as live oaks in North America. In addition to *Q. virginiana,* there are encina, also known as California live oak and coast live oak (*Q. agrifolia*), canyon live oak or maul oak (*Q. chrysolepsis*), and interior live oak (*Q. wislizeni*). Holm oak or holly oak (*Q. ilex*), which has leaves resembling those of holly, is the most widespread European evergreen species. Bamboo-leaved (or -leaf) oak, also known as Chinese evergreen oak and Japanese evergreen oak (*Q. myrsinifolia*), found only in eastern Asia, is an evergreen species with narrow, smooth-edged leaves. There are also semievergreen oaks, such as laurel oak (*Q. laurifolia*) and willow oak (*Q. phellos*). Semievergreen trees retain some but not all of their leaves throughout the year.

One evergreen oak produces cork, which is one of the most familiar commodities in the world. The cork oak (*Q. suber*) grows in southern Europe and North Africa. Cork oak produces a very thick layer of cork (see "How wood forms" on pages 94–97), and removing cork encourages the living tree to lay down more. Cork oaks live to a great age.

Beeches (*Fagus* species) have a much more restricted distribution. There are only 10 species, and only one of these, American beech (*F. grandifolia*) is native to North America. European beech (*F. sylvatica*) and oriental beech (*F. orientalis*) are the equivalent species in western and eastern Europe respectively. Japanese beech (*F. crenata*) is an important forest tree in Japan.

Southern beeches (*Nothofagus* species) are the second most important timber trees of the Southern Hemisphere, after the mainly tropical and subtropical eucalypts (*Eucalyptus* species). Some are deciduous and others evergreen. There are 35 species of southern beeches, occurring naturally in New Guinea, New Caledonia, temperate Australia and New Zealand, and in Chile and southern Argentina. Wood from myrtle beech (*N. cunninghamii*), native to southeastern Australia, is used for flooring and to make furniture. Roble (*N. obliqua*), ruil (*N. alessandri*), and Dombey's southern beech or coigue (*N. dombeyi*) are commercially important in South America. Southern beeches have been planted extensively in Europe to replace elms lost to Dutch elm disease (see "Diseases and parasites of trees" on pages 132–135).

Sweet chestnuts (*Castanea* species) are deciduous trees that occur naturally only in the Northern Hemisphere. There are 12 species. American chestnut trees (*C. dentata*) were once widespread in North American forests, yielding high-quality timber and the best of all chestnuts, but chestnut blight has rendered the species almost extinct. The European sweet chestnut (*C. sativa*) grows naturally in southern Europe. The Romans introduced it to Britain, where it is sometimes known as the Spanish chestnut, perhaps—although no one can be sure—because until then chestnuts were imported from Spain. Other chestnut species grow in China and Japan.

Alders (*Alnus* species), birches (*Betula* species), hornbeams (*Carpinus* species), and hazels (*Corylus* species) all belong to the family Betulaceae—the birch family. Alders are 35 species of small deciduous trees that grow on wet ground, beside rivers and lakes. Their male flowers are catkins and their woody fruits look like small pinecones. Native Americans used to make canoes by hollowing out the trunks of red or Oregon alder (*A. oregona*), and the wood chippings were used to smoke fish. The most widespread North American species are American green alder (*A. crispa*), which grows in the East, and Sitka alder (*A. sinuata*), which grows in the West, from Alaska to northern California. Wood from black alder (*A. glutinosa*), also called common alder and European alder, is used for carving and was once used to make clogs. It may also have been used in making Stradivarius violins.

Birches are small, hardy deciduous trees that grow best in northern temperate regions. There are about 60 species. They also bear catkins, but unlike alder catkins, birch catkins shatter when they are ready to release their windborne pollen. Many birches have attractive bark. The waterproof bark of the paper birch or canoe birch (*Betula papyrifera*) peels off like sheets of paper. Native Americans formerly used it to cover canoes. This is the most widespread North American birch. Silver birch (*B. pendula*) is one of the most common European species. "Silver" refers to the color of its bark and *"pendula"* to the way the tips of its branches hang down. Downy birch (*B. pubescens*) is also widespread. Oil obtained from the bark of downy birch is used in Russia to tan leather, giving Russian leather a characteristic smell.

American hornbeam (*Carpinus caroliniana*) is the only one of the 35 species of hornbeams that is native to North America. It is grown as an ornamental tree because of its fall colors, and it occurs naturally on the eastern side of the continent. Hornbeams are deciduous trees that produce very hard, dense wood. Wood from the common European hornbeam (*C. betulus*) is still used to make the levers between the keys and hammers in pianos, as well as butchers' blocks, pulleys, and similar items that must withstand hard wear. It was once used to make the cogwheels in mills and yokes for oxen.

Hazels are 10 species of deciduous shrubs or small trees that often occur in the understory of temperate forests in the Northern Hemisphere. They are widely cultivated for ornament or for their nuts, and also for poles produced by coppicing (see the sidebar "Coppicing and pollarding" on page 195). American hazel or filbert (*Corylus americana*), a shrub up to 10 feet (3 m) tall, is the most popular ornamental hazel. Nuts from cultivated hazels are called filberts. In Europe *C. maxima,* a tree native to southeastern Europe, yields the best filberts. In Britain, large filberts grown mainly in Kent are sometimes sold as "cobnuts." The native British and northern European hazel is *C. avellana,* which grows to about 20 feet (6 m) tall. Turkish hazel (*C. colurna*), native to southeastern Europe and southwestern Asia, is a much bigger tree, reaching about 80 feet (25 m). Farther east there are Chinese hazel (*C. chinensis*), which is very similar to Turkish hazel, and Tibetan (*C. tibetica*) and Japanese hazel (*C. sieboldiana*), both of which grow to 15–25 feet (4.5–7.5 m).

Typical animals of temperate forests

Many traditional folktales are set in the vast, seemingly endless forests that once blanketed northern Europe (see "Forests in folklore" on pages 167–169). The animals that feature in those stories are forest animals and, of all those animals, bears are the fiercest.

Brown bears (*Ursus arctos*) once inhabited the Eurasian forests from Scandinavia eastward to the Pacific, patches of forest in southern Europe and western Asia, and the forests of northwestern North America. Despite this, encounters between people and bears were never common. A brown bear is a big animal that needs a large area of forest in which to forage for food, so bears were always widely scattered. In addition, most bears avoid contact with humans, except where they are attracted to food that has been discarded around human settlements. In these places bears may have learned to associate the smell of humans with food, making encounters more likely. This is undesirable, because an urgent need to defend their cubs and repel rival adults makes all bears aggressive. Combined with poor eyesight that makes it easy for them to mistake a human for a juvenile bear in an upright, challenging posture, their inclination to attack makes them unpredictable and therefore dangerous. The resulting persecution, together with changes in land use that have divided what was once continuous forest into patches too small to support bears, has greatly reduced the bear population. The brown bear is still the most widely distributed of all bears, but large populations now survive only in northwestern North America and Russia.

There are several subspecies of brown bears. Grizzlies (*U. a. horribilis*) and Kodiak bears (*U. a. middendorffi*) are the biggest. An adult male grizzly weighs up to 800 pounds (365 kg) and eats up to 30 pounds (14 kg) of food a day. Male Eurasian brown bears (*U. a. arctos*) usually weigh less than 600 pounds (272 kg). Brown bears feed on roots and burrowing animals, which they dig up with their long claws, and on leaves, berries, honey, fish, deer, and sometimes farm livestock. Despite their name, not all brown bears are brown. Their fur ranges in color from cream through many shades of brown to black.

Black bears (*Ursus americanus*) occur only in North American forests—and they may be white or brown rather than black. They are smaller than brown bears and eat a similar diet.

Bears breed very slowly. Female grizzlies raise no more than six or eight cubs in their whole lives, and black bears raise no more than about 12. Consequently, killing bears quickly reduces the population. Since bears need such a large area to find food, it is easy to see why they have vanished from most of the territory they once occupied.

Wild boar (*Sus scrofa*) still roams through most of the forests of continental Europe and Asia, but it is not found in North America. It became extinct in Britain in the 17th century; in modern times, however, a market has developed for its meat, leading to the introduction of farmed boars. Some of these animals escaped, and they have now reestablished themselves in the wild in parts of southern England. Wild boars feed mainly on roots, nuts, and other plant material, but will also eat earthworms and other small animals. Adult males are often solitary. Groups of wild boar consist either of bachelor males or of sows with their young. Ordinarily, wild boars live an unhurried existence, walking slowly across the forest floor as they search for food and resting frequently. Despite their relaxed appearance, anyone encountering wild boar should give them a wide berth. They are highly aggressive if disturbed, can run fast when they need to, and they are capable of inflicting serious wounds with their powerful tusks.

Rivers that flow through forests, and the ponds and lakes associated with them, are the home of the beaver. Because of demand for their fur, North American beavers (*Castor canadensis*) suffered greatly from hunting—wars were fought over access to the areas where they were trapped—but they are now protected and have been reintroduced where they had become extinct. Today they are found throughout North American forests, and they have been introduced in parts of Europe and Asia. Steps are also being taken to reintroduce the European beaver (*C. fiber*) in the forests it once inhabited. Formerly found throughout Europe and western Asia north of the Caspian Sea, the European beaver survives today only in isolated parts of France, Germany, Scandinavia, and Russia.

Beavers mate for life and devote a great deal of care to the young, called kits, which remain with their parents for up to two years. Each family builds a dam across a stream, using sticks, bigger branches, and stones, all held together with mud. The beavers then tunnel into the bank of the stream and extend the tunnel upward as the water level rises behind the dam. When the tunnel breaks the surface, the beavers cover it with sticks and mud. As the water level continues rising, the beavers raise the dam wall and also the roof of the chamber in which they sleep and where the kits are born. All the family except for the kits work to build and maintain the dam and dwelling, called a lodge. The rising water usually surrounds the lodge, so eventually it becomes an artificial island in the middle of the pond. The drawing shows a beaver lodge and dam.

During spring and summer the beaver family feeds on plants around the pond, but in the fall they start to store woody plant material to feed them through the winter. The

dam   water level   lodge   water level

food store is situated on the bottom of the pond, within easy underwater access from the entrance to the lodge. In summer beavers often dig canals to link ponds and feeding areas.

Beavers are rodents that live in and beside water. Above them are rodents that live in the trees, leaping from branch to branch and running effortlessly up trunks and headfirst down them. Squirrels are marvelously agile, and the most widespread squirrel of temperate forests is the gray squirrel (*Sciurus carolinensis*), a North American species that was introduced to Britain on several occasions between 1876 and 1930. It is now common in most of England and Wales, but occurs only in the central part of Scotland. It is also found in parts of eastern Ireland. Gray squirrels inhabit broad-leaved forests, especially where oak, hickory, and walnut are the dominant trees. They eat nuts of all kinds, as well as tree leaves, buds, pollen, and fungi.

Foresters regard squirrels as pests because they strip bark from trees, causing considerable damage. The squirrels strip bark to find the sweet sap flowing through the vascular tissue just below the outer bark (see "How wood forms" on pages 94–97). They invariably choose the trees with the thickest sap—those that the forester considers the best trees—and ignore the others. The eastern chipmunk *(Tamias striatus)* is

Beaver lodge and dam. Inside their lodge the beavers live above the water, but the entrance to the lodge is below the surface.

Chipmunks are lively, inquisitive forest animals. They feed on nuts, berries, and all kinds of seeds. This is an eastern American chipmunk (Tamias striatus). (Courtesy of Gerry Ellis, Minden Pictures)

also a squirrel, and very familiar because it is naturally inquisitive and is not afraid of humans. It does not damage trees.

Deer also strip bark from trees in order to eat it. They also eat buds, shoots, leaves, and flowers of a wide variety of plants. Most deer are forest animals. They are seen in open country, but they seldom stray far from the forest edge. The biggest deer of the temperate forest is the red deer (*Cervus elaphus*), standing about four feet (1.2 m) tall at the shoulder, which is found throughout Europe, Asia, and North Africa. Some zoologists consider the red deer to be the same species as the North American wapiti or elk, but others regard the wapiti as a separate species, *C. canadensis*. The white-tailed deer (*Odocoileus virginianus*) is smaller, up to 3.3 feet (1 m) tall at the shoulder, and highly adaptable. It occurs in forests, brushland, and swampy areas from southern Canada to Brazil and Peru. The roe deer (*Capreolus capreolus*) is very similar but stands only about three feet (0.9 m) tall. It occurs throughout Europe and Asia.

CHAPTER 7

HISTORY OF TEMPERATE FORESTS

Forest clearance in prehistory

When Europeans first began to explore North America it was natural for them to assume that the landscapes they saw had existed since the dawn of time. In the east there were forests, and beyond the forests the interior of the continent was a sea of tall grasses and bright flowers. The French called it a meadow, for which the French word is *prairie*.

The tallgrass prairie was vast, but it had not existed since the dawn of time. Sediments taken from the beds of lakes on the prairie contain tree pollen. Until about 5,000 years ago there were groves of trees set in the grassland, making it an open forest.

Scientists are not sure why the landscape changed, but the most likely explanation begins with a change in the climate. Between 5,000 and 6,000 years ago the weather became much drier. Trees need moisture, and as the rainfall decreased they became more scattered. Grasses are more tolerant of dry conditions, so they thrived. The prairies became established.

That was not the end of the story, however, because about 4,000 years ago the climate changed again. This time it became cooler and moister. Trees returned and the boundary between the forests and the prairies moved westward. Open forest should have become established over much of the prairies, and it would have if humans had not intervened.

Grassland fires have always been common. Grass withers and dries during dry weather, and then it ignites easily. Storms were as common then as they are now, and lightning started fires that swept before the wind. Herds of grazing animals moved ahead of the fire, and this made them easier for skilled hunters to kill. Native Americans aided the process by starting fires deliberately to drive game into ambushes.

When the fires died down, fresh grass and other non-woody plants flourished in the ashes, improving the pasture. There was more food for the grazing animals, so their numbers increased, and that meant there was more food for the hunters. The herds became huge and the people lived well, but the forest never returned. Fire and trampling by livestock destroyed tree seedlings until the soil's stock of tree seeds was exhausted and there were no mature trees to replenish it. More recently, the prairie has been converted to farmland.

It was not only the North American prairies that were formed in this way. Many scientists suspect that large parts of the South American pampa and Eurasian steppe also resulted from this combination of fire and trampling by game. To this day, people inhabiting the African savanna use fire to maintain the grassland for the benefit of the livestock on which they depend.

Forest is the natural type of vegetation over most of the lowlands of northwestern Europe, but it is not the vegetation that travelers see today. Europe is farmed intensively and fields have replaced most of the original forests.

Clearance of the British forest began about 5,500 years ago and it was farmers, not hunters, who were responsible. Knowledge of farming—the cultivation of plant crops—spread across Europe from what is now Turkey. By about 6,000 years ago it had reached the Atlantic and Channel coasts and soon afterward it entered Britain, carried by people who had to cross the open sea to reach British shores. At the end of the Wisconsinian (Devensian) ice age (see the sidebar "Holocene, Pleistocene, and late Pliocene ice ages and interglacials" on page 13), melting ice sheets and glaciers released so much water that the sea level rose rapidly. About 8,000 years ago water flooded low-lying land between what are now England and France, creating the English Channel.

The early farmers grew wheat, barley, and other plant crops and kept pigs, cattle, and possibly sheep and goats as well. They probably practiced *swidden* farming. This involves clearing an area of ground to grow crops. After a year or two, when the soil becomes depleted of nutrients, weeds proliferate out of control, and crop yields decline, the farming family moves to a new area, clears the ground, and starts over.

Swidden farmers revisit the same areas, working in a cycle, usually of five to 10 years.

Farmers would not have allowed the animals onto their cultivated ground, where they would have destroyed the crops. Pigs are forest animals and would have foraged for themselves in the forest. Cattle would have grazed in the forest clearings, but they fed mainly by browsing on the tree leaves and shoots within their reach. Their herders would have augmented this food supply by climbing into the trees and cutting down browse from higher branches. As they fed, the cattle trampled tree seedlings and damaged bark, sometimes severely enough to kill trees, thus enlarging their clearings. If the farmers kept sheep they would have needed to clear forest to provide pasture for them, because sheep are grazers, not browsers.

About 5,000 years ago a sharp reduction in the number of elm trees (*Ulmus* species) occurred over most of northwestern Europe, in an episode called the elm decline. No one knows just why this happened. Disease or a severe pest infestation might have caused it (see "Diseases and parasites of trees" on pages 132–135), but alternatively it might have resulted from a change in farming technique. Farmers might have started keeping their cattle in pens to protect them from predators such as wolves and to prevent them from wandering into the forest and disappearing. That would have made their farming more efficient, but it would also mean the animals were no longer able to find their own food. The farmers would have had to gather food and bring it to them, as is done for cattle raised in beef lots. Farmers would have collected browse, perhaps seeking out elm twigs and leaves because cattle find these especially palatable. Removing foliage before the trees flowered would have greatly reduced the amount of pollen they produced—and scientists know about the elm decline because of the reduction in the amount of pollen they find in the soil (see "Using pollen and beetles to study the past" on pages 157–161). It may be, therefore, that the number of trees remained fairly constant and it was only their output of pollen that decreased.

What is certain is that it was farmers who cleared the European forests. This sounds like a formidable task, but it is surprisingly easy. European farmers used axes with blades made of chert—the stone called *flint* when it is found embedded in chalk—fixed to ashwood handles. Some years ago, Danish scientists fixed a wooden handle to a genuine 4,000-year-old ax blade of this type and found they could cut down 100 trees before the blade needed sharpening. On another occasion it took three men using axes with blades of polished stone just four hours to clear about 718 square yards (600 m^2) of birch forest, helped by the fact that as one tree fell it often brought down others.

Using pollen and beetles to study the past

Flower pollen consists of microscopically small grains produced by the anthers (see the sidebar "What is a flower?" on page 90). Borne by the wind or clinging to the bodies of animals, pollen travels from the male organs of one flower to the female organs of another. It is a hazardous journey, and flowers produce copious amounts of pollen to allow for the fact that most never reaches its intended destination.

Pollen grains are extremely tough, however. Each one is encased in a coat called an exine that is almost indestructible. Of all the countless trillions of pollen grains that set off each year in search of a female flower to fertilize, most fall by the wayside, onto the ground, into rivers and lakes, or into the sea, and are lost. But a few grains fall onto wet mud or sink to the bed of a lake or pond, where the acid conditions preserve them. The cells inside the pollen grain survive for only a short time, but the exine can remain unaltered for thousands of years.

The exine has two layers. The inner layer, called the nexine, is smooth, but the outer layer, called the sexine, is sculptured, with patterns of pores, grooves, or spines. Pollen grains also vary in shape and size. Some are spherical, others oval, and they range in size from less than 10 μm (0.0004 inch) to 250 μm (0.01 inch) across. The shape and size of the pollen grain and the markings on its surface are unique to each plant family and, in some cases, to particular species.

Scientists are able to extract pollen grains from soils and sediments and identify the type of plants that produced them. Pollen from grasses and other herbs can usually be identified to the family level, trees and shrubs to the level of genus, and a few plants to the species level.

Radiocarbon dating

Most carbon atoms have nuclei composed of six protons (particles carrying a positive charge) and six neutrons (particles carrying no charge); this is written as $^{12}_{6}C$ or simply ^{12}C, the "12" referring to the mass of the nucleus. Nitrogen nuclei have seven protons and a mass of 14: $^{14}_{7}N$. Chemical elements are defined by the number of protons in the nuclei of their atoms.

Cosmic radiation—high-energy particles from space—strike air molecules, and this bombardment releases neutrons. Occasionally a neutron strikes a nitrogen atomic nucleus and replaces one of its protons. The nitrogen atom now has six protons, but a nucleus with six protons is not nitrogen but carbon: $^{14}_{7}N$ has been transformed into $^{14}_{6}C$. This is carbon-14, or ^{14}C, and because it is radioactive it is also known as radiocarbon.

Plants use both ^{12}C and ^{14}C in photosynthesis, so both forms of carbon are present in all living tissue. Only ^{12}C is stable, however. Being radioactive, ^{14}C decays back to ^{14}N at a slow and very precise rate. After 5,700–5,760 years, half of the ^{14}C in a sample will have decayed.

While an organism is alive the amount of ^{14}C in its tissues is constantly replenished, so the ratio of ^{12}C to ^{14}C in its tissues is the same as the ratio in the atmosphere. After it dies, however, the organism no longer absorbs ^{14}C, and the ^{14}C in its tissues steadily decays, altering the ratio of ^{12}C to ^{14}C. Scientists can measure this ratio in small samples of material and use it to calculate the amount of ^{14}C that has decayed and therefore the age of the sample. The calculated age is reported as so many *radiocarbon years BP* ("BP" means "before present," "present" being taken as 1950).

Although cosmic radiation constantly produces ^{14}C in the atmosphere, the rate at which it does so varies slightly. Scientists have been able to check radiocarbon dates against dates measured by counting the annual growth rings in very ancient trees, to allow them to convert radiocarbon years into calendar years.

Radiocarbon dating measures the age of material up to about 70,000 years old. If the sample is older than that, so much of the ^{14}C has decayed that it is impossible to measure the $^{12}C:^{14}C$ ratio accurately. The method can be used only with samples from material that was once alive. As well as the remains of plants and animals, this also includes wood and cloth.

The operation begins by drilling out a core of soil or sediment, then laying out the material on a bench. The ages of tiny fragments of organic material present in the core are calculated from the amount of radioactive carbon-14 present in their cells (see the sidebar), allowing the core to be labeled with the age at each level from the surface downward. Scientists then know when the pollen at each level was produced.

By studying the pollen, scientists reconstruct the type of plants that were growing at different times: the vegetational history of the site. This is displayed graphically in the form of a *pollen diagram,* like the example in the illustration. A pollen diagram devotes one column to each of the most abundant species in the sample. Each column is graduated vertically with the depth, in this case starting 39 inches (100 cm) below ground level. Horizontally it shows the amount of pollen for that species as the percentage of the total pollen present, known as the *relative pollen frequency* (RPF). Some pollen diagrams show the *absolute pollen frequency* (APF), which is the

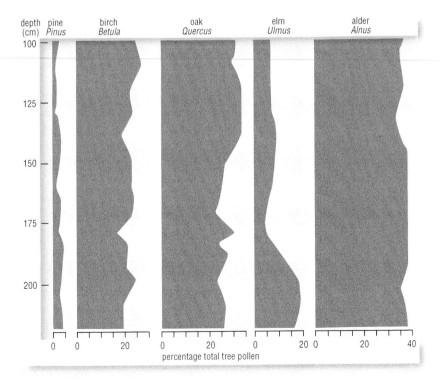

A pollen diagram, showing the percentage of the total pollen contributed by five tree species at each depth. The diagram shows how the vegetation has changed over time.

number of pollen grains present. The shading makes it is easy to see the proportion of plants at each level. In the drawing, for example, at a depth of 60 inches (150 cm), the forest was 40 percent alder (*Alnus* species), 30 percent oak (*Quercus* species), 25 percent birch (*Betula* species), 10 percent elm (*Ulmus* species), and 5 percent pine (*Pinus* species).

Alder grows on riverbanks and on wet ground and birch is a species found in northern forests, where the climate is cool. The preponderance of alder suggests that at the time corresponding to soil at a depth of 60 inches the site was wet, perhaps marshy, and the climate was cool and fairly rainy. Pollen diagrams must be interpreted with care, however, and the obvious interpretation may not be accurate. In this case it is important to know that alder and birch trees produce more than twice as much pollen as the other species growing at the site; adjust the count for those species and the picture changes. Probably the forest was mainly oak with birch and elm and occasional pine trees, and alder growing where the ground was wet.

Paleoecologists and paleoclimatologists—scientists who study past environments and past climates, respectively—have another tool to help them: beetles. Beetles are everywhere, and there are at least 350,000 species. Of all the animals living in a forest, approximately three-quarters are beetles. Individual beetles do not travel very far, and most species survive only within a narrow environmental range. If the climate is too warm, too cool, too wet, or too dry for them, they disappear, so if the climate changes the beetle community will also change. Some species will die out and others will take their place. A representative sample of the beetle population in a particular place is therefore an excellent guide to the climate.

The ancestors of beetles had two pairs of wings, but in beetles the front pair have become modified and are now *elytra*—tough wing cases that open to allow the wings to be used and that protect the delicate hind wings when the insect is not flying. Even insects that have lost their hind wings in the course of their later evolution still retain elytra. Like pollen grains, beetle elytra are very tough and are often preserved in soils and lakebed sediments.

Beetle elytra are more useful indicators than pollen, because they are easier to interpret. Elytra are unlikely to be carried far from where the insect died, so they really do represent the beetles living at the site. Pollen, on the other hand, is blown by the wind, and pollen from some trees travels farther than pollen from others. Consequently, unlike beetle elytra, the pollen preserved at a site may not give an entirely true picture of the plants that once grew there.

Forests in the days of ancient Greece and Rome

In about 2000 B.C.E., people using tools and weapons made of bronze, an alloy of copper and tin, entered Greece from the north. They were called the Hellenes, or Greeks, and they mingled and intermarried with the original inhabitants of Greece, who used stone tools. Their migration took place in three stages, the last in about 1100 B.C.E., and the culture the immigrants established developed into the civilization of ancient Greece.

The migrants brought with them their stories of gods, goddesses, and heroes. Many of those stories are set in forests or forest clearings, places where mortals might encounter gods and goddesses, as well as lesser woodland spirits such as pans and satyrs (later called fauns by the Romans)—beings who were half human and half goat. Forests must have been familiar places to the people who told and listened to such stories, and who worshipped gods who lived in the forest. In fact, in those days forests covered 84 percent of the land area of Greece.

The forest was not to last. Farmers needed land to grow food, and as agriculture expanded the area of forest decreased. Mountainsides were cleared first. The land was fertile and food was plentiful, but as immigration continued and the population increased, farming spread into the lowlands, where more trees were felled to make way for cropland. The success of agriculture made farmland valuable. Neighboring communities quarrelled over boundaries and outsiders attacked, attempting to seize land. Repeated conflicts drove people out of northern Greece, and many of these migrants headed south to find new ways to earn a living in the city of Athens. But the soils of southern Greece were poorer than the soils of the north and they were unable to support the expanding population. The Athenians had no choice but to establish colonies elsewhere to accommodate people their own farms could not feed.

Athenian expansion resulted in war with neighboring states. There was an age of wars that reached its climax during the lifetime of Pericles (c. 495–429 B.C.E.), an Athenian statesman who was largely responsible for the establishment of the Greek Empire and the development of Greek democracy. Greece comprises a peninsula and many islands, and in order to wage war the Athenians needed a navy. Their ships were built from wood, and by the time of Pericles the timber for shipbuilding had to be imported. The forests of southern Greece had been cleared and the northern mountainsides were bare. Soil eroded from the mountains, washed away by the rains, and erosion created the dramatic, harsh landscapes of modern Greece.

More than half of the original Greek forest has gone. Today forests cover almost 14,000 square miles (36,000 km²), amounting to 27 percent of the total land area of Greece, and 97 percent of the forest is natural, rather than plantation (see "Plantation forestry" on pages 199–202). The Greek forests are now expanding. Their area increased by 9 percent between 1990 and 2000.

Greek civilization spread throughout the lands surrounding the eastern Mediterranean. The mightiest empire of the ancient world was not Greek, however, but Roman. Immigrants from central Europe had begun settling in Italy in about 1600 B.C.E., and at its peak in 400 C.E. the Roman Empire stretched from Jordan in the east to the Atlantic Ocean in the west, and from North Africa and Egypt in the south to Britain in the north.

Roman power expanded by military conquest and by trade, and the expansion made many Romans extremely wealthy. Roman aristocrats invested their money in land, establishing large rural estates, and as land prices rose, speculators bought and sold farms in the hope of making a quick profit. Small farmers found life difficult, much as they do today in the face of competition from large agricultural corporations. The wealthy landowners seldom farmed the land themselves. They employed bailiffs to manage their estates and there were slaves to do the hard work.

The first immigrants found forests covering 94 percent of the land area of Italy and, being farmers, they set about clearing areas to grow food. The process continued, until eventually almost two-thirds of the original forest had disappeared. Today forests cover approximately 39,000 square miles (101,000 km^2), which is 33 percent of the land area of Italy. Almost all of the forest is natural rather than plantation. As in Greece, the forested area is increasing. Between 1990 and 2000 it expanded by 3 percent.

How North America nearly lost its forests

Forests cover 33 percent of the land area of the United States and 45 percent of Canada. The U.S. forests represent 5 percent of the world's forests and the Canadian forests amount to 10 percent, so 15 percent of the world's forests are located in North America. The Canadian forests cover 1.6 million square miles (4.18 million km^2) and those of the United States occupy 1.2 million square miles (3 million km^2).

It is a vast area, but it used to be even greater. European settlers cleared parts of the forests to make space for farming and they used the seemingly inexhaustible supply of timber for construction and fuel—fuel for industrial as well as domestic use. Wood was also a source of charcoal (see the sidebar "Charcoal and how it is made" on page 182) and of certain industrial raw materials, such as potash. Potash, also called pearlash, is potassium carbonate (K$_2$CO$_3$). It is used in the manufacture of glass and soap and in the processing of wool. Nowadays there is an industrial process for making potassium carbonate, but in the 18th century it was obtained from wood ash and in the 1790s potash from burned forest timber was one of Vermont's most important exports.

Forests began to disappear during the 17th century, but the process accelerated during the 19th. The rate of clearance was dramatic. A good example of this is Cadiz, a small town in Wisconsin with a population of 863 and a land area of 36.4

George Perkins Marsh

George Perkins Marsh (1801–82) was one of the founders of the conservation movement and the author of *Man and Nature,* one of the most influential books on the subject ever published.

   Marsh was born in Woodstock, Vermont, on March 15, 1801, the son of a prominent attorney and politician. A frail child, with eyesight so poor that it often prevented him from reading, Marsh had an exceptional memory and much of his early education consisted of remembering information that was read to him. He entered Dartmouth College to study languages and had mastered several by the time he graduated in 1820. Marsh specialized in Scandinavian languages and later wrote a grammar of Icelandic, but he also learned other European languages. By the time he was 30 he was able to speak 20 languages. After graduating he spent a year teaching Greek and Latin at a military academy, but he found he disliked teaching and left it to enter his father's office and study law. He was admitted to the bar in 1825 and established a practice in Burlington, Vermont, while continuing to study languages in his free time. In 1828 he married Harriet Buell; she died in 1833. Marsh's second wife, whom he married in 1839, was Caroline Crane, a writer and German translator.

   Marsh entered politics in 1835, as a member of the Vermont executive council—the equivalent of the state senate. He entered Congress in 1843 as a Whig. In 1849 President Zachary Taylor appointed him to be minister resident in Turkey, where he served until 1854, when he returned to Vermont. While in Turkey he led a diplomatic

square miles (94.3 km^2). In 1881 the town had 33.7 square miles (87.2 km^2) of forest. By the following year, 1882, this had decreased to 10 square miles (25.8 km^2), by 1902 to 3.2 square miles (8.4 km^2), by 1935 to 1.6 square miles (4.2 km^2), and by 1950 to 1.2 square miles (3.2 km^2). Only 3.6 percent of the original forest remained by the 1950s, and the surviving forest was divided into small patches.

   In the United States as a whole, approximately 177,680 square miles (460,300 km^2) of the original forest had been cleared by 1850. The rate of clearance then accelerated and a further 297,670 square miles (770,900 km^2) of forest had disappeared by 1910. Between 1600 and 1920 the United States

mission to Greece in 1852–53. He served on the Vermont state railway commission from 1857 to 1859 and lectured in philology—the scientific study of languages—at Columbia University in 1858 and 1859 and at the Lowell Institute, Boston, in 1859 and 1860.

Marsh joined the recently formed Republican Party and in 1861 President Lincoln appointed him as the first U.S. ambassador to Italy. That was the year Italy united into a single kingdom, rather than a number of small states. Marsh remained in this post until his death at Vallambrosa, near Florence, Italy, on July 23, 1882.

During his years in the lands bordering the Mediterranean, Marsh saw for himself the erosion that had resulted from deforestation centuries earlier. He also studied some of the numerous texts that had already been written on the environmental effects of human activities. Marsh determined to write a general account of the ways in which people had altered the natural environment over the centuries and to issue a warning of the dangers that might lie ahead. His book *Man and Nature* was published in 1864. It aroused little interest, so he revised it and in 1874 published a second edition with a new title, *The Earth as Modified by Human Action: Man and Nature*. Some of his warnings sound very modern. Marsh wrote: "But we are, even now, breaking up the floor and wainscoting and doors and window frames of our dwelling, for fuel to warm our bodies and seethe our pottage, and the world cannot afford to wait till the slow and sure progress of exact science has taught it a better economy."

His book set out the case for conservation, but it did much more. It presented a deep insight into history and the way societies and civilizations develop.

lost 29 percent of its original forest, almost all by conversion to farmland.

The settlers believed that by clearing away the forest they were improving the land. They were "taming the wilderness" by transforming it into productive fields and orchards. Few people thought this could be anything but beneficial.

One person who questioned the wholesale alteration of landscapes was George Perkins Marsh (1801–82), the studious, thoughtful son of a Vermont attorney and congressman (see the sidebar). The Marsh family lived in a large house on the slopes of Mount Tom, in Woodstock. Mount Tom had once been forested, as had an estimated 95 percent of Vermont, but almost all of the trees on Mount Tom had been removed by the time George Marsh was old enough to play on the hillside. When he was older, he noticed that clearing the trees from Mount Tom had allowed the rain and wind to remove topsoil, which had been washed down the slope and into the rivers, making them shallower and destroying the habitat for many of the fish. At the same time, the loss of topsoil reduced the fertility of the hillside fields. In a speech he gave to a Vermont agricultural society in 1847 Marsh warned of the dangers of deforesting steep hillsides and described the way forests were being managed more sustainably in Europe.

George Perkins Marsh was one of the founders of the conservation movement, and his ideas became very influential. He was not alone in observing the harmful effects of deforestation. As early as the 18th century, French colonial administrators sought to prevent further deforestation in Mauritius, and the British established forest reserves in Tobago in 1764 and St. Vincent in 1791. The British began to draw up plans for managing the forests of India in 1847. Marsh's book *Man and Nature* provided scientists and early conservationists with powerful support for their own campaigns. The foresters managing the Indian forests were known as "conservators," and that title is still used in Britain.

In his own country, Marsh's work contributed to the arguments favoring the establishment of national parks, starting with Yellowstone, which opened on March 1, 1872. In 1877 the secretary of the interior, Carl Schurz, proposed that permanent forests be retained in public ownership. The system of U.S. forest reserves was authorized in 1891.

Eventually the rapid deforestation of the United States was checked, and since 1920 the forested area has increased. It was not concern for the forests that halted the clearance, however, but changes in farming. Until the early 20th century, approximately one-quarter of all farmland was being used to feed the horses, mules, asses, and oxen that provided transport and powered plows and other farm machines. With the introduction of automobiles, tractors, and other farm machinery, draft animals were no longer required, freeing the land to grow crops for human consumption. In effect, a 25 percent increase in the available land was achieved without plowing an additional acre or felling a single tree. More recently, agricultural advances have allowed food production to increase faster than population growth, making it possible to take some land out of agricultural production.

Large areas of Canadian forests were also cleared to provide farmland, but the clearance was on a much smaller scale than that in the United States. Canada is sparsely populated and much of its land is unsuitable for farming. Consequently only 6 percent of the original Canadian forest area has been converted to farmland.

Forests in folklore

Little Red Riding Hood set out one day to deliver meat and wine to her grandmother, who lived half an hour's walk away, deep in the forest. When she arrived, a wolf had taken grandmother's place. The story is not really about little girls, grandmothers, and wolves, of course. It has much deeper meanings. But it all takes place in a forest—in fact, a German forest, and the little girl's name was Rotkäppchen, "Little Red Cap," in the version written down by the brothers Grimm.

Forests are portrayed in folktales as mysterious and potentially dangerous. It is easy to become lost—the forest plays tricks on travelers—and when shelter appears, it may not be all that it seems. Remember Hansel and Gretel, who found shelter with a witch who used candy as bait to trap children that she then cooked and ate. Wolves and bears prowled the forest, and murderous robbers might be hiding behind every tree.

In the stories, a journey through a forest symbolizes the journey of life. It is difficult to find the true path, there are countless dangers and distractions, and, all too often, apparent solutions to life's problems turn out to be traps that lead the traveler into still greater hazard. Truth, love, courage, ingenuity, and loyalty will guide and protect the traveler, however. Hansel and Gretel are saved because they protect each other and are able to outwit the witch, and Beauty in "Beauty and the Beast" is able to see that the fearsome appearance of the Beast hides a true and noble heart. When she falls in love with him she sees the handsome prince that he really is. Beauty and her Beast lived in a French forest; *La Belle et la Bête* is a French story.

There were also honest people living in the forest, but these were invariably poor. Hansel and Gretel were the children of a woodcutter so poor that he could barely put food on the table when times were good. People lived in the forest because they had no choice. They had no land to grow food, no trade to practice in the city, and therefore no means of earning a living. Forest dwellers might cut wood for sale or make charcoal (see page 182), or they might try to sell furniture or other wooden items they made by hand, but it was a poor way to earn a living. Some were outlaws, unable or unwilling to pay heavy fines or avoiding justice for crimes they had committed. There were also gangs of criminals who robbed the wealthy—but not to give to the poor.

Villagers gathered fuel and timber from the woodlands nearby, but the remoter parts of the forest were of no value to them. There was no food to be had there—game such as deer was the property of rich landowners and the punishment for stealing it was severe.

Poverty drove people to abandon children. Hansel and Gretel were left in the forest to perish from hunger, by their stepmother who could think of no other way to save her husband and herself from starvation. Snow White was another child abandoned by her stepmother. "Babes in the Wood" is a story based on "The Children in the Wood," a ballad that was probably written in about 1595. It is one of several similar stories that appeared at about that time. All of them tell of a man who dies, leaving his property to his infant son and daughter and the children to the care of his brother, their uncle. The uncle hires assassins to take the children into the forest and kill them so he can acquire their inheritance. One of the assassins relents, killing his companion and leaving the children to their fate. The infants die and are buried in the leaves by a robin redbreast. The assassin is later caught and confesses.

Fear and mistrust of forests was widespread in medieval Europe and it persisted for a long time, but the stories also allow for hope. A stroke of good fortune can end poverty. A passing prince may fall in love with the woodcutter's beautiful daughter and marry her, transporting the entire family to live in the palace. A poor man may save the life of a rich man, and be rewarded. A fairy or magical animal may show the way to endless wealth.

Russian folktales describe the forest differently. The Russian forest is so vast and familiar that people regard it as an obstacle to the traveler, but not as mysterious or dangerous. Russian stories are set in lands far away, beyond the edges of the forest. They have plenty of magic, in the form of birds and mammals that talk and involve themselves in human affairs, and although there are evil monsters in the forest, they do not lie in wait to leap upon passing travelers.

In the West, however, some of the dangers were genuine. In the 10th century someone called Acehorn built a refuge near Filey in Yorkshire, England, where travelers could find shelter if they were being attacked by wolves. In 1712 Viscount Weymouth cleared part of Selwood Forest in Somerset, in the west of England, and built a church on the land in order to drive out the criminal gangs that had been operating there. The English word *savage* is derived from the French *sauvage,* which comes originally from the Latin *silvaticus,* meaning "woodland," so a savage is someone who dwells in the forest.

Europeans who settled in North America took with them the images they had acquired from these ancient children's tales. When they encountered the forest that stretched endlessly before them, what they saw was a desolate wilderness haunted by wild beasts and wild men. They set about clearing it to make a land where civilized people could live in safety.

History of forestry

John Evelyn (1620–1706) was a man who loved trees and who had studied the cultivation and uses of plants in Paris as part of his education. The author of about 30 books, from the age of 11 Evelyn also kept a diary that gives us a detailed description of life in 17th-century London. John Evelyn was a founding member of the Royal Society of London—today

Britain's national scientific society and equivalent to the U.S. National Academy of Sciences. Although he only occasionally held an office at the royal court, Evelyn was often in the company of the king and other members of the royal family.

At the time England was on the verge of war with the Netherlands (war actually broke out in 1665), and King Charles II was very worried about the state of the British navy. In 1662 the commissioners of the navy asked the Royal Society to examine and comment on the extent of the depletion of English timber suitable for shipbuilding over the past 20 years. The task was passed to John Evelyn and three other fellows of the society. Evelyn compiled and expanded their comments. In his diary entry for October 15, 1662, he wrote:

> *I this day delivered my* Discourse concerning Forest-Trees to the Society, *upon occasion of certain queries sent us by the Commissioners of his Majesty's Navy, being the first book that was printed by order of the Society.*

He continued to expand on the ideas in his discourse, and the resulting book, published in 1664, was called *Sylva, or a Discourse of Forest-Trees, and the Propagation of Timber in His Majesties Dominions.* Two other works, called *Pomona* and *Kalendarium Hortense,* were included with it. *Pomona* gave instructions for growing apple trees to supply cider apples, and *Kalendarium Hortense* was a horticultural almanac listing the tasks to be undertaken in the garden each month. *Sylva* itself was written as a manual for the owners of large estates and gave instructions for growing a variety of trees and utilizing their timber.

Sylva was the first textbook on forestry, and its publication marked the start of commercial forestry. Evelyn's book remained the standard work on forestry for the next 150 years. An enlarged second edition of *Sylva* was published in 1670, and a third edition, enlarged still further, was published in 1679. The 1679 edition also included "Terra," a section on different soils and their treatment. A fourth edition appeared in 1706, shortly after Evelyn's death, with what was now called *Silva* enlarged again and another section added, called "Acetaria," on plants suitable for use in salads. There was a fifth edition in 1729, and in 1776 an edition of just *Silva* appeared, edited and revised to make it much more scientific. That version of *Silva,* with "Terra" added, went through several more editions, the last appearing in 1825.

Landowners had always managed their forests, encouraging trees to grow from seed to replace those that were felled and planting trees to fill gaps, and some had even planted blocks of trees all of the same species. The first such block was planted in 1580 when Lord Burghley (1520–98), first minister to Queen Elizabeth I, planted 13 acres (5.26 ha) of oaks in Windsor Forest, near London. These were to replenish timber used to build ships during the war with Spain that lasted from 1585 until 1603, and to provide for the future.

Evelyn was proposing something quite new, however, at least for England. His idea was to plant entire forests on land where no forest stood previously. Trees were to be grown as a crop and their timber sold for profit. Evelyn and his supporters calculated the amount by which planting forests would increase the value of estates.

Despite Evelyn's enthusiasm, however, many English landowners continued to believe that forests were wasteland and that clearing trees improved the land. British landowners planted at least 50 million trees between 1760 and 1835, but most of these were ornamental species grown to adorn the landscaped parklands that were fashionable among the extremely wealthy. The Germans, on the other hand, began planting forests of coniferous trees much earlier, the first near Nuremberg in 1368. When in 1895 the British prime minister, William Ewart Gladstone (1809–98), visited the German chancellor, Prince Otto von Bismarck (1815–98), Bismarck presented him with an oak sapling to plant back at home.

It was not until World War I, when Britain had to import timber through a partial blockade of its seaports, that Evelyn's lesson was really learned. The Forestry Commission was established in 1919 as a British government agency charged with acquiring land and planting forests to create a state forest large enough to provide a strategic reserve of timber (see "Plantation forestry" on pages 199–202).

The first forest reserves were established in the United States at the end of the 19th century (see "How North

British geography

The names *England, Britain, Great Britain, United Kingdom,* and *British Isles* are often used as alternatives for the same country, but in fact they have quite different meanings.

Britain, a name first used in about 325 B.C.E., is the island comprising the Kingdom of England, the Kingdom of Scotland, and the Principality of Wales.

England and Wales were joined politically in 1301, when Edward I made his son prince of Wales, a title held ever since by the eldest son of the reigning sovereign.

In 1604 King James VI of Scotland inherited the crown of England, becoming James I of England and often known as James I and VI. This united the crowns of England and Scotland; the two parliaments were united in 1707. The country was then called the Kingdom of Great Britain or the United Kingdom.

The Kingdom of Ireland was joined to Britain by the Act of Union in 1801, and the name became the United Kingdom of Great Britain and Ireland. In 1922, 26 counties of Ireland separated from the United Kingdom to become the Irish Free State; the name was later changed to Éire (Gaelic) or Ireland (English), but the country is often called the Republic of Ireland.

Great Britain is the island of Britain together with its more remote offshore islands, including the Outer Hebrides, off western Scotland, and the Orkney and Shetland Isles, to the north of Scotland. The name refers to the fact that the island contains two kingdoms (and is therefore "great," that is, "large"). It also distinguishes Britain the island from Brittany (meaning "little Britain") in France; in French *Bretagne* is Brittany and *Grande Bretagne* is Great Britain.

The United Kingdom consists of Great Britain and the province of Northern Ireland; the full name is the United Kingdom of Great Britain and Northern Ireland. This is the official name of the country, often abbreviated to U.K., but in certain situations, such as sports, the country is called Great Britain, and car licence plates carry the national identifier "GB" (although many Scottish drivers use "Sco" or "Ecosse").

The Channel Islands, lying close to the Cherbourg Peninsula, France, and the Isle of Man—the large island between Northern Ireland, Scotland, and England—are self-governing British dependencies. They are not parts of Great Britain or of the United Kingdom, and they are not members of the European Union.

The British Isles is the geographic name for the islands of Britain, Ireland, the Channel Islands, the Isle of Man, and all the smaller associated islands.

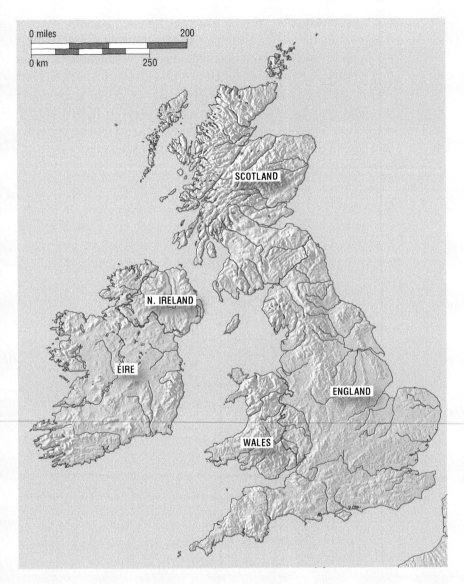

Great Britain and the United Kingdom. Éire is also known as the Republic of Ireland.

America nearly lost its forests" on pages 163–167), although the main purpose of the reserves was to protect watersheds from erosion, rather than to supply timber. Careful management, with controls on logging and time allowed for natural regeneration, could be relied on to sustain the timber supply. Today plantations account for only 7 percent of the total forested area of the United States, although two-thirds of the total area is managed as commercial forest. More than half of all Canadian forests are managed commercially, but there are only a few experimental plantations.

European plantations are more extensive. They account for 30 percent of the total forest area in Europe as a whole and for almost 70 percent of the forest area of the United Kingdom (see the sidebar "British geography" on page 172 for an explanation of the different names applied to Britain).

CHAPTER 8

USES OF TEMPERATE FORESTS

Renewable and nonrenewable resources

A resource is anything people can use to provide something needed or desired. It could be money deposited in a bank. When a person plans a vacation, she may start by examining her bank account to see whether she has enough money, or resources, to pay for it. A builder preparing to erect a group of houses will need to ensure that the necessary materials—timber, cement, bricks, slates, and so forth—will be available as they are required. These materials are also resources.

Slates are made from a particular type of rock obtained from quarries. Slate is plentiful, but eventually slate quarries are exhausted. This does not mean that all the slate has been removed, but only that the best and most accessible slate—cheapest to remove and most valuable to sell—has gone. It is possible to imagine a time when all the slate quarries in a particular part of the world, or even in the entire world, are exhausted. Slate will then exist only on the roofs of buildings and in the other items, such as pool table tops, made from slate. These can be recycled, but as they break and have to be discarded the amount of usable slate steadily decreases until finally the world runs out of slate. It is a highly improbable scenario, but not altogether impossible, because although slate is forming now, it is forming much more slowly than the rate at which it is being used. True slate, as opposed to flagstones and other materials used for roofing that are often called "slate," forms when a mixture of mud and volcanic ash is heated and compressed over millions of years by movements of the rocks forming the Earth's crust. It is a process that is going on all the time, but it happens very slowly. Consequently slate is being used much faster than it is being replaced.

A material such as slate that is being used faster than it can be replaced is said to be a *nonrenewable resource*. Petroleum, gas, and coal—the so-called fossil fuels—are nonrenewable resources; they are forming constantly, but much more slowly than they are being burned. Metals are obtained from the ground. A few, such as gold and some copper, occur in the pure or "native" form, but most are chemically bound in rocks called "ores." Chromium, for example, which is used to make certain types of high-quality steel, is obtained mainly from the mineral chromite, $FeCr_2O_4$, which is a compound of iron (chemical symbol Fe), chromium (Cr), and oxygen (O). Iron is obtained mainly from the mineral hematite, Fe_2O_3. Native copper is very rare, and most copper is obtained from ores such as chalcocite, also called copper glance (copper sulfide, Cu_2S), and chalcopyrite or copper pyrites ($CuFeS_2$). Metal ores are still forming, but not at anything like the rate at which they are mined and used. They are therefore nonrenewable.

Mining companies know how much of the fuel or mineral their mines contain, so they can calculate how soon they will need to abandon each mine and move elsewhere. In preparation for that day they explore and identify the location of their next generation of mines. The measured quantity of the resource in existing and next mines is called a "proven reserve." If the amount is calculated on the basis of the type and structure of the rocks, but not measured directly, it is an "inferred reserve." If the presence of the resource is suspected because of the rock formations, it is called a "potential reserve."

The fact that a resource is nonrenewable does not mean it is likely to run out any time soon. If it should be in short supply, its price will rise and this will provide an incentive for companies to explore more vigorously and to consider reopening mines that are not exhausted but had become too expensive to work. Increased demand for a resource usually increases the size of the reserves. Due to increased demand between 1950 and 1970, for example, the reserves of ores for tin increased by 10 percent, for copper by 179 percent, for aluminum by 279 percent, and for chromium by 675 percent.

Nevertheless, it is possible in principle that one day a non-renewable resource will be completely exhausted and the world will have to learn to live without it.

Trees are different, because when one tree is felled another can be planted to replace it. With proper management, a forest can continue supplying timber and smaller cuts of wood for thousands of years without even diminishing in size. Wood is a *renewable resource,* as are cotton, silk, wool, and any type of food.

Many people suggest that modern industrial societies should be much thriftier in their use of nonrenewable resources to ensure that enough remains to satisfy the needs of future generations. This sounds like common sense, but unfortunately there is no way of predicting what the needs of future generations will actually be. Huge amounts of copper were formerly used to make telephone landlines and submarine cables, and at one time many people feared that the world would run out of copper. Instead, fiber optics are replacing copper wires, cell phones are replacing landline telephones, and intercontinental communications are often transmitted by radio via satellites, reducing the demand for copper. Similarly, a century ago coal was being mined in such large amounts that, vast though the reserves were, it surely must have seemed that all the mines would be exhausted before many more years had passed. What actually happened was that cleaner and cheaper oil and gas became the more important fuels, fuel efficiency increased, and many coal mines were closed—not because they were exhausted, but because they were no longer required. As technology changes, so do the resources on which society depends, and since technological change is unpredictable, there is no way to say what resources will be needed decades from now.

Renewable resources will last forever, but the distinction between renewable and nonrenewable resources is less straightforward than it seems. Forests renew themselves, but if we decide to increase our use of forest products we will need to plant more forests. That requires land and the supply of land is limited.

Rather than emphasizing the relative merits of renewable and nonrenewable resources, the more sensible approach is to use whichever is most appropriate for the task in hand, but to use it carefully, with the minimum waste.

Forests for fuel

Today most energy is obtained from fossil fuels—coal, gas, and oil. Nuclear power provides smaller amounts, hydroelectric power is important in certain countries, and there are parts of the world where people still burn peat in their homes and in power stations to generate electricity. Peat consists of partly decomposed plant material; it has to be cut from the ground and dried before it can be burned.

At one time wood was the most important fuel. Wood fires provided the only heating inside buildings. They cooked all the meals and were the only means of heating water. Although coal became popular in Europe in the Middle Ages, it was available only in the cities and there were attempts to ban it because smoke from coal fires polluted the air. Country people burned wood, as they had always done. Coal, gas, and oil did not become economically important until the 19th and 20th centuries: At the start of the Industrial Revolution, in the 18th century, water mills powered the machines.

Despite the rise of alternative fuels, wood has not been completely displaced. In the world as a whole, people burn approximately 61.4 billion cubic feet (1.74 billion m^3) of wood each year. Wood is a more important fuel in less industrialized countries than it is in the industrialized countries, but it makes a significant contribution even in the most advanced countries. The table shows the amount of fuelwood burned each year in a number of industrialized countries and the amount burned per person. The highest rate of consumption is found in Russia and the United States. Canadians and Russians, with the world's biggest forests, burn more wood per person than do people in any other industrial country.

Throughout history, wood has always been easy to obtain and it is easy to burn. It is a convenient fuel, but if the wood fire is to burn cheerfully and give out enough heat to warm the room, the wood must be chosen carefully. Live oak, Pacific madrone or madroña (*Arbutus menziesii*), and walnut are among the best trees for fuel. Each of these delivers more

Fuelwood consumption per year

Country	Total consumption		Consumption per person	
	cubic feet	cubic meters	cubic feet	cubic meters
United States	2.6 billion	74.6 million	8.92	0.26
Russia	1.8 billion	52.3 million	12.42	0.36
France	389.7 million	11 million	6.52	0.18
Italy	201 million	5.7 million	3.52	0.10
Germany	90.4 million	2.5 million	1.09	0.03
United Kingdom	8.2 million	232,000	0.14	0.004
Japan	9.4 million	266,000	0.07	0.002
Canada	4.4 million	12.6 million	14.1	0.4

Figures include wood burned for all purposes, including power generation, and in all forms, including charcoal.

Sources: *Encyclopaedia Britannica Book of the Year 2004*; Earthtrends, 2003.

than 156,000 Btu of energy per cubic foot (6 GJ/m^3; 1 GJ = 1 billion joules). Pine, poplar, and willow deliver only about 94,000 Btu per cubic foot (3.5 GJ/m^3).

Wood is a fibrous material that absorbs water. Freshly cut wood, called green wood, is at least 50 percent water by weight and can consist of two parts of water for one part of wood fiber. Drying reduces the water content to between 15 percent and 20 percent. Even when dried, however, wood is a bulky fuel. One ton of wood, dried to about 20 percent moisture content, has a volume of about 124 cubic feet (3.2 m^3/tonne). One ton of coal has a volume of about 10 cubic feet (0.25 m^3 per tonne). Its bulk means that fuelwood is expensive to transport. Consequently, most fuelwood is burned close to its source.

Chemically, wood fiber is 48.5 percent carbon, 43.5 percent oxygen, and 6.0 percent hydrogen, with 0.5 percent nitrogen and 1.5 percent noncombustible solids. Combustion is the oxidation of carbon and hydrogen, producing carbon dioxide (CO_2) and water (H_2O), respectively. This is the reaction that releases energy. Fully oxidizing one pound of carbon releases approximately 14,500 Btu (33.7 MJ/kg; 1 MJ = 1 million joules) and oxidizing one pound of hydrogen releases about 62,000 Btu (164 MJ/kg). The oxygen that wood contains is released when the wood burns, but it contributes nothing to the release of energy; effectively it dilutes the real fuel, which is carbon. One ton (2,000 pounds) of wood contains 970 pounds (485 kg/tonne) of carbon, but one ton of black coal contains 1,540 pounds (770 kg/tonne). This dilution of its carbon means that wood has a much lower *energy density* than coal.

When wood is set alight, at first the fire gives off almost no warmth. This is because the heat is used to vaporize water, and vaporization absorbs latent heat (see "Evaporation and transpiration" on pages 66–69), lowering the temperature of the wood. When the temperature of the wood rises above about 500°F (260°C) it begins to break down chemically, releasing a number of gases. These include carbon monoxide (CO), carbon dioxide (CO_2), ethanoic acid (also called acetic acid, CH_3COOH), and methanoic acid (also called formic acid, $(H)COOH$), together with creosote, which is a complex mixture of compounds. Because the gases vaporize at quite low temperatures they are known as *volatiles*. They do not ignite, however, until the temperature rises above about 540°F (280°C). Then the volatiles start to burn, and that is when the fire gives off most of its heat. As it burns, the temperature of the fire continues to rise. It typically reaches between 900°F (480°C) and 1,200°F (650°C) in the white-hot center of the fire, but the temperature in the flames is only 200°F (93°C) to 400°F (204°C). This is cooler than the ignition temperature because the gases ignite closer to the hot center of the fire and cool as they rise. This is called *primary combustion*.

As the fire burns it also generates more volatiles, known as *secondary gases*. These include methane (CH_4) and methanol (CH_3OH). The secondary gases do not burn, either because the temperature of the fire is too low to ignite them, or because in the heart of the fire there is too little oxygen available for oxidation. The secondary gases will burn only when the temperature is higher than 1,100°F (593°C) and there is just enough air to support combustion, but not too much. Air is a mixture of 78 percent nitrogen and 21 percent oxygen, with small amounts of other gases. Oxygen supports combustion—oxidation—but nitrogen does not. If there is too much air at the heart of the fire, the nitrogen absorbs a large proportion of the heat, lowering the temperature of the mixture of oxygen and secondary gases.

It is possible to design a furnace that will burn all of the volatiles and achieve temperatures higher than 1,100°F (593°C), but a wood fire cannot provide the temperatures needed to melt iron. Copper melts at 1,982°F (1,083°C), so copper can be melted from its ore in a skillfully prepared and managed wood furnace. Tin melts at 450°F (232°C). These low temperatures allowed people to alloy copper and tin to make bronze. Wood was the only fuel needed during the Bronze Age. Iron presented a more difficult problem, however, because it melts at 2,795°F (1,535°C). Smelting and forging iron called for temperatures higher than could be achieved in a wood-fired furnace. A new fuel was required.

The new fuel was *charcoal*. It is made by heating wood in airless conditions (see the sidebar), a process industrial chemists call *destructive distillation*. The high temperature drives off all the moisture from the wood and also most of the oxygen, leaving the carbon and remaining hydrogen much more concentrated and thereby increasing the energy density of the fuel. Charcoal is an impure form of carbon, and burning it releases at least 50 percent more heat than burning a similar volume of wood. It ignites easily and burns cleanly, and if a bellows is used to force air through the fire it will burn at up to 3,000°F (2,980°C). Charcoal made metallurgy possible, and it is still used in some places as a fuel for blast furnaces. Today, though, charcoal is used mainly as a fuel for barbecues.

Logging and timber

Wood taken from a forest is known as *roundwood*, and data for roundwood production include wood that is of every kind and destined for every use. Tall, thick tree trunks and branches are included, and so are the stumps and roots of felled trees if these are ripped from the ground. The wood may retain its bark or have the bark removed, and when it leaves the forest the wood may be round in shape, split into half-round lengths, or squared. It is all called roundwood.

Charcoal and how it is made

Charcoal is made from small sticks and branches by the process of *destructive distillation,* or heating in the absence of air. Oak makes the best charcoal, but the bark must be removed first because oak bark contains large amounts of sulfur and produces choking fumes when it is heated. Today charcoal is manufactured industrially, but traditionally it was made in clearings in the forest.

Short pieces of wood would be stacked around the bottom of a pole about 6.5 feet (2 m) tall that stood in the center of a shallow, circular pit approximately 14.75 feet (4.5 m) in diameter. Longer sticks were piled around the short ones, with all the sticks sloping inward. More sticks were added, almost to the top of the central pole, until the stack was dome-shaped. The stack was then covered with bracken, leaves, and finally turf, and the pile tightly sealed with a coat of mud made from earth mixed with ash and water.

Once the mud had dried, the central pole would be withdrawn and a small amount of charcoal dropped down the hole through the stack. Sufficient burning charcoal was then dropped into the hole to ignite the charcoal and wood in and surrounding the base of the hole. As soon as the person igniting the stack saw flames, the top of the hole was sealed with mud.

White smoke soon started to appear from the stack. The emerging smoke revealed cracks in the mud sealing the stack; these had to be repaired. From time to time the charcoal maker would remove the mud sealing the central hole to check conditions inside. It was important that the wood inside did not catch fire; if flames were seen, the worker poured water into the hole to extinguish them.

After one or more days the smoke emerging from the stack turned blue, indicating that the process was complete. The stack was then left to cool. Once it was cool the charcoal was ready for use.

While one stack was smoldering, the next stack was being built and charcoal from the preceding stack was being bagged for sale.

Making charcoal was hard, dirty work, and charcoal makers, who lived in the forest, were always filthy and disheveled. They were also desperately poor. Village people often feared and despised them, but metallurgy would have been impossible without the fuel they produced.

(opposite page) *Malagasy women making charcoal in Madagascar.* (Courtesy of Frans Lanting, Minden Pictures)

Once removed from the forest, the wood may be sent to factories to be made into paper and other industrial products. It may be sold to builders for use in construction. Companies or individual craftspersons may buy it to make furniture, cabinets, and ornaments. The wood may be burned as fuel or made into charcoal (see "Forests for fuel" on pages 178–181). Regardless of the way it is used, it is all roundwood. It is not bought and sold as roundwood, however, but as timber, lumber, or wood.

The terms *timber, lumber,* and *wood* are often used interchangeably, but in fact each word has a distinct meaning; they are not synonyms. *Timber* is a very ancient word. Originally it meant a building and this meaning expanded to include any kind of building material, including material used to build ships—hence the old sailors' exclamation: "Shiver my timbers!" In English law, timber also means the live trees more than 20 years old growing on an area of land, especially oak, ash, and elm. Sawmills define timber as wood cut into sections that are not less than 5×5 inches (12.7×12.7 cm) in cross section. *Wood* consists of material used to make furniture, ornaments, and other small items. *Lumber* consists of felled trees that have been stripped of their branches and cut into logs of a length that can be transported conveniently.

At the time it is cut, wood contains a large amount of water. This accounts for at least half of its weight, and if the timber is left lying on the ground in wet weather it can consist of one part of wood to two parts of water. Also, different trees produce wood of widely differing densities. Consequently, roundwood is measured and sold by volume rather than weight, and it is dried before it is sold to the final user. Drying, or seasoning, takes place at the sawmill after the timber has been cut into planks or boards.

The international unit of volume is the cubic meter (m^3), but in the United States lumber is often sold by the board foot (bd. ft.). The units *cubic foot* (ft^3), *standard,* and *cord* are also used. A board foot is a length of wood one inch thick, 12 inches wide, and 12 inches long (2.5 cm $\times$ 2.5 cm $\times$ 30 cm); 424 board feet = 1 m^3. A standard is equal to 1,980 board feet. A cord (so called because it was originally meas-

Roundwood production, 2000

Rank	Country	Cubic meters (thousands)	Cubic feet (thousands)	Board feet (thousands)
1	United States	500,434	17,670,324	212,184,000
2	China	291,330	10,286,862	123,523,000
3	Canada	185,659	6,555,619	78,719,416
4	Russia	158,100	5,582,511	67,034,400
5	Sweden	61,800	2,182,158	26,203,200
6	Finland	54,263	1,916,026	23,007,512
7	France	50,170	1,771,503	21,272,080
8	Poland	25,652	905,772	10,876,448
9	Germany	21,907	773,536	9,288,568
10	Japan	19,031	671,985	8,069,144
11	New Zealand	17,953	633,920	7,612,072
12	Turkey	17,767	627,353	7,533,208
13	Latvia	14,488	511,571	6,142,912
14	Spain	14,810	522,941	6,279,440
15	Czech Republic	14,441	509,912	6,122,984
16	Switzerland	10,428	368,213	4,421,472
17	Ukraine	10,008	35,338	4,243,392
18	Portugal	9,878	348,792	4,188,272
19	Norway	8,173	288,589	3,465,352
20	United Kingdom	7,451	263,095	3,159,224

Includes both hardwood and softwood species.

Source: *Encyclopaedia Britannica Book of the Year 2004.*

ured using a length of cord) is a pile of wood 8 feet × 4 feet and four feet high (2.4 m × 1.2 m × 1.2 m); 1 cord = 128 cubic feet = 3.6 m^3.

The table lists the annual production of roundwood for the 20 temperate countries with the largest output, ranked in order of their production. It shows that the United States is by far the world's largest producer.

Chipboard, fiberboard, and paper

As well as felled timber in the form of tree trunks and large branches, the term *roundwood* includes smaller branches and even the stumps and roots of felled trees. It is not possible to cut this type of material into pieces suitable for use in construction, but it is not wasted. Along with waste wood from sawmills—small ends of logs and planks, split and broken pieces, shavings, and even sawdust—it can be made into board.

Chipboard, also called particle board, has many uses. Cabinet interiors are made from it, with a door of solid wood. It is used to make upholstered furniture, for interior walls in buildings, and for cladding to protect exterior walls.

As the name suggests, chipboard is made from wood chips. These are dried and then sorted according to size. Chips of similar size are mixed with heat-setting glue, and the mixture is spread in molds. A second layer, comprising chips of a different size, is laid on top of the first layer, and the mold is filled with three or more layers, each comprising chips of a different type. The top and bottom surface layers are usually thinner than the inside layers and are made from smaller chips. When the mold is full, the material is pressed into sheets, heated to set the glue, and allowed to cool. The sheets are then sanded and their edges trimmed, after which they are cut to the required size and shape.

Fiberboard is made from waste material from sawmills and factories that make wooden products. It is used mainly for surfacing interior walls, insulation, and draftproofing. Its manufacture begins by pounding and grinding the raw material until it becomes a mass of fibers. These are mixed with water and glue and spread continuously onto a mesh drum. The continuous sheet of fiber is known as a "web." The drum rotates against a solid roller, pressing the mixture to squeeze out excess water. The web then passes between drying rollers to remove more water, after which it is cut into sheets. The sheets are either dried completely or pressed and heat-treated, depending on the quality required. Hardboard is fiberboard with a density of more than 50 pounds per cubic foot (800 kg/m^3). Boards with densities between 19 pounds per cubic foot and 50 pounds per cubic foot (300–800 kg/m^3) are classed as semi-hard. The density of soft board is less than 22 pounds per cubic foot (350 kg/m^3).

Each year the world production of chipboard and fiber-board is approximately 5.3 billion cubic feet (151.4 million m³). Almost one-third of the world total—1.8 billion cubic feet (51 million m³)—is produced in North America, the United States manufacturing about 1.4 billion cubic feet (40 million m³). Europe produces almost as much as North America—1.7 billion cubic feet (48 million m³).

Paper is made in very much the same way as fiberboard. Most paper is made from softwood—wood from coniferous trees—but ash, beech, and poplar are also used. The wood is chopped into small chips, which are ground to fiber, and the fiber is mixed with water to form pulp. Bleach and whiteners such as kaolin (china clay) are added to whiten the pulp, and dyes are added if the paper is to be tinted. The pulp is sprayed continuously onto a rotating mesh, forming a web. After it leaves the mesh, the web passes between rollers that press and dry it.

All the wood destined for pulping in Europe and North America is grown in plantations (see "Plantation forestry" on pages 199–202), using fast-growing tree species, especially Sitka spruce (*Picea sitchensis*). Paper manufacture threatens no forests, and although economizing in the use of paper may reduce the pollution caused by paper manufacture, it will not help to conserve forests.

The annual world production of paper and paperboard, such as cardboard, amounts to approximately 344 million tons (313 million tonnes). Of that total the United States produces 96 million tons (87 million tonnes), Canada 22 million tons (20 million tonnes), and Europe 104 million tons (94 million tonnes).

Paper is extensively recycled. Ordinary households are learning to leave their old newspapers and magazines at collecting centers, but most recycling takes place in offices and commercial premises where large amounts of paper are used. Printing factories, for example, trim sheets after they have been printed, and the trimmings are collected and recycled. In the world as a whole, about 139 million tons (126 million tonnes) of paper are recycled every year. The United States recycles 45 million tons (41 million tonnes), Canada

1.6 million tons (1.5 million tonnes), and Europe 43 million tons (39 million tonnes).

Veneers and plywood

The most beautiful wood is also the rarest and most expensive. Only the wealthiest people were ever able to afford furniture made from it, but many centuries ago a way was found around this difficulty, allowing cabinetmakers to produce furniture that looked exactly like furniture made from the costliest materials. The solution was called *veneer* and it was practiced as early as Roman times. The technique fell into disuse during the Middle Ages but was revived by French craftsmen in the 17th century and quickly spread throughout Europe.

Veneer is the craft of cutting a very thin slice of expensive wood and using it to cover the surface of an article made from inferior wood. Nowadays veneer is often used to hide defects in the cheap pine from which some furniture is made, and the veneer itself may be plastic rather than made from wood.

Any attractive wood can be used as veneer. The French furniture makers of the 17th century liked to use ebony and were known as *ébénistes,* but by the 18th century mahogany, walnut, box, almond, pear, and cherry were among the woods being used. Veneer makes economical use of expensive material and greatly improves the appearance of the articles it covers.

The process begins by slicing a sheet from a block of wood. The slice may be cut by saw, but it is often taken from a round log that turns in a lathe, the slice being removed in a single sheet and the cut spiraling toward the center of the log. After sanding, the sheet is usually 0.03–0.06 inch (0.8–1.6 mm) thick. The log is soaked in water before being cut to make it easier to work and reduce the risk of splintering, and the wet sheet of veneer is easy to flatten. When dry, the sheet is cut to the required shape, glued to the surface it is intended to cover, and placed in a press until the glue has set. If the surface is molded, the veneer is pressed onto it using sandbags that take the shape of the molding. Pressing and drying take only a few minutes.

Veneer is also used to make *plywood*. Plywood is light, but very strong; compared with solid wood it is much less prone to splitting when sawn, drilled, or nailed; and it is produced in large sheets of very consistent quality. It is used to make cabinets, chests of drawers, and closets. Floors and partition walls that are required to bear no structural load are often made from plywood, as are the walls of many trailers and mobile homes. Until fiberglass displaced it, plywood was used to make the hulls and decks of small boats as well as parts of the fuselage and wings of airplanes. The Mosquito, a famous twin-engined British fighter-bomber of World War II, had an airframe made from wood and covered with plywood.

Plywood veneer is usually 0.03–0.1 inch (1–3 mm) thick, and the sheets are glued together with thermosetting resins to make laminated boards that are pressed, dried, and cut to the required size. If the plywood is to be used outdoors, water-resistant resins such as phenol-formaldehyde are used to hold the veneers together; urea-formaldehyde resin is used for indoor plywood. Phenol-formaldehyde resists cold water, hot and even boiling water, seawater, and dry heat. It is the adhesive used in making marine plywood for boats.

The board may consist entirely of sheets of veneer, or of veneer on the upper and lower surfaces with a thicker layer of sawn lumber between them; this is known as *lumber-core plywood*. *Sandwich board* consists of two layers of plywood separated by a thicker layer of a light material, such as foam plastic, balsa wood, or paper honeycomb. The plywood bears the load and the sheet is very light, and extremely strong for its weight. Most plywood is of all-veneer construction.

Some applications, such as boatbuilding and furniture-making, require the plywood to be shaped. This is done by bending and gluing the veneers in a single operation.

Each plywood veneer is laid with its wood grain running at right angles to the veneer beneath it. This makes the construction very strong and it also eliminates almost completely the problems that arise with the shrinking and swelling of wood as its moisture content changes. The grain usually runs in the same direction on both the outer veneers, so plywood usually has an odd number of layers, or *plies*. Three-ply plywood is probably the most widely used, but five-ply is much stronger and more rigid. Finished plywood sheets are from 0.12 inch (3 mm) to 1.2 inches (30 mm) thick.

Small wood and its uses

In the days when sailing ships were made from wood, oak (*Quercus* species) was considered the best source of shipbuilding timber. Oak is strong, and once the timber had been thoroughly soaked to make it swell and seal all the joints, a ship built from oak was completely watertight. The wood did not deteriorate after prolonged immersion in water.

Shipbuilding and construction once consumed large amounts of timber, but forests yielded small pieces of wood as well as whole trunks, and small wood has always had many uses. Even today, every modern home contains furniture, ornaments, and everyday utensils such as wooden spoons and chopping boards that are made from wood.

Oak was not used only for shipbuilding. The durability of oak wood makes it suitable for other outdoor uses. It makes excellent fence posts and gates, and it is the best wood for making the staves of wooden barrels. Barrels are used to store liquids, so they are kept permanently wet.

Oak also has indoor uses, of course. Its attractive grain and the ease with which it bends make it a good material for making furniture.

Elm is another wood that survives immersion in water, especially if it remains immersed all the time, rather than being alternately wet and dry. Water pipes were once made from elm and some of them remained in use for more than two centuries. Waterwheels and the wooden piles supporting jetties were often made from elm.

Beech wood does not last long outdoors, but it is strong and resists compression. Both American (*Fagus grandifolia*) and European (*F. sylvatica*) beech are used to make wood blocks for floors, furniture, and high heels for shoes. Kitchen utensils, such as wooden spoons and breadboards, are often made from beech, as are the stocks for rifles and shotguns. Bentwood chairs are made from beech.

Nowadays the slats of most venetian blinds are made from plastic, but before plastic was introduced they were made from American basswood (*Tilia americana*), which has a long, straight grain. This is also the wood used to make piano keys, topped with plastic today but formerly with ivory from elephant tusks.

Quaking aspen (*Populus tremuloides*) of North America and European aspen (*P. tremula*) also have wood with a straight grain. In medieval times arrows were made from aspen. Because of their straight grain, wooden matches are made from various *Populus* species, known as poplars, cottonwoods, and aspens—despite the fact that the wood is nonflammable. Matchsticks are impregnated with paraffin wax to make them burn. Its nonflammability made it the preferred wood for brake blocks on horse-drawn vehicles because friction with the wheel did not make it smolder, far less burst into flames. *Populus* wood does not splinter, which makes it suitable for boxes and crates, and also for the pallets on which goods are stacked to be carried by forklift trucks.

Tool handles, oars, and sports equipment such as hockey sticks and baseball bats (now often made from aluminum) must withstand shock. Ash (*Fraxinus* species) is often used, but hickory (*Carya* species) is the most popular wood for making tool handles. Cricket bats, however, are made from a variety of white willow (*Salix alba caerulea*) known, not surprisingly, as "cricket-bat willow." Hornbeam (*Carpinus* species) is even tougher than ash and hickory; it used to be called "hard-beam." Mallet heads and the wooden pulley-blocks and cogwheels used in windmills and watermills were made from hornbeam.

Rulers, set squares, and similar mathematical instruments must be straight-edged and hard enough to withstand repeated friction from pencils and pens drawn along their edges. Modern instruments are made from metal or plastic, but they used to be made from boxwood, the wood from box trees (*Buxus* species). Boxwood is very hard and, as its name suggests, the very finest boxes are made from it. The wood is an attractive yellow color and can be carved with delicate designs. Woodblocks once used in printing were usually made from boxwood.

Stringed instruments, such as guitars, violins, violas, cellos, and basses, have backs and bellies made from maple (*Acer* species), usually either sugar maple (*A. saccharum*) or sycamore maple, also known as European sycamore (*A. pseudoplatanus*). Sheets of maple wood, planed to a very precise thickness and bent to produce exactly the right shape, make the best resonating chamber, but maple has other uses. Sugar maple is pale pink in color and often has an attractive grain. Sports equipment and furniture are made from it. European sycamore is used to make kitchen utensils and chopping boards.

CHAPTER 9

MANAGING TEMPERATE FORESTS

Traditional management

Paper, chipboard, fiberboard, plywood, timber for building houses, wood for making furniture, tools, ornaments, and countless other items all come from forests. Even today, when most Americans and Europeans live in towns and cities, we still need forests. Throughout most of history, people lived in small, rural communities where they were even more dependent on forest products. As well as raw materials, forests supplied them with fuel and even with some of their food. Villagers collected wild berries and nuts and allowed their pigs to forage in the forest for fallen fruit, nuts, and acorns. Where the forest canopy was fairly open (see "Structure of a temperate forest" on pages 123–127) and sufficient light reached the forest floor, people gathered grass and bracken for use as bedding for themselves and their livestock.

Forests have always been used, and when a tree was felled no part of it was wasted. Leaves were fed to livestock, bark was used to tan leather, galls were dried and ground to make ink, and small sticks were used for kindling. In Europe, most forests were privately owned, but local people were allowed to enter them for specific purposes, such as gathering fuel, cutting vegetation for bedding, or allowing pigs to forage. Some forests, called wasteland, were owned and used by the whole community.

Such an important resource had to be protected. Each area of forest was enclosed by a strong fence or by a deep ditch and high bank. The barrier kept out livestock that might trample seedlings or, worse, might kill trees by nibbling the bark all around them. This is called ringbarking or girdling, and it is invariably fatal to the tree. It kills the tree by severing the xylem and phloem vessels that lie just beneath the bark (see "Differences between conifers and flowering plants" on pages 87–89). Ringbarking prevents water and nutrients from reaching the part of the tree above the cut and sugars from reaching the parts below it.

The stock of trees had to be sustained. It was essential that whenever a tree was felled another tree replaced it. This usually happened naturally, as a sapling previously shaded by the mature tree grew rapidly to close the gap in the canopy. If there was no suitable sapling, however, one had to be planted.

Nevertheless, there is a limit to the amount of timber a community needs. Buildings, bridges, and other large pieces of civil engineering last a long time. People have a much greater need for small wood to make tools, furniture, lath to repair ceilings and walls, fences, and especially for fuel. A way of producing regular crops of small poles was discovered at least 6,000 years ago: Traces of the method have been found in peat of that age in Somerset, England. The technique is called coppicing (see the sidebar), and it was in widespread use in England by the time of the Norman invasion in 1066.

Beginning in the late 18th century, the rapid expansion of manufacturing based on the factory system greatly increased the demand for iron and steel. More and more iron foundries were built and the ironmasters who owned them needed a regular, reliable supply of fuel. Coal had not yet become the predominant fuel. In the first decades of the Industrial Revolution, the ironmasters contracted with local landowners to supply charcoal (see the sidebar "Charcoal and how it is made" on page 182). Coppicing was the only management system capable of supplying charcoal regularly in sufficient amounts, and the technique spread throughout Britain, eventually reaching the Highlands of Scotland.

Coniferous trees die when they are felled, and therefore cannot be coppiced, but most broad-leaved species are suitable. Hazel (*Corylus avellana*) was popular, especially for making fences. Sweet chestnut (*Castanea sativa*) was also coppiced for fence poles called pales and was often used to make the fences enclosing forests—hence the expression "beyond the pale." Willow (*Salix* species) was coppiced for basket-

Coppicing and pollarding

Cutting a tree close to the ground will not necessarily kill it. Indeed, many tree species are invigorated by this treatment. Called coppicing, it is a traditional technique used in forest management.

A tree trunk consists of the dead heartwood surrounded by the sapwood, which forms a layer just inside the bark. The sapwood is the only part of the trunk that is alive, and if the trunk is sliced through, the sapwood will continue to grow. The trunk will not regenerate, because the heartwood is dead, but many small shoots will arise from the sapwood around the edge of the stump—called the stool. These shoots will grow into straight poles, called underwood.

The rate of coppice growth varies according to the species, but many species produce a dense crop of poles within about five years. When they reach a suitable size, the poles are cut at the point where they emerge from the stool. More poles grow to take their place, and the coppiced trees are cropped in a rotation, with an average gap of 12–15 years between cuts, although coppice rotations can be as little as four or as much as 30 years. A coppiced stool will continue to produce underwood for many years; coppicing often makes trees live longer than they would otherwise.

Deer and cattle will eat tender young coppice shoots, so a different technique is needed in places where these animals are present. That technique is called pollarding. It is identical to coppicing, except that the tree is cut about 6.5 feet (2 m) above ground level. The remaining part of the trunk is called a bolling. Shoots grow upward from the top of the bolling, just as they do from a coppice stool, but they are out of reach of animals that might damage them. Like coppicing, pollarding extends the life of the tree. Trees lining city streets are often pollarded to prevent them from growing too large.

making. Oak (*Quercus* species), alder (*Alnus* species), field maple (*Acer campestre*), and hornbeam (*Carpinus betulus*) are among the other species that were frequently coppiced.

Although small wood from coppiced woodland may have been the most important forest product, it was not the only one. Large lumber was still needed and its production was often combined with coppicing in a system called "coppicing with standards." Individual trees selected for their high quality—especially the length and straightness of their trunks—

were allowed to grow to their full size, while the trees surrounding them were coppiced. The tall trees, known as the standards, benefited from not being shaded by surrounding trees. They were felled as they were needed and the forest was managed to ensure that the supply of standards was always sufficient for local needs.

From about 1800, landowners began to alter the composition of their coppiced forests by removing some species and planting others to replace them. Chestnut and hazel came to predominate in the coppiced forests of southern and eastern England, and oak coppice in the north.

Coppicing produces a highly artificial forest, but the system greatly encourages biodiversity (see "What does *biodiversity* mean?" on pages 138–141). Coppiced trees never grow big enough for form a canopy, and consequently the forest floor is well lit in some places and shaded in others, and the clumps of coppice poles provide shelter from the wind. This is an ideal habitat for many plant species, and coppice woodland supports a rich variety of herbs and small shrubs.

During the middle decades of the 20th century it was fashionable in Britain to clear broad-leaved forest and replant with fast-growing coniferous species. Conservationists responded by protecting as much broad-leaved woodland as they could and by reintroducing coppicing, which had almost died out. As coppice poles became available there was a revival in crafts using small wood, and coppicing is now fairly widespread. Nowadays it is practiced mainly for conservation reasons, however, rather than as a system of forest management.

Park woodland

Most cities have parks where people can walk, play games, or just sit and enjoy the view. In fine weather many workers spend their lunch breaks in a nearby park. Parks have open areas covered with grass, borders growing shrubs and flowers, paths, and trees. Parks have many trees. Parks have so many trees, in fact, that they are considered a type of woodland, called park woodland.

Parks have a long history. Thousands of years ago, the first farmers in Northern Europe developed an "in-field, out-field" system. The in-fields were small, irregular in shape, and surrounded the farm buildings. They were cultivated all the time. The out-fields formed an outer circle beyond the in-fields. Out-fields were larger than in-fields and were cultivated in a rotation, growing cereals, root crops, and from time to time being left fallow. Both in-fields and out-fields were enclosed by walls, fences, or hedges, and each out-field was called a "park." A park was an enclosed area of ground some distance from the farmhouse.

Wealthy landowners later extended this meaning of "park" by applying it to the land some distance from the house where owner's family and friends could ride, walk, or rest in

Orchards imitate woodland, which is more open than closed forest. This is an olive grove, where the olive trees (Olea europaea) are widely separated, allowing other plants to grow between them. (Courtesy of Cisca Castellijns, Foto Natura, Minden Pictures)

the shade of a tree. The park was managed but not used to grow crops. It was open, with scattered trees, and it was enclosed to define the boundary of the property and to keep out livestock. By the 18th century this type of park was becoming fashionable, and creating one was a way to increase the value of an estate. Entirely artificial landscapes were made by shifting earth, making lakes, planting grass, and establishing small groves of trees, often with cattle and sheep grazing between the groves. The farm that supplied food for those living on the estate and the gardens supplying flowers, fruits, and vegetables were usually not visible from the best rooms in the owner's house. The view from the house looked across formal gardens to the park beyond.

Not all parks were used for recreation, however. Parks—enclosed areas—were also created to keep animals such as fallow deer (*Dama dama*), red deer or wapiti (*Cervus elaphus*), wild pigs (*Sus scrofa*), and cattle. These parks had to be surrounded by tall, dense hedges or fences to prevent the animals escaping. Fallow deer are sometimes called "park deer."

Livestock will destroy tree seedlings and damage mature trees. In some parks the trees were pollarded to protect them (see the sidebar "Coppicing and pollarding" on page 195). Alternatively, the trees could be confined to small areas of closed forest, protected by fences and separated by areas of open grassland.

Not all farmers could afford anything so grand as a park, but they could and did plant trees for entirely practical reasons. Trees provide shelter from the wind, rain, and snow in winter and they give shade in summer. They were planted in the open countryside for the benefit of cattle and sheep, and also around houses and churches. Trees appeared in villages and in the cities, and by the middle of the 18th century there were tree nurseries to supply almost every town and large village in England. As well as native trees, the nurseries sold species imported from other parts of the world, such as European sycamore (*Acer pseudoplatanus*), holm oak (*Quercus ilex*), London plane (*Platanus acerifolia*), and horse chestnut (*Aesculus hippocastanum*). The popularity of attractive imported trees grew steadily in England from the 16th century until the early 19th.

Trees were planted in groves as components in carefully designed but artificial landscapes. Farmers planted trees because it was fashionable to do so, but also to provide shade and shelter. Exotic trees were often planted singly, to show them off to their best advantage. Villagers planted trees around their cottages. In towns and cities, trees appeared in private gardens and lining streets.

By the 19th century most European towns had parks for public recreation and most rural estates had parks for private recreation. The parks consisted of expanses of grassland, with trees growing singly or as groups—park woodland.

Plantation forestry

Park woodland could not supply significant quantities of timber, and British landowners began planting forests of timber trees. Few planted native broad-leaved species, however, because these grow slowly and would not repay the cost of planting within the lifetime of the person making the capital investment. They preferred fast-growing species, mainly conifers. The output was still insufficient for the nation's needs, however, and the major expansion in plantation forestry in Britain began in 1919 with the establishment of the Forestry Commission, a government agency charged with creating and then managing state-owned forests (see "History of forestry" on pages 169–174).

Today there are approximately 7,440 square miles (19,280 km^2) of plantations growing timber in the United Kingdom, compared with 3,340 square miles (8,660 km^2) of natural forest. With its much bigger area of natural forest, the United States is less reliant on plantations. It has 62,700 square miles (162,380 km^2) of plantations and 810,000 square miles (2.1 million km^2) of natural forest.

Plantations produce trees as a crop, so plantation forestry is like farming, but with a much longer period between planting and harvesting. A plantation forest must produce crops of trees regularly and reliably. To achieve this, the forest is divided into compartments bounded by permanent features such as roads or rivers. Each compartment contains several stands of trees. All the trees in a particular stand are the same age, but each stand is a different age. Once the plantation is fully mature, each year there will be some stands ready to harvest.

Timber is measured by volume (see "Logging and timber" on pages 181–185) and the yield of a plantation can be estimated in advance, before a single tree is planted, because the average rate of growth is known for different species. The amount by which a tree increases in volume each year is known as the mean annual increment (MAI). The MAI rises rapidly at first, then slows, and finally reaches a maximum value. The maximum MAI for a stand of trees is known as the yield class for that stand. A stand of coniferous trees, for example, may reach a maximum MAI of 30 cubic meters per hectare (429 cubic feet per acre), giving the stand a yield class of 30. Some broad-leaved trees have a yield class as low as four.

Knowing the yield class helps foresters decide which species to grow. When they have decided on the species, the foresters will also know how soon the trees will be ready to harvest and the annual sustainable yield the forest will deliver once harvesting commences. Armed with that information, managers can calculate the capital investment the forest will need and the rate of return it will yield. They will also know how many workers they will need for each stage in the operation and when they will need them, and what machines will be used and when. Operations can be planned many years in advance.

The planning of a new plantation begins with a detailed survey of the site. The survey will produce a map that marks roads, railroads, power lines, rivers, ponds, and other permanent features as well as contours showing hills and valleys. There will also be aerial photographs to accompany the map; these are often stereoscopic, providing three-dimensional views. Once the map is completed, the boundaries of the forest compartments can be marked on it, as well as the roads and tracks that will provide access for machinery.

Firebreaks must also be planned. In the event of fire, firebreaks help prevent the fire leaping from one stand to another. They must be at least 33 feet (10 m) wide and contain nothing that will burn readily.

Climate is important, and the survey includes details of the average amount and distribution of rain and snow, average temperatures through the year, and average wind directions and speed. Cotton flags are sometimes used to measure the wind speed. Distributed at various points around the site, flags, all made from the same thickness and quality of cloth, will become increasingly tattered as they flap in the wind. The rate at which the wind destroys them identifies the places that are sheltered and those that are exposed to the strongest winds, where trees may be blown down. The shape of the forest edge and the species planted there can be adjusted to reduce the risk of wind damage in the exposed areas.

Plantations produce timber, but they are also communities of plants and animals, and they should be managed in such a way as to maximize their value as wildlife habitat. Trees should not be planted on riverbanks, for example, but the riverbanks left to be colonized naturally. Stands of trees native to the area should be planted among the commercial stands of "exotic" species. It is desirable to provide nesting boxes for birds and bats. Forests also attract visitors, who need roads and paths suitable for walking, biking, and horseback riding; toilets; and information boards. The locations for these must be decided and marked on the site map.

Once planning is complete, the foresters can leave the office and start work. The site may need to be cleared and the land drained—an operation that involves huge machines cutting deep trenches. Then the first blocks can be planted with tree seedlings that have spent one or two years in seedbeds and a similar time in orchards. These will be the first trees to mature and be harvested. Once they are growing well, the next set of blocks is planted, and then more. It will take several years to plant the entire area. As the stands grow, dead trees must be replaced, woody undergrowth cleared away, and some branches pruned to improve the quality of the timber.

Finally, up to 60 years after planting, the trees in the first stand are ready to harvest. First, though, the routes the machines will follow into the stand are clearly identified and marked on the ground, and the stand is divided into sections. One or two workers are assigned to fell all the trees in each section and the operation is planned so the distance between felling teams is not less than double the height of the tallest tree. The first trees are cut so they all fall in the same direction and the next trees to be cut fall at right angles across them. This arrangement makes it easier to remove the branches—a task called "snedding"—and lift the trunks. Machines called forwarders lift whole trunks and load them onto trailers, or *skidders*—machines that hold one end of the trunk and drag it along the ground.

The lumber is taken away to the sawmill, the immense machines rumble away to another part of the forest, and the forest block is left bare. Soon the foresters will return to prepare the ground for the next crop.

What are lichens?

Some look like tiny shrubs, others resemble flattened leaves, and there are those that look like a smear of paint. All of them are lichens. They grow on rocks, the roofs of buildings, and the trunks and branches of trees. In some forests they festoon tree branches.

People often suppose that lichens are a type of moss, but they are not. Strictly speaking they are not plants at all. A patch of lichen consists of millions of single-celled organisms living inside a fungus. This kind of close relationship, from which both partners benefit, is known as *mutualism*.

Mushrooms, toadstools, and molds are all fungi, but the part of the fungus that you see is the *fruiting body*—the structure the fungus produces when it is time for it to release spores for reproduction. The main part of the fungus exists as minute threads called *hyphae* (singular *hypha*) that form a network called a *mycelium*. The fungus absorbs nutrients through its hyphae.

In a lichen, photosynthesizing cells are lodged among the hyphae, just below the lichen's upper surface. Depending on the species of lichen, these cells are either algae or cyanobacteria, and they may live as separate cells or be joined together to form fine filaments. The fungus is the main part of the lichen, and the scientific name of the lichen is taken from that of the fungal partner.

Pest control

Trees are plants, and like all plants they provide food for animals. Because they are so large and support so many animals—as well as mosses, lichens, and even ferns that grow in moist hollows where large branches emerge from the trunk—trees are complete ecosystems in their own right. The older the tree, the more time there is for species to arrive and become established, and some trees live to a great age. Oak trees (*Quercus* species) can live for more than 1,000 years, which is time enough to accumulate a bewildering diversity of living things.

Windsor Forest, near London, England, contains oak and beech (*Fagus sylvatica*) woods in which the trees are 300–1,000 years old. These woods support more than 2,000 species of

---

The fungus protects its photosynthesizing partner. Its hyphae retain water and dissolved minerals and produce pigments that shade the photosynthesizing cells from intense sunlight. The hyphae also secrete acids that assist in the uptake of minerals, and in some species the hyphae secrete poisons that prevent the lichen from being eaten. The algal or cyanobacterial partner produces sugars by photosynthesis, some of which are used by the fungus. As well as reproducing by means of fungal fruiting bodies, lichens also release *soredia,* structures comprising a few fungal cells together with a few algal or cyanobacterial cells that will grow if they fall onto a suitable surface. Releasing soredia is a type of asexual reproduction, meaning that it does not involve the fertilization of an egg by sperm.

Lichens are extremely tough organisms. They can survive prolonged drought, and when water becomes available they can absorb more than 10 times their own weight and resume their growth immediately. Some individual lichens are thousands of years old. Most species of lichens cannot tolerate sulfur dioxide, however, and disappear in areas where the air is polluted. This sensitivity makes them useful indicators of polluted air.

There are more than 25,000 species of lichens. These can be divided into three groups on the basis of their appearance. *Foliose* lichens are loosely attached to the tree or rock surface and have a flattened, leaflike appearance. *Fruticose* lichens are attached to the surface at only one point; some are upright and shrublike, others hang down like tassels. *Crustose* lichens are firmly attached to the surface and look as though they have been smeared onto it.

invertebrate animals and approximately 1,000 species of fungi. An individual oak tree in Windsor Forest may shelter more than 400 species of invertebrates—including the larvae of 200 species of butterflies and moths—and more than 300 species of lichens (see the sidebar). A single beech tree may harbor more than 300 species of invertebrates. The Windsor oak trees are English or pedunculate (*Q. robur*) and durmast or sessile oaks (*Q. petraea*). These are typical of temperate-forest oaks. A much younger, but nevertheless mature specimen of Oregon white oak (*Q. garryana*) supports nearly 200 species of invertebrates, more than 100 species of lichens, and approximately 30 species of mosses and liverworts.

Some of the invertebrate animals feed on the tree itself, eating leaves, fruits, seeds, or sap they obtain by burrowing beneath crevices in the bark. Other invertebrates hunt the plant-eaters, and there are birds that hunt the insects.

A tree is able to resist most of the attacks from the plants, animals, and fungi living on its surface. It can even survive the manipulation of its chemistry that takes place when certain insects and mites inject its leaves a substance that induces the leaf to produce new tissue in the form of a *gall*. A gall is a growth inside which the insect or mite lays its eggs and the larvae develop, feeding on the gall tissue. Many species of insects induce gall formation, but the most abundant are parasitic wasps, none more than about one-quarter of an inch (8 mm) long and most much smaller. There are hundreds of species of gall mites, all belonging to the family Eriophyidae, and they are less than 0.01 inch (0.25 mm) long. (Mites are not insects but arachnids, related to spiders and scorpions.) Oaks are especially attractive to gall wasps, and a single oak leaf may carry more than 100 galls. But galls do not harm the tree.

Some attacks are much more serious, however (see "Diseases and parasites of trees" on pages 132–135), and although trees are able to defend themselves and recover from injury, their ability to do so is not limitless. There are moths and sawflies that are capable of stripping a tree of all its leaves, and certain fungi that will destroy a tree from the inside. Gypsy moths (*Lymantria dispar*) will defoliate oak trees, for example.

Insects also transmit diseases by transporting fungal and bacterial spores and viruses into the plant tissue. For instance, the tiny beech scale insect (*Cryptococcus fagisuga*), up to 0.04 inch (1 mm) long, lays its eggs in cracks on the bark of beech trees (*Fagus* species). When the eggs hatch, the larvae feed on the bark. Beech scale insects themselves may weaken the tree, but more seriously they introduce a fungus (*Nectria* species) that spreads around the tree. The fungal infection can kill it. Other insects and fungi then invade the dead tree and they, too, can spread disease to nearby trees.

Healthy trees are better able to withstand disease and insect attack than are trees with dead or dying tissues and wounds where dead limbs have fallen away. Wounds and patches of decaying tissue provide sites for infection, and once a tree is sick it can infect its neighbors.

Old-growth forests suffer more from disease and pest attacks than do plantation forests. This is because plantation forests consist entirely of young trees that are felled before they are old enough to succumb. Old-growth forests contain many old and dying trees that infect others. This does not mean that the forest as a whole is sick. It is entirely natural in any community that old individuals die from diseases or insect infestations that may infect others, injuring or even killing them. Trees die, but in dying they make space for young trees and the life of the forest continues. Even the loss of an entire species, such as elms through Dutch elm disease and chestnuts through chestnut blight, does not destroy the forest. Other species fill the gaps left by the one that has gone. In a natural forest, insects, fungi, bacteria, and viruses that feed on trees are not pests, but simply part of the community. The damage that they do becomes important only when it reduces the value of the harvest that people are able to take from the forest.

Because insects transmit many tree diseases, if an insect infestation becomes widespread in a commercial forest—natural or plantation—it must be treated. The only practicable treatment is to kill the insects, and the only way to achieve that is likely to be by spraying insecticide from the air. This is expensive, and even when the operation is conducted with great care there is an inevitable risk to harmless insects.

Modern insecticides do not persist for long in the environment and are only mildly poisonous to wildlife other than the species against which they are directed. Nevertheless, spraying is a last resort, and of all the pesticide used in temperate regions only about 2 percent is sprayed over forests.

Modern disease control is achieved more cheaply as well as more safely through hygiene, which involves felling seriously infected trees, removing them from the area, and burning them. Although spraying to kill the insect or fungus may save single trees grown for ornament, fungal damage will have reduced the value of the wood, so this treatment is seldom feasible in a forest. Effective pest control relies on a detailed knowledge of the life cycle of the pest, which allows pesticide to be applied at the stage in its life when the target insect is exposed and vulnerable.

In some cases it is possible to use predators to control pest populations. There is, for example, a species of ladybug, *Chilocorus stigma,* that feeds on the beech scale insect, and a fungus, *Nematogonum ferrugineum* (also called *Gonatorrhodiella highlei*), that parasitizes the *Nectria* fungi that cause beech bark disease. This type of biological control is effective only in certain cases, however, and it can go wrong. The introduced predator may simply die out, or, much more seriously, it may attack beneficial species, becoming a pest in its own right.

An alternative method of biological control uses scent attractants. The females of many species of flying insects release chemical substances called *pheromones* into the air to attract males for mating. The males are extremely sensitive to them—males of some species can detect them up to one mile (1.6 km) away, and male gypsy moths can detect them at concentrations as low as one part in 100 quadrillion (10^{17}). Scientists have been able to analyze some insect pheromones and make them in large enough quantities for use in pest control. Released into the air at the time when the pest insects are preparing to mate, they will lure males into traps. Trapped males may be killed or exposed to radiation that sterilizes them without otherwise harming them and then released. The sterile males mate normally, but their female partners produce no fertile eggs. Known as the *sterile-male technique,* this works with insect species in which the females mate only once each season.

Pests and diseases must be controlled in commercial forests and plantations. Pesticides will remain in use for the foreseeable future, but a combination of hygiene to prevent infection and more advanced methods of regulating insect populations mean that foresters are becoming less reliant on them.

Modern forestry

Forests grow on land that someone or some organization owns, and the landowner usually seeks to sell enough lumber and small wood at least to pay for the management of the forest. Conservation groups also own forests and manage them in ways that enhance their value for wildlife. In both cases, outsiders used to be regarded as intruders. They were not welcome, either because they might damage the forest—by lighting fires, for example, or trampling rare herbs—or disturb the wild animals.

Commercial forestry is less profitable than agriculture, so where trees and farm crops compete for the same land the trees usually lose. This means that commercial forest plantations are sited on *marginal land*—land that will not grow farm crops. Plantations are set on hillsides and in the uplands. Forest trees can survive in such places, but conditions are harsh and trees grow slowly. Profits are small and the plantations are unpopular for several reasons: Their exposed locations makes them visually intrusive; planting in rectangular blocks makes them ugly; when a compartment is harvested the area is left as a wilderness of tree stumps and bare earth; and plantations support less wildlife than permanent forests.

Over several decades of the 20th century, objections to these aspects of plantation forestry and demands for access to privately owned forests came from naturalists, horse riders, and hill walkers—literally millions of members of clubs, societies, associations, and conservation groups across Europe and North America. Landowners, including the government agencies responsible for European state-owned forests, needed an additional, noncommercial reason for maintaining the forests and the naturalists, riders, and walkers supplied it. The landowners responded by opening the forests to the public.

Visitors to the forests needed certain facilities. There had to be adequate paths and maps, for example. Providing these was straightforward, but people also wished to see some of the plants and animals living in the forest, and that called for modifications to the way the forests were managed. Little by little, "forestry" transformed itself into "silviculture."

Silviculture is the management of a forest for the benefit of the plants and animals living in it, regardless of whether or not all or part of the forest is being exploited commercially. As well as being a source of timber, the forest in the silvicultural approach becomes a public amenity.

Planting methods change. Instead of planting endless rows of closely spaced trees, all of the same species and the same age, the planting is less regular, more widely spaced, and includes a greater variety of tree species. The resulting forest is more interesting to look at, and more light penetrates through it, encouraging a more varied community of herbs on the forest floor.

All forests have paths and tracks to allow access for forestry vehicles. When subcompartments are thinned, the trees growing along the edges of some tracks can be removed and not replaced. This produces a wide strip of ground on either side of the track that can be left for wild plants to colonize.

Increasing the variety of plants and allowing more light to penetrate to the forest floor make the forest more attractive to wildlife. More insects arrive, including colorful butterflies, and birds arrive to hunt them. Mammals find food and shelter inside the forest. Nesting boxes for birds and roosting boxes for bats, attached to trees, help increase the bird and bat populations.

Surveyors identify areas that are especially important for wildlife, such as small ponds, marshy areas, and sheltered hollows, during the very first stages of planning for a forest on a new site. Those areas, as well as sites of geological or archaeological importance, are marked on the maps and managed differently from the remainder of the forest in order to preserve them.

When trees are felled for their timber, foresters nowadays prefer to allow natural regeneration to fill the gaps. They plant tree seedlings only where there are no suitable young trees growing from seeds dropped by the mature trees. This practice maintains the forest while allowing it to develop a more natural composition.

Forests are managed in this way even in remote areas that visitors never reach. The new approach accepts that, regardless of their location, forests are more than sources of timber. Their importance as wildlife habitat is fully recognized, and forest workers have welcomed the change. After all, they spend most of their working lives inside the forest. They are familiar with and care about the forest's inhabitants. Certain species must be excluded or their numbers limited in order to protect the trees (see "Pest control" on pages 203–207), but most plants, fungi, and animals cause no harm and are welcome.

Modern forest management combines timber production with conservation and the provision of recreational facilities for the visiting public.

CHAPTER 10

HEALTH OF TEMPERATE FORESTS

Are the temperate forests disappearing?

If farmers are unable to make a profit from the sale of their produce they will go out of business and farms will close. With fewer farms, food production will fall, and as the amount of food reaching the market decreases the price of food will increase. Higher prices will make farming more economically attractive and more people will be tempted to become farmers. There will be an endless cycle of "boom and bust."

Governments cannot allow this to happen, because if food prices rise, working people will demand higher wages, but they will not accept lower wages when food prices fall. Large fluctuations in food prices destabilize the economy, so governments try to keep prices constant, with only minor and predictable seasonal variations. They achieve this by subsidizing agricultural production. Subsidies to farmers take many forms, but they all have the same goal: to ensure that farmers keep on producing the commodities people want to buy.

Throughout most of the 20th century, while governments were introducing subsidies to stabilize food prices and maintain the profitability of farming, agriculture itself was changing. New machinery was introduced to increase the efficiency of cultivation and harvesting. The new machines—especially tractors—performed work that was previously done by horses and, in some regions, oxen. Land that had formerly grown food for draft animals was released to produce food for people. Agricultural chemicals boosted crop growth and reduced losses to pests, weeds, and fungal diseases. Output increased dramatically during the second half of the 20th century, and the subsidies guaranteed that increasing output did not lead to falling prices. Throughout the temperate regions of Europe and North America, agriculture became so productive that farmers were producing more food than people could eat. There were surpluses.

Agricultural subsidies keep food prices artificially low. This is a major source of friction between rich countries and poor countries that cannot afford to subsidize their farmers to the same extent. But the subsidies also have another effect: By encouraging overproduction they reduce the demand for more agricultural land and make it possible to take land out of farming altogether. Land that was once farmed can be converted to other uses—such as forests.

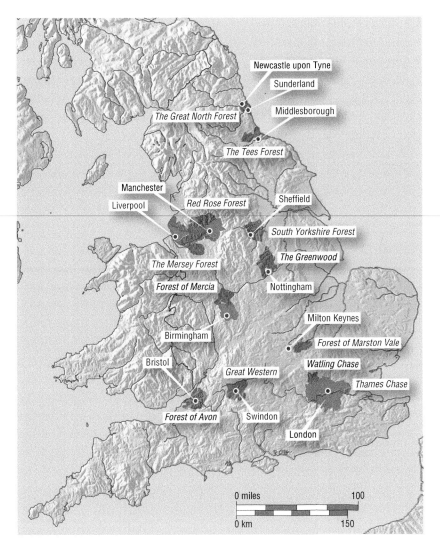

English Community Forests. Community Forests are planned to serve the people living in major cities.

The rise in agricultural productivity has coincided with the recognition that forests are havens for wildlife and that they can provide valuable recreational opportunities to city dwellers, becoming the "lungs of the city." Forests were once seen as obstacles in the way of farming. Today they are highly valued, and the area of temperate forest is expanding.

In England, government agencies, local government, and volunteer organizations are collaborating in a program to establish 12 Community Forests. Each forest will serve the people of a major city; the map shows their locations. The forests provide opportunities for leisure activities and are an educational resource for city schools. At the same time, they transform the landscape, in many places revitalizing abandoned industrial sites. In Scotland (see the sidebar "British geography" on page 172) natural forests, such as the Argyll Forest in the west of the country, are protected as tourist attractions, as local amenities, and for their value as wildlife habitat. Between 1990 and 2000 the area of natural forests in the United Kingdom increased by 16 percent.

Forests are also expanding in the United States. During the 1990s the area of natural forest increased by 1 percent and the area of plantations also by 1 percent. The United States now has approximately the same area of forest that it had in 1920. This means that the rapid deforestation of the 19th and early 20th centuries has been arrested.

According to figures collected by the UN Food and Agriculture Organization (FAO), during the 1990s the total area of all the world's forests decreased by approximately 386,000 square miles (1 million km^2), from 15.1 million square miles (39 million km^2) to 14.7 million square miles (38 million km^2). That is a decrease of 9.4 percent, and equivalent to a loss of 0.22 percent a year.

The loss was not spread evenly across the world, however. While tropical forests diminished in size, forests outside the Tropics—including the northern coniferous forests (called boreal forest or taiga) as well as temperate forests—expanded. Globally, 0.9 percent of the area of natural forest outside the Tropics was cleared during the 1990s and the land converted to other uses, but the forests also expanded onto unforested land by an area equal to 2.6 percent. That amounts to an increase in area of approximately 6,600 square miles (17,000 km²) each year between 1990 and 2000. The expansion was due to new planting, in projects such as the Community Forests in England, and the regeneration of forest on land that had been taken out of agriculture. Plantation forests also expanded during the 1990s, by 12,000 square miles (31,000 km²). This added 1.2 percent to the Earth's total forest area. When the increases in area of natural and plantation forests are combined, the temperate and boreal forests expanded by 2.9 percent during this period. The table shows how the area of forest changed between 1990 and 2000 in each continent, with the change in the most extensively forested temperate countries shown in parentheses.

Far from disappearing, temperate forests are expanding, and in coming years they are likely to continue expanding. Improvements in agricultural productivity have released land that was once needed to grow food, providing space for forests. This change has coincided with the growing public appreciation of forests. Forests support a wide variety of plant and animal species (see "Why biodiversity matters" on pages 142–144) and they attract visitors to walk, bike, and ride

Forest area changes, 1990–2000

Region	Total forest, 1990		Total forest, 2000		Rate of change (% per year)	Forest as % of land area
	000 miles²	000 km²	000 miles²	000 km²		
Africa	2,712	7,025	2,509	6,498	–0.8	22
Asia	2,130	5,514	2,115	5,478	–1.0	49
China	561	1,454	631	1,635	+1.2	17
Oceania*	777	2,013	763	1,976	–0.2	23
Europe	3,979	10,305	4,012	10,392	+0.1	46
Russia	3,282	8,500	3,287	8,513	0	50
N. America & Caribbean	1,802	4,667	1,817	4,706	+0.1	26
Canada	944	2,446	944	2,446	0	27
Central America	341	883	304	787	–1.1	43
South America	3,563	9,227	3,419	8,856	–0.4	50

*Oceania comprises Australia, New Zealand, and the small islands of the South Pacific Ocean.

Source: FAO Global Forest Assessment, 2000.

horseback through them. Forests are more popular than they have ever been, and in the temperate regions of the world they are highly treasured. They will not vanish.

Acid rain

In the late 1960s and early 1970s, Swedish and Norwegian scientists noticed that the rain falling on their countries was becoming increasingly acidic. Scientists in the eastern United States and Canada observed the same phenomenon at about the same time.

At first the problem centered on damage to buildings, statues, and public monuments made from limestone and sandstone. Acid was eroding the surfaces, leaving them pitted. Then lakes began to suffer. Their waters became clear as the microscopic organisms disappeared, and fish were dying. Finally, forest trees were affected. German environmentalists called it *neuartige Waldsterben* ("new form of forest death") and suggested that up to 10 percent of the country's forests were sick or dying. Forests were also suffering in parts of Central Europe, Britain, and North America.

The damage was blamed on "acid rain." In fact, it was rather more complicated. Industrial furnaces, especially in power plants, were burning coal that contained relatively large amounts of sulfur. The sulfur entered the air as sulfur dioxide (SO_2), which then drifted with the wind. The acid reaching Scandinavia came from Britain, Germany, Poland, and Russia. Most German acid rain was produced in Germany. In North America the culprits were power plants and factories in the U.S. Midwest. Depending on the atmospheric conditions, the airborne SO_2 reacted with other substances in various ways, but all of the reactions led to the conversion of the SO_2 to sulfuric acid (H_2SO_4). This was the source of most of the acid.

Very high temperatures allow atmospheric nitrogen to be oxidized to nitric oxide (NO) and nitrogen dioxide (NO_2). Some industrial furnaces generate temperatures high enough for this reaction, but most of the NO and NO_2 are produced in high-compression gasoline engines—the engines in modern cars. Fertilizer manufacture also releases some NO_2. Both of these nitrogen oxides react with other atmospheric gases. Several reactions take place and all of them lead to the production of nitric acid (HNO_3).

Acid can damage plants directly when it is deposited on their leaves through *dry deposition* (when droplets of acid in dry air collide with a leaf surface), *acid mist,* and *acid snow.* All of these are more harmful than acid rain, which usually falls on only the upper surfaces of leaves and then runs off them onto the ground. Acid mist coats both upper and lower leaf surfaces, and snow lies on plant surfaces until it melts. Although acid rain gets the blame, it is the least harmful; "acid precipitation" is a better term because it is more comprehensive.

Acid precipitation also affects soil chemistry in two ways. Increasing soil acidity slows the rate at which organic matter decomposes. Decomposition releases nutrients, so slowing their release deprives tree roots of the nutrients they need, thus harming the trees. By a process called *mass action,* acids introduce hydrogen ions carrying positive charge (H^+) that displace magnesium (Mg^+) and calcium (Ca^+), which are essential plant nutrients. This is a serious problem in soils derived from hard rocks such as granite. (It is much less of a problem for soils developed from sedimentary rocks, such as chalk or limestone. Most sedimentary rocks are derived from the shells of marine organisms made from magnesium and calcium carbonates, so sedimentary soils usually contain enough of these elements to prevent the soil being overwhelmed by hydrogen ions; this is called *buffering*.) Mass action can also liberate aluminum ions (Al^+) that react with soil water, releasing more hydrogen ions and further increasing the soil acidity. The overall effect is to starve plant roots of essential nutrients. This is much more harmful to trees than direct damage to their leaves. It slows growth rates and makes trees less able to combat disease and pest attacks.

Nitrogen also reaches the ground in acid precipitation. Nitrogen is an essential plant nutrient and stimulates plant growth, but in a forest this can be harmful. Many forests grow on land that is poor in plant nutrients. Adding nitrogen makes plants grow more vigorously, but because the other nutrients they need are in short supply, the plants' "diet" is unbalanced. The nutritional imbalance interferes with the processes by which plants prepare for dry conditions. This makes them less able to survive summer drought and winter cold, when the soil water is frozen and plant roots cannot absorb it.

Although the problem was serious, it was exaggerated during the 1980s due to an error in the way the effect was estimated. Damage was first observed in Norway spruce (*Picea abies*), and trees were believed to be suffering if they lost more than 10 percent of their needles. Since almost one-third of spruces had lost more than 10 percent of their needles, the damage appeared to be severe and very widespread. Foresters then pointed out that perfectly healthy trees often lose more than 10 percent of their needles. When the assessment was revised, the damage was seen to be less serious. Rather than killing entire German forests, as the name *Waldsterben* ("forest death") suggests, a survey in 1986 found that 1.6 percent of German forest trees of all species were severely affected and 17.3 percent were moderately badly affected. In 1999, approximately 25 percent of all European forest trees had lost more than 25 percent of their foliage and therefore were suffering moderate damage or worse.

Environmental groups in the United States, Canada, and Europe campaigned for measures to address the problem in the only way practicable: by reducing acid emissions. In 1979 governments signed the Geneva Convention on Long-Range Transboundary Air Pollution, and the convention came into force in 1983. It lays down the general principles and goals that allow nations to cooperate in reducing the emission of air pollutants that drift across international frontiers. It was followed by eight more specific agreements, called "protocols," to reduce air pollution. The convention has been highly successful.

Emissions of sulfur dioxide in the United States fell by 37.5 percent between 1980 and 2000, from 26.4 million tons (24 million tonnes) to 16.5 million tons (15 million tonnes). They are predicted to reach 15.4 million tons (14 million tonnes) by 2010. European emissions fell 56 percent, from 65 million tons (59 million tonnes) to 28.6 million tons (26 million tonnes), over the same period and are expected to reach

20 million tons (18 million tonnes) by 2010. In fact, sulfur dioxide emissions had already been falling for some time before acid rain damage began to cause concern, so the steps taken to reduce emissions reinforced an existing downward trend. In contrast, Asian emissions, which were 16.5 million tons (15 million tonnes) in 1980, are expected to rise to 87 million tons (79 million tonnes) by 2010.

Nitrogen oxide emissions are also rising, due mainly to increasing use of nitrogen fertilizer on farms. The rising number of automobiles also contributes to nitrogen oxide emissions, but to a lesser extent, because vehicles are now fitted with *catalytic converters*—devices that remove most pollutants from exhaust emissions.

Forests are recovering from the harm caused by acid precipitation, but the recovery is slow. Slow progress is inevitable because most of the damage arose from changes in the chemistry of water moving through the soil, and this takes time to correct. Meanwhile there is a danger that unless Asian emissions are curbed, damage to forests will increase in that part of the world.

Forest clearance and climate

Farmers plant trees to shelter their fields from the wind. A *shelter belt*—a row of trees planted at right angles to the direction of the prevailing wind—absorbs some of the energy of the wind as the air expends its energy pushing against the trees. The diagrams on page 218 show how this works. In the upper picture the trees are planted close together, forming a dense barrier. Some of the wind flows back from the barrier as though reflected, forming an eddy, and more of the wind forms a second eddy on the downwind side of the trees, but most of the wind blows over the top of the barrier. There is very little wind immediately behind the trees because the wind cannot blow through the barrier, but the wind soon recovers its strength. By a distance equal to 10–15 times the height of the barrier it has regained about 90 percent of its force. If the trees are more widely spaced, as shown in the lower drawing, the wind can penetrate the barrier, but is slowed by it. Although the wind speed on the downwind side

*How a
shelter belt works*

of the trees is greater than it would be behind a denser barrier, the effect continues for longer. The wind does not recover to 90 percent of its original strength for a distance equal to 15–20 times the height of the barrier. If the shelter belt is neither too dense nor too open it is possible to reduce the wind speed for a distance up to 40 times the height of the trees.

A shelter belt is a barrier only a few trees deep, and a forest has a much greater effect on the wind. Suppose the wind outside the forest is blowing at 20 MPH (32 km/h). Inside the forest, 100 feet (30 m) from the edge, the wind speed will be 12–16 MPH (19–26 km/h), and 400 feet (120 m) from the edge it will be about 1.2 MPH (2 km/h). In the calm center of the forest, the trees have absorbed almost the whole of the wind's energy. The wind also blows around and over the top of the forest, but it is much weaker on the downwind side than on the exposed side. Forests shelter the land downwind of them as well as the ground they occupy.

Not surprisingly, when a forest is cleared the local climate becomes windier. This increases the risk of soil erosion (see "Forest clearance and soil erosion" on pages 225–227). More surprisingly, perhaps, clearing a forest also makes the climate foggier and dustier. Fog consists of droplets of water that are so small they fall very slowly, and most of them are lifted by air eddies before they can reach the ground. The droplets remain airborne and the fog drifts slowly on the wind. Dust particles behave in the same way—until they enter the forest. A forest acts as a filter. As the wind carries water droplets and dust particles through a forest, the trees trap many of them and the reduction in the wind speed holds them inside the forest long enough for them to fall to the ground. Conditions are often foggy or dusty upwind of a forest, but the air is clear and fresh on the downwind side. Remove the forest and the fog and dust will affect a larger area.

Forests also influence the air and ground temperatures. At night the ground radiates the heat it absorbed during the day and its temperature falls. On cloudy nights some of this radiated heat is reflected by the clouds, so the air remains warm, but on clear nights the radiation escapes and the ground becomes much colder. If the air is still, a *boundary layer* of air next to the ground becomes cold enough for its moisture to condense or freeze, producing dew or frost. Condensation and freezing release latent heat (see "Dew and frost" on pages 65–66), which the ground surface absorbs, warming it a little. Inside and on the sheltered downwind side of a forest, the air is still, so these are places where dew and frost are likely to form. But remove the forest and the wind increases. Close to the ground the moving air is turbulent, rolling and eddying as it crosses the uneven surface, and constantly drawing air from higher levels to mix with the air next to the ground, preventing a layer of still air from forming. Dew and frost cannot form under these conditions, so removing the forest makes dew and frost less common. If there is no dew or frost, however, there is no release of latent heat to warm the ground. In winter ground frosts will occur earlier and they will be harder.

Forests shade the ground. On a hot, sunny day, the air inside a forest will feel cool. If the forest is cleared, the shade will be lost, so summer days will likely be hotter. At night and in winter, trees absorb much of the heat that is radiated from the ground. Without the trees, that effect will be lost and the ground temperature will fall faster and farther. Summer days may grow warmer, but the nights may be cooler and the cold of winter will last for longer.

Clouds often form above forests. This is because trees move large quantities of water from the ground to the air by transpiration (see "Evaporation and transpiration" on pages 66–69) and by the evaporation of rainwater from leaves and bark. The air inside a forest is more humid than the air outside; the difference is greatest in summer. The clouds that form above the forest often release rain, so the forest causes some of the precipitation that falls on it. If the forest is cleared, this effect will disappear. Air moves horizontally, carrying moisture and clouds with it, so clearing a forest may have little effect on the amount of rain and snow that fall, but if the forest is cleared over a very large area it is likely that the climate will become drier.

Without the evaporation of rainwater from tree surfaces, more of the rain that falls will reach the ground, and without transpiration less soil water will be returned to the air. If the ground is well drained, the overall effect is likely to make the ground drier, but if the drainage is poor the ground may become wetter.

If temperate forests are cleared from a large area, the climate of that area will change. Weather will be windier and probably drier, and there will be a bigger contrast between summer and winter temperatures and between day and night temperatures. Fogs may be more frequent. Depending on the drainage, the ground may be drier or wetter. If it is drier there may be dust storms.

How will forests respond to global warming?

Since about 1880 the average air temperature over the whole world has risen by about 1.25°F (0.7°C). Approximately half of this warming occurred between 1880 and 1940. It was entirely natural and was probably the final part of the recovery from a cold period called the Little Ice Age that had lasted since the 16th century. From 1940 until the middle of the 1970s the average temperature fell very slightly. Then in 1976–77 there was a sudden jump in temperature of about

0.5°F (0.3°C), after which the temperature remained steady until the early 1990s, when it began rising again.

At present Earth's average temperature is increasing at a rate of about 3°F (1.7°C) per century. The warming is not distributed evenly. It is strongest in the northern latitudes of the Northern Hemisphere, and especially in northwestern North America—Alaska and the Yukon—and northeastern Siberia. There is very little warming in the Southern Hemisphere, except for the Antarctic Peninsula, which has been growing warmer for several decades, most probably due to changes in the circulation of water in the Southern Ocean. Where it has occurred, the warming has had the effect of raising winter and nighttime temperatures much more than summer and daytime temperatures, so the difference in temperature between summer and winter and daytime and nighttime is growing smaller.

All of the rise in temperature that has happened since the late 19th century can be called global warming, but it is the warming since the 1970s that worries many scientists. Part of the warming is natural, but it is also highly likely that humans have been contributing to it by releasing into the air gases, known as *greenhouse gases,* that absorb long-wave radiation. This is known as the greenhouse effect or, more correctly, the *enhanced greenhouse effect* (see the sidebar).

Climate scientists estimate the way temperatures may respond to the continued accumulation of greenhouse gases by means of extremely complex mathematical models they construct on the fastest and most powerful supercomputers in the world. There are many of these models and they are improving all the time, but they are still unable to predict what the consequences of the change in climate will be for any particular region. It is not yet possible to calculate how the change may affect an area the size of the United States, far less any smaller region. The scientists hope they may achieve this within the next few years.

Still, there are a few clues. At present the air contains less carbon dioxide than plants are able to use. Many commercial growers increase the carbon dioxide concentration in the air inside their greenhouses in order to stimulate plant growth. Plants (outside greenhouses) are responding to the increasing atmospheric concentration of carbon dioxide by growing bigger. At the same time, milder winters and warmer nights mean the first frosts of autumn occur later than they used to do, and the last frosts of spring happen earlier. This has extended the growing season. In North America the start of spring, marked by the date of the last frost, is now four to 12 days earlier than it was in about 1980, and autumn weather, marked by the date of the first frost, begins one to seven days later. In Europe spring begins four to eight days earlier and autumn begins 14–22 days later.

Warmer weather makes water evaporate faster, a higher rate of evaporation makes more cloud form, and more cloud

The greenhouse effect

When any object is warmer than its surroundings, it emits electromagnetic radiation, such as light or heat. The wavelength of that radiation is inversely proportional to the temperature of the object emitting it: The hotter the body, the shorter the wavelength of its radiation. This is because the amount of energy carried by electromagnetic radiation is greatest when the wavelength is shortest, meaning that more wave crests and troughs pass a stationary point in the same interval of time. Astronomical bodies such as stars and planets are surrounded by space, which is very cold. The Sun is hot and radiates most intensely at short wavelengths. Its radiation warms the surface of the Earth, which then emits radiation at a much longer wavelength because it is relatively cool.

Some of the sunshine falling on the Earth is reflected into space by clouds and pale-colored surfaces such as snow and desert sand. Some is scattered by particles and tiny droplets in the air and returns to space without reaching the surface. The surface of land and sea absorbs approximately 51 percent of the solar radiation reaching Earth. The absorbed energy warms the material that absorbs it.

During the day the Earth absorbs solar radiation—sunshine—faster than it loses heat by radiating it away, and so its temperature rises. By late afternoon the surface is radiating heat at about the same rate as it is absorbing it; during the night it continues to radiate, but because the Sun is no longer shining, the Earth's surface temperature falls. It continues to fall until about one hour before dawn, when the first light appears in the sky.

While air is transparent to incoming short-wave solar radiation, it is less so to outgoing long-wave radiation because certain gases—principally water vapor, carbon dioxide, and means more rain and snow. In other words, a warmer climate is also a wetter climate, and the weather today is becoming cloudier and wetter. In eastern North America, for example, the temperature has not risen, but precipitation has increased. More snow falls in winter, and because the snow is deeper it takes longer to melt in spring.

Warmer and wetter weather does not necessarily benefit plants, however. If the climate becomes a great deal warmer, water will evaporate from the soil faster than it falls as rain, making the soil grow steadily drier, and once the soil is thoroughly dry the rainfall will decrease. So a very much warmer climate is a drier climate. Provided the climate warms by less

methane—absorb radiation at these wavelengths. This absorption of energy warms the air. It is called the greenhouse effect because, in a similar fashion, the glass of a greenhouse allows the sunshine to enter but the warm air inside the greenhouse is unable to escape, so the air inside the greenhouse becomes much warmer than the air outside.

The greenhouse effect is entirely natural. The absorbed radiation warms the air, which radiates at longer wavelengths, and energy escapes into space each time it is radiated at a wavelength no gas absorbs, 8.5–13.0 μm, known as the *atmospheric window*. The departure of the outgoing energy is delayed but not prevented. Without the greenhouse effect the average air temperature at ground level would be approximately 34°F (1°C); in fact, the average surface temperature is 59°F (15°C).

At present, human activities are enhancing the greenhouse effect by releasing certain "greenhouse gases," especially carbon dioxide, into the air. We release carbon dioxide (CO_2) whenever we burn a carbon-based fuel such as coal, oil, or gas. Combustion (burning) is a chemical reaction in which carbon (C) is oxidized (combined with oxygen, O), releasing energy and creating carbon dioxide as a by-product:

$$C + O_2 \rightarrow CO_2 + heat$$

Most climate scientists agree that the accumulation of greenhouse gases is producing a rise in the average temperature over many parts of the world. They disagree over the extent to which this presents a serious problem. At present the average temperature is increasing at about 2.3°F–3.2°F (1.3°C–1.8°C) per century. It seems probable that the average temperature in the early 22nd century will be 1.8°F–3.6°F (1°C–2°C) higher than it is today.

than about 3.6°F (2°C) conditions will become wetter; if the rise in temperature exceeds this threshold they will become drier. If the temperature continues to increase at its present rate of about 3°F (1.7°C) per century, the weather in the coming decades will become wetter, but some time in the 22nd century the increase may exceed the threshold. Of course, the present rise in temperature may not be sustained.

This is an estimate for the whole world, however, and the world is not warming evenly. The rise in temperature affects mainly the temperate and high-latitude Northern Hemisphere, where the threshold may be reached before the end of the 21st century.

As northern latitudes grow warmer and probably wetter, the change will favor temperate forests. If nature were left to take its course, the broad-leaved, deciduous forests typical of the northeastern United States and northwestern Europe would expand their range northward, replacing the southern part of the boreal forest. The boreal forest would also expand northward. The belt of tundra across northern Canada and Eurasia would become narrower—it cannot expand northward, because the Arctic Ocean lies to the north.

If the climate should become warmer but drier, the broad-leaved, deciduous forests would not fare so well. They prefer moist summers and wet winters. As they retreat, coniferous forests will replace them. Coniferous trees are more tolerant of dry conditions. They flourish in the north, where the ground is frozen for most of the long winter and their roots cannot absorb water. But they also flourish around the Mediterranean and in parts of the United States that have a dry summer, such as the mountains of Colorado, Arizona, and New Mexico.

Many scientists believe that a continued rise in temperature will sooner or later bring harmful consequences. Humans may adapt to the changes or seek to avert them by reducing emissions of greenhouse gases. That is the aim of the Kyoto Protocol, an international agreement drawn up in 1997 that commits the governments that have signed it to taking steps to reduce emissions by target amounts set for each country.

Forest clearance and soil erosion

Tree roots push their way through the soil, reaching far in search of water and nutrients. The roots of the herbs growing between the trees are engaged in the same pursuit. All these roots form an intricate network belowground. When the plants die, their roots decompose, leaving behind the tunnels they made and once occupied. Small animals are able to move through the larger of these tunnels, and air penetrates all of them. Meanwhile the decayed material of the roots becomes part of the soil, along with the decomposed remains of leaves, twigs, and wood.

Plants supply the materials that sustain the animals, fungi, bacteria, and other microbes living in the soil. These organisms feed on the plant material, working it over and breaking it down. Together the plants, animals, and microorganisms make the soil, and they continue to make it for as long as their community endures.

If the forest is cleared, the supply of plant material ceases. This may not matter. The trees may soon be replaced, or the land may be converted to fields to grow crops. But there are dangers facing land that is left bare for too long.

Trees move large amounts of water from the soil and into the air (see "Evaporation and transpiration" on pages 66–68). When the trees are removed, that movement ceases. Rain and melted snow drain downward into the soil and join the groundwater. Groundwater eventually transports the water to a river, but the movement is slow (see "How water moves through a temperate forest" on pages 29–33). If a forest grows on fairly level ground in a region of high precipitation, removing the trees may mean the water drains vertically downward faster than the horizontal movement of the groundwater can carry it away. Under these circumstances the water table will rise, and after a time the ground will be waterlogged. This may harm the next crop of trees by making the soil cold and airless at the level the roots try to penetrate. The remedy—which is expensive—is to plow the land and install drains to remove the surplus water.

On sloping ground the soil may start to erode. Soil is naturally irregular in texture, and soil particles stick together to form lumps. Raindrops falling onto bare soil knock particles free from the lumps; repeated impacts wash fine soil grains into tiny hollows and crevices in the surface, eventually filling them and sealing the soil beneath an impermeable cap. Rain then no longer penetrates the soil. Instead it washes over the surface, washing away the surface layer little by little but resealing the surface with small particles as it does so. The flowing water finds its way into natural depressions, carrying soil with it, widening and deepening the depressions until they form *rills*—small channels. Further enlargement by water turns rills into *gullies*—channels the size of small streambeds—that flow with water only after heavy rain, carrying soil with them. This downhill transport of soil is called "erosion."

Washing away surface soil is a gradual process, but under certain circumstances erosion can happen faster, carrying all of the topsoil rather than wearing away the surface layer. It is then called "mass wasting."

Water draining downward through soil eventually meets a layer of rock, clay, or some other impermeable material. Immediately above the impermeable layer the accumulating water may turn the soil to mud. If the impermeable layer is fairly close to the surface and if the ground slopes steeply, the mud may start to flow downhill, carrying the overlying soil with it. Often the movement is quite slow, the soil shifting a little farther with each heavy fall of rain in a process called "soil creep," but, left unchecked, eventually it will strip away all of the soil, exposing bare rock.

Creep is one form of mass wasting, but there are others that are much more dramatic and dangerous. The layer of liquid mud may detach the entire layer of topsoil from the impermeable material on which it lies. All of the topsoil will then slide downhill, riding on the lubricating layer of mud. If the mud layer is close to the surface, the slide will carry all of the surface soil, vegetation, and debris of all kinds, accelerating as it gathers momentum. This is a landslide. If the soil is extremely sodden, all of it may slide as a mudflow. Both landslides and mudflows are catastrophic events that can block or carry away roads and demolish homes.

Even without mudslides, erosion due to deforestation can remove large amounts of soil. A study in England found that sandy soil eroded at a rate of eight tons per acre (17.7

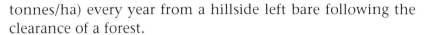

tonnes/ha) every year from a hillside left bare following the clearance of a forest.

Foresters understand the risks of erosion on hillsides and seek to prevent it. The first step is to plan the harvesting operation in such a way as to leave as small an area of bare ground as possible. As soon as the lumber has been removed, machines dig trenches at right angles to the slope. The trenches are not meant to transport water, but only to collect water flowing downhill and hold it long enough for the water to soak into the ground. Work to prepare the ground for the next tree crop begins with *scarification*. This operation breaks up the soil using machines that chop up and scatter the *brash*—small branches and foliage—left after harvesting. Scarification leaves a very uneven surface that water penetrates easily. Finally, except on very well drained ground, machines dig soil from hollows to make mounds on which the new tree seedlings are planted. This also breaks up the surface and improves drainage.

Forest clearance and agriculture are the two principal causes of soil erosion. Some erosion is unavoidable, because this is a natural geological process that becomes serious only when soil is removed faster than new soil can form. Good land management reduces the risk of unacceptably high rates of erosion.

Sustainable forest management

During the 1960s many people began to fear that the resources on which society depends were being used up at a rate that would soon cause some of them, particularly oil and metal ores, to be exhausted. Also, those resources that renew themselves naturally (see "Renewable and nonrenewable resources" on pages 175–178) were being consumed faster than they were being replenished.

The fear was not new. In the middle of the 19th century, mining geologists were warning that the supply of coal was not infinite, although the known reserves were so large that most people could not conceive of them ever being exhausted. In 1864 George Perkins Marsh (see the sidebar on page 164) warned of the dangers of clearing forests.

Eventually the concerns about the depletion of minerals and fuels—the nonrenewable resources—and the degradation of renewable resources such as farmland led to the idea of sustainability. The term first appeared prominently in *World Conservation Strategy: Living Resource Conservation for Sustainable Development* (1980). This was a document published jointly by the International Union for Conservation, Nature, and Natural Resources (IUCN), the World Wildlife Fund (WWF), the UN Environment Program (UNEP), the UN Food and Agriculture Organization (FAO), and the UN Educational, Scientific and Cultural Organization (UNESCO). *World Conservation Strategy* called on governments to devise resource conservation strategies for their own countries. It had little effect, but the word *sustainable* caught the imagination of environmentalists and, through them, of politicians.

Sustainability was defined in another document, *Our Common Future,* the report of the World Commission on Environment and Development. (The United Nations established this independent body in 1983 under Gro Harlem Brundtland, then the prime minister of Norway, and the commission prepared the way for the UN Conference on Environment and Development—the Earth Summit—held in Rio de Janeiro in 1992. *Our Common Future* outlined the matters to be debated at the conference.) It said: "Humanity has the ability to make development sustainable—to ensure that it meets the needs of the present without compromising the ability of future generations to meet their own needs." (*Our Common Future,* p. 8.)

A commercial forester might take this to mean that a forest should produce a crop of trees each year and continue doing so indefinitely. But that is how forests have been managed in Europe since medieval times, so it is hardly original. A more imaginative interpretation follows from a different definition of *forest.* If the forest is seen as a community of living organisms rather than simply as so much standing timber, then to be sustainable its management must preserve the entire community—the biodiversity of the forest. Such management does not preclude commercial exploitation. Trees and small wood can still be taken from the forest, but in ways that cause the least possible disturbance to other organisms.

Plantation forests (see pages 199–202) supply timber and relieve the pressure on natural forests. Today they, too, are managed in ways that are more consistent with the aims of conservation. British plantations once consisted almost exclusively of coniferous trees that do not grow naturally in Britain. It takes time for those trees to mature and many coniferous plantation still remain, but as the old plantations are cleared, stands of more varied species are planted to replace them.

Plantations are less popular in countries with much larger expanses of natural forest. There, timber is cut from the natural forest, but the forests are then encouraged to regenerate naturally from seeds shed from the forest trees. Where that is impractical, plantations replace cleared forest. Areas of old-growth forest—managed or unmanaged forest that has been standing for more than 200 years—are being identified and marked for protection. In Britain, ancient woodland—growing on land that is known from documentary evidence to have been forested since before 1600—is also protected.

Insensitive logging still occurs, some of it illegal, but attitudes are changing. Temperate forests are now regarded as much more than "timber factories." They are popular for recreation, education, and conservation. Any plan to clear a forested area is certain to meet strong local opposition, and if the forest is especially beautiful, extensive, or rich in wildlife, the opposition will be national or even international. It may be too early to say that every temperate forest is managed in a sustainable fashion, but the trend is clearly in that direction.

CONCLUSION: WHAT FUTURE FOR TEMPERATE FORESTS?

Long, long ago forests of oak, elm, beech, chestnut, maple, ash, poplar, linden, birch, and many other species blanketed most of the lowlands of Europe. Similar forests covered much of the northeastern United States. Many of those forests have gone, cleared by long-dead settlers to make way for farms.

Farms were needed, of course. People must be fed—and so must the draft animals that helped the farmers till the land. But forests have always been needed. Most furniture, house frames, floors, and everyday tools are made wholly or partly from wood. This book is made from paper manufactured from what were once trees growing in a forest. Wood was once the only fuel that heated every home, from the king's palace and the baron's castle to the villager's cottage. It cooked everyone's meals, and the only way to obtain hot water for washing was to place a cauldron over a wood fire. Many people burn wood to keep warm even today. We may boast of living in the "Information Age," but the truth is that we live in the Wooden Age, and we always have.

Nowadays a new use has been found for our forests, based on a deeper understanding and appreciation of the way they function. Forests are seen not simply as sources of raw materials and fuel, but as living communities of plants, animals, fungi, and organisms so small they can be seen only with the aid of a microscope. The forest reveals itself as a wonderland of diversity, a community of living organisms so vast and complex as to be barely comprehensible.

Most North Americans and Europeans now live in cities. The countryside and its forests are remote from the sidewalks, subways, city blocks, and suburban sprawl, and city parks are pale imitations of genuine countryside. This makes the forests still more special—and valuable. The forest is a place to visit. It is where families can walk, children can play, and naturalists can observe what is around them. It is where scientists can study the planet we all share, and where students can learn.

As well as supplying raw materials, forests within reach of cities are also amenities, places where people can relax, play, or be refreshed.
(Courtesy of Fogstock)

Throughout much of the Tropics, forests are being cleared, although strenuous efforts are being made to halt the clearances. In temperate regions, on the other hand, the forests are expanding. Forests that have stood for centuries, known as old-growth forests in most of the world and as ancient woodland in Britain, are protected. The protection is not always effective and valued forests are sometimes lost, often through illegal logging, but conservation bodies are increasingly vigilant and the chainsaws can no longer enter the forest unchallenged.

It seems certain, therefore, that the temperate forests will survive long into the future. Changes in the climate may alter their composition, but forests are not static; their composition is changing all the time. Trees come and go, but the forest will remain. Of that we may be certain.

SI UNITS AND CONVERSIONS

UNIT	QUANTITY	SYMBOL	CONVERSION
Base units			
meter	length	m	1 m = 3.2808 feet
kilogram	mass	kg	1 kg = 2.205 pounds
second	time	s	
ampere	electric current	A	
kelvin	thermodynamic temperature	K	1 K = 1°C = 1.8°F
candela	luminous intensity		
mole	amount of substance	cd	mol
Supplementary units			
radian	plane angle	rad	$\pi/2$ rad = 90°
steradian	solid angle	sr	
Derived units			
coulomb	quantity of electricity	C	
cubic meter	volume	m^3	1 m^3 = 1.308 yards^3
farad	capacitance	F	
henry	inductance	H	
hertz	frequency	Hz	
joule	energy	J	1 J = 0.2389 calories
kilogram per cubic meter	density	kg m^{-3}	1 kg m^{-3} = 0.0624 lb. ft.$^{-3}$
lumen	luminous flux	lm	
lux	illuminance	lx	

(continues)

233

(continued)

UNIT	QUANTITY	SYMBOL	CONVERSION
meter per second	speed	m s^{-1}	1 m s^{-1} = 3.281 ft s^{-1}
meter per second squared	acceleration	m s^{-2}	
mole per cubic meter	concentration	mol m^{-3}	
newton	force	N	1 N = 7.218 lb. force
ohm	electric resistance	Ω	
pascal	pressure	Pa	1 Pa = 0.145 lb. in^{-2}
radian per second	angular velocity	rad s^{-1}	
radian per second squared	angular acceleration	rad s^{-2}	
square meter	area	m^2	1 m^2 = 1.196 yards^2
tesla	magnetic flux density	T	
volt	electromotive force	V	
watt	power	W	1W = 3.412 Btu h^{-1}
weber	magnetic flux	Wb	

Prefixes used with SI units

PREFIX	SYMBOL	VALUE
atto	a	$\times 10^{-18}$
femto	f	$\times 10^{-15}$
pico	p	$\times 10^{-12}$
nano	n	$\times 10^{-9}$
micro	μ	$\times 10^{-6}$
milli	m	$\times 10^{-3}$
centi	c	$\times 10^{-2}$
deci	d	$\times 10^{-1}$
deca	da	$\times 10$
hecto	h	$\times 10^2$
kilo	k	$\times 10^3$
mega	M	$\times 10^6$

PREFIX	SYMBOL	VALUE
giga	G	$\times 10^9$
tera	T	$\times 10^{12}$

Prefixes attached to SI units alter their value.

SOIL CLASSIFICATION: ORDERS OF THE SOIL TAXONOMY

Entisols   Soils with weakly developed horizons, such as disturbed soils and soils developed over alluvial (river) deposits.

Vertisols   Soils with more than 30 percent clay that crack when dry.

Inceptisols   Soils with a composition that changes little with depth, such as young soils.

Aridisols   Soils with large amounts of salt, such as desert soils.

Mollisols   Soils with some horizons rich in organic matter.

Spodosols   Soils rich in organic matter, iron, and aluminum; in older classifications known as a podzol.

Alfisols   Basic soils in which surface constituents have moved to a lower level.

Ultisols   Acid soils in which surface constituents have moved to a lower level.

Oxisols   Soils rich in iron and aluminum oxides that have lost most of their nutrients through weathering; old soils often found in the humid Tropics.

Histosols   Soils rich in organic matter.

Reference Soil Groups of the Food and Agriculture Organization of the United Nations (FAO)

Histosols   Soils with a peat layer more than 15.75 inches (40 cm) deep.

Cryosols   Soils with a permanently frozen layer within 39 inches (100 cm) of the surface.

Anthrosols   Soils that have been strongly affected by human activity.

Leptosols   Soils with hard rock within 10 inches (25 cm) of the surface, or more than 40 percent calcium carbonate within 10 inches (25 cm) of the surface, or less than 10 percent of fine earth to a depth of 30 inches (75 cm) or more.

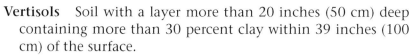

Vertisols   Soil with a layer more than 20 inches (50 cm) deep containing more than 30 percent clay within 39 inches (100 cm) of the surface.

Fluvisols   Soils formed on river (alluvial) deposits with volcanic deposits within 10 inches (25 cm) of the surface and extending to a depth of more than 20 inches (50 cm).

Solonchaks   Soils with a salt-rich layer more than six inches (15 cm) thick at or just below the surface.

Gleysols   Soils with a sticky, bluish gray layer (gley) within 20 inches (50 cm) of the surface.

Andosols   Volcanic soils having a layer more than 12 inches (30 cm) deep containing more than 10 percent volcanic glass or other volcanic material within 10 inches (25 cm) of the surface.

Podzols   Pale soils with a layer containing organic material and/or iron and aluminum that has washed down from above.

Plinthosols   Soils with a layer more than six inches (15 cm) deep containing more than 25 percent iron and aluminum sesquioxides (oxides comprising two parts of the metal to three parts of oxygen) within 20 inches (50 cm) of the surface that hardens when exposed.

Ferralsols   Soils with a subsurface layer more than six inches (15 cm) deep with red mottling due to iron and aluminum.

Solonetz   Soils with a sodium- and clay-rich subsurface layer more than three inches (7.5 cm) deep.

Planosols   Soils that have had stagnant water within 40 inches (100 cm) of the surface for prolonged periods.

Chernozems   Soils with a dark-colored, well-structured, basic surface layer at least eight inches (20 cm) deep.

Kastanozems   Soils resembling chernozems, but with concentrations of calcium compounds within 40 inches (100 cm) of the surface.

Phaeozems   All other soils with a dark-colored, well structured, basic surface layer.

Gypsisols   Soils with a layer rich in gypsum (calcium sulfate) within 40 inches (100 cm) of the surface, or more than 15 percent gypsum in a layer more than 40 inches (100 cm) deep.

Durisols   Soils with a layer of cemented silica within 40 inches (100 cm) of the surface.

Calcisols   Soils with concentrations of calcium carbonate within 50 inches (125 cm) of the surface.

Albeluvisols   Soils with a subsurface layer rich in clay that has an irregular upper surface.

Alisols Slightly acid soils containing high concentrations of aluminum and with a clay-rich layer within 40 inches (100 cm) of the surface.

Nitisols Soils with a layer containing more than 30 percent clay more than 12 inches (30 cm) deep and no evidence of clay particles moving to lower levels within 40 inches (100 cm) of the surface.

Acrisols Acid soils with a clay-rich subsurface layer.

Luvisols Soils with a clay-rich subsurface layer containing clay particles that have moved down from above.

Lixisols All other soils with a clay-rich layer within 40–80 inches (100–200 cm) of the surface.

Umbrisols Soils with a thick, dark colored, acid surface layer.

Cambisols Soils with an altered surface layer or one that is thick and dark colored, above a subsoil that is acid in the upper 40 inches (100 cm) and with a clay-rich or volcanic layer beginning 10–40 inches (25–100 cm) below the surface.

Arenosols Weakly developed soils with a coarse texture.

Regosols All other soils.

Note: A *basic* or alkaline soil is one containing more hydroxyl ions (OH⁻) than hydrogen ions (H⁺); an *acid* soil contains more H⁺ ions than OH⁻ ions. Acidity is measured on the pH scale, a logarithmic scale expressing the activity of H⁺ ions in solution, where pH 7.0 is a neutral reaction. A basic soil has a pH greater than 7.0; an acid soil has a pH lower than 7.0.

GEOLOGIC TIME SCALE

Eon/ Eonothem	Era/ Erathem	Subera	Period System	Epoch/ Series	Began Ma*
		Quaternary	Pleistogene	Holocene	0.11
				Pleistocene	1.81
Phanerozic	Cenozoic	*Tertiary*	Neogene	Pliocene	5.3
				Miocene	23.03
			Paleogene	Oligocene	33.9
				Eocene	55.8
				Paleocene	65.5
	Mesozoic		Cretaceous	Upper	99.6
				Lower	145.5
			Jurassic	Upper	161.2
				Middle	175.6
				Lower	199.6
			Triassic	Upper	228
				Middle	245
				Lower	251
	Paleozoic	Upper	Permian	Lopingian	260.4
				Guadalupian	270.6
				Cisuralian	299
			Carboniferous	Pennsylvanian	318.1
				Mississippian	359.2
			Devonian	Upper	385.3
				Middle	397.5
				Lower	416
		Lower	Silurian	Pridoli	422.9
				Ludlow	443.7
				Wenlock	428.2
				Llandovery	443.7
			Ordovician	Upper	460.9
				Middle	471.8

(continues)

(continued)

Eon/ Eonothem	Era/ Erathem	Subera	Period System	Epoch/ Series	Began Ma*
				Lower	488.3
			Cambrian	Furongian	501
				Middle	513
				Lower	542
Proterozoic	Neoproterozoic		Ediacaran		600
			Cryogenian		850
			Tonian		1000
	Mesoproterozoic	Stenian			1200
			Ectasian		1400
			Calymmian		1600
	Paleoproterozoic	Statherian			1800
			Orosirian		2050
			Rhyacian		2300
			Siderian		2500
Archean	Neoarchean				2800
	Mesoarchean				3200
	Paleoarchean				3600
	Eoarchean				3800
Hadean	Swazian				3900
	Basin Groups				4000
	Cryptic				4567.17

Source: International Union of Geological Sciences, 2004.

Note: *Hadean* is an informal name. The Hadean, Archean, and Proterozoic eons cover the time formerly known as the Precambrian. *Quaternary* is now an informal name and *Tertiary* is likely to become informal in the future, although both continue to be widely used.

*Ma means millions of years ago.

GLOSSARY

adiabatic   a change in temperature that involves no exchange of heat with an outside source

adventitious   arising from an unusual part of the plant. Roots that emerge from NODES are said to be adventitious

air mass   a large body of air, covering most of a continent or ocean and extending to the TROPOPAUSE, in which atmospheric conditions are fairly constant throughout

alga   an organism (a protist) that performs PHOTOSYNTHESIS; it may be single-celled or multicelled. Seaweeds are algae

alternation of generations   two stages in the life cycle of a plant. The DIPLOID generation is called a SPOROPHYTE and the HAPLOID generation a GAMETOPHYTE

ambrosia beetle   a member of a group of beetles that feed on ambrosia, a sweet substance produced by certain FUNGI

angiosperm   a flowering plant

anther   the structure in a male flower, situated at the tip of a FILAMENT, where POLLEN is produced

anthophyte   a flowering plant; flowering plants were formerly classified in the division Anthophyta

anticyclone   a region in which the atmospheric pressure is higher than it is in the surrounding air

aquifer   an underground body of permeable material (e.g., sand or gravel) lying above a layer of impermeable material (e.g., rock or clay) that is capable of storing water and through which the GROUNDWATER flows

auxin   a hormone-like substance produced by a plant that promotes growth by making cells at the tips of branches grow longer

axil   the angle where a leaf joins the stem or a small branch joins a larger one

bedrock   the rock lying below the ground surface over a large area

biomass   the total mass of all the living organisms present in a given area

biome the largest biological community recognized, comprising a type of vegetation (e.g., temperate forest) together with the other organisms associated with it, occupying a large geographical area.

blocking the situation that occurs when an ANTICYCLONE or area of low pressure becomes stationary, obstructing the passage of weather systems which are forced to move around it

bootlace fungus *see* HONEY FUNGUS

boreal pertaining to the north

boundary current an ocean current that flows northward or southward close to the coast of a continent and parallel to it. Eastern boundary currents carry cold water southward on the eastern side of ocean basins (not along the eastern coasts of continents). Western boundary currents carry warm water northward on the western side of ocean basins

boundary layer the layer of a gas or liquid adjacent to a solid surface within which the characteristics of the gas or liquid are strongly influenced by proximity to the surface

bract a modified leaf that forms part of a flower

brash small branches and leaves that are cut from a tree trunk before the trunk is removed from the forest

broad-leaved describes the leaves of flowering plants, which are broad compared with the needles or scale leaves of CONIFERS

browse to feed on the leaves and shoots of living plants; leaves and shoots that are cut in order to be fed to livestock

calyx the collective name for the SEPALS

canopy the forest cover, more or less shading the floor, formed by the touching and overlapping branches and foliage of adjacent trees

capillarity (capillary attraction) the movement of water against gravity through a fine tube or narrow passageway

capillary attraction *see* CAPILLARITY

capillary fringe the region immediately above the WATER TABLE into which water rises by CAPILLARITY

carpel the female reproductive organs of a plant, comprising the STIGMA, STYLE, and OVARY

carrying capacity the largest population of a particular species that an area of environment can sustain

cecidium *see* GALL

charcoal a form of impure carbon used as a fuel, made by heating wood in airless conditions

chestnut blight a disease of chestnut trees caused by the fungus *Endothia parasitica* that was introduced to North America from Asia and by 1940 had killed most American chestnut trees

chipboard an industrial and construction material manufactured in sheets from compressed wood chippings

chlorophyll the pigment present in the leaves and sometimes stems of green plants that gives them their green color. Chlorophyll molecules trap light, thus supplying the energy for PHOTOSYNTHESIS

chloroplast the structure in plant cells that contains CHLOROPHYLL and in which PHOTOSYNTHESIS takes place

chromosome one of the threads of DNA found in the nucleus of a cell. Each chromosome carries some of the organism's genes, and the full complement of chromosomes (a number that varies according to species) contains the full set of genetic instructions (the genome) for that organism

climax the final stage in a plant SUCCESSION in which the plant community reaches a stable equilibrium with the environment

companion cell a modified PARENCHYMA cell that is linked to a SIEVE CELL

condensation the change from gas to liquid

conifer a GYMNOSPERM plant that produces seeds in cones, releasing them when the cone scales open

continental drift the movement of the continents in relation to one another across the Earth's surface

coppice the practice of cutting trees close to ground level in order to stimulate the growth of poles; an area of woodland that has been managed by coppicing

CorF *see* CORIOLIS EFFECT

Coriolis effect (CorF) the deflection due to the Earth's rotation experienced by bodies moving in relation to the Earth's surface; bodies are deflected to the right in the Northern Hemisphere and to the left in the Southern Hemisphere

cork (phellem) a layer of protective tissue, comprising dead cells, that forms immediately beneath the outer surface of the trunk and branches of a woody plant

cork cambium *see* PHELLOGEN

corolla the collective name for all the PETALS of a flower

cotyledon a seed leaf; the leaf that emerges from a germinating seed

crown   the branches and foliage at the top of a tree

crown fire   a forest fire that reaches the crowns of the trees, leaping from tree to tree

cuticle   a thin, waxy outer coat that protects the leaves and stem of a plant

cyclone   *see* DEPRESSION

deciduous   describes parts of a plant or animal that are shed at the same season each year

denitrification   the conversion by bacteria of nitrate or nitrite to a gas, principally nitrogen and nitrous oxide (N_2O)

depression (cyclone)   a region along a weather front where the atmospheric pressure is lower than it is in the surrounding air

destructive distillation   the process of heating organic material in the absence of air in order to drive off VOLATILES, leaving a more concentrated carbon fuel

detritivore   an organism that feeds on DETRITUS

detritus   fragments of dead plant and animal material that forms a layer on the surface of the ground

dew-point temperature   the temperature at which water vapor condenses to form dew or cloud droplets

diploid   describes a cell containing two sets of CHROMOSOMES, or an organism made up of such cells

disjunct distribution   the occurrence of related species in places separated by major geographical barriers, such as an ocean or mountain range

dominant   the species comprising the most prominent plants in a community or the species with the most influence of the character of the community

drip line   the line surrounding a tree that is formed by water dripping from the tips of leaves

dry adiabatic lapse rate   *see* LAPSE RATE

Dutch elm disease   a disease of elm trees caused by the fungus *Ophiostoma ulmi,* carried into the tree by elm bark beetles, mainly *Scolytus scolytus* and *S. multistriatus*

ecological energetics   the study of the flow of energy through ECOSYSTEMS

ecological pyramid   a diagram representing feeding relationships within an ECOSYSTEM as a series of bands, all the same thickness but varying in width, with PRODUCERS at the base and CONSUMERS stacked above them

ecology   the scientific study of the relationships among organisms inhabiting a specified area and between the organisms and the physical and chemical conditions in which they live

ecosystem   a clearly defined area or unit within which living organisms and their physical and chemical surroundings interact to form a stable system

edge effect   the occurrence of more species in the area where two ECOSYSTEMS overlap than are found in the two separate ecosystems combined, because the overlap area provides conditions suitable for species that could not survive in either ecosystem

elytra (sing. elytron)   the hardened forewings of a beetle that give the beetle its characteristic appearance when not flying and that rise to allow the hind wings to open when the beetle is in flight

elytron   *see* ELYTRA

embryo   a young plant contained within a plant seed, or a young animal contained within a fertilized egg or other reproductive structure. (In humans an embryo is called a fetus after the first eight weeks of pregnancy)

emergent   a forest tree that stands taller than those around it

ephemeral   short-lived

epizootic   a disease epidemic in nonhuman animals

equinox   March 20–21 and September 22–23, when the noonday Sun is directly overhead at the equator and day and night are of equal length everywhere in the world

ethene   *see* ETHYLENE

ethylene (ethene)   a gas (C_2H_4) produced by plants that functions as a hormone, controlling such processes as seed germination, cell growth, fruit ripening, and aging

evaporation   the change from liquid to gas

evapotranspiration   EVAPORATION and TRANSPIRATION considered together

evergreen   describes a plant that bears leaves at all times of year; although it sheds its leaves, it does not shed all of them at the same time

exine   the tough outer coat of a POLLEN grain

Fennoscandian ice sheet   the ice sheet that covered northern Europe during the last GLACIAL

Ferrel cell   part of the general circulation of the atmosphere in which air rises in about latitude 60° in both hemispheres, moves toward the equator at high altitude, subsides in about latitude 30°, and flows away from the equator at low level

fertilization   the union of male and female GAMETES to produce an EMBRYO

fiberboard　material manufactured in sheets from waste material from sawmills and factories making wood products that is ground into a mass of fibers

filament　the stalk of the STAMEN of a flower, bearing an ANTHER at its tip

fire climax　*see* PYROCLIMAX

firestorm　a fire so intense that the air drawn in to replace hot air rising by convection moves at gale force, carrying with it loose material that fuels the flames

floret　*see* INFLORESCENCE

flowering plant　*see* ANGIOSPERM

food chain　a set of feeding relationships in which each in a sequence of organisms feeds on the preceding member

food web　a diagram that shows the inhabitants of an ECOSYSTEM linked by lines between species and the species on which they feed; an array of FOOD CHAINS

forb　a herbaceous plant other than a grass

forest limit　*see* TREE LINE

front　the boundary between two AIR MASSES

Fungi　one of the kingdoms of biological classification, comprising non-photosynthesizing organisms that feed by absorbing organic substances from their surroundings and reproduce by SPORES

gall (cecidium)　a growth or swelling on the roots, stem, or leaves of a plant caused by bacterial or fungal infection or by attack from mites, nematodes, or insects

gamete　a sex cell, i.e., a spermatozoon or ovum

gametophyte　the HAPLOID stage in the life cycle of a plant. In simple plants, such as mosses, the gametophyte is the visible plant; in GYMNOSPERMS and ANGIOSPERMS the gametophyte is inconspicuous

girdling　*see* RINGBARKING

glacial　a period when polar ice sheets advance; an ice age

greenhouse effect　the absorption and reradiation of longwave radiation emitted by the Earth's surface by molecules of water vapor, carbon dioxide, ozone, and several other "greenhouse gases," warming the air

ground fire　a fire that burns across the ground surface, affecting only HERBS and the lower parts of trees and shrubs

groundwater　underground water that flows through an AQUIFER

gymnosperm　a seed plant in which the OVULES are carried naked on the scales of a cone. Coniferous (i.e., cone-bearing) trees are the most abundant gymnosperms

habitat   the living place of a species or community

Hadley cell   the tropical part of the general circulation of the atmosphere. Air rises over the equator, moves away from the equator at high altitude, subsides over the subtropics, and flows toward the equator at low altitude

haploid   describes a cell nucleus that contains only one set of CHROMOSOMES

heartwood   the central part of a tree trunk, made from dead cells

herb   a small, nonwoody plant in which all the parts above ground die back at the end of each growing season

holdfast   the structure by which a seaweed or other ALGA is attached to a solid surface

honey fungus (bootlace fungus)   the most serious of all fungal parasites of trees. It spreads throughout the tree, eventually killing it

hoof fungus   *see* TINDER FUNGUS

humidity   the amount of water vapor present in the air

humus   decomposed plant and animal material in the soil

hypha   one of the minute threads that form the main part of a fungus

ice storm   wind-driven rain that falls through air and onto surfaces below freezing temperature, where it freezes on contact, forming thick layers of ice

inflorescence   a mass of small but complete flowers (called *florets*) growing together and giving the appearance of a single flower. Sunflower and grass "flowers" are inflorescences

interglacial   a period of warmer weather between two GLACIALS

Intertropical Convergence Zone (ITCZ)   the region where the TRADE WINDS from either hemisphere meet (converge)

isobar   a line drawn on a weather map to join points on a surface (not necessarily the ground surface) of equal air pressure

ITCZ   *see* INTERTROPICAL CONVERGENCE ZONE

jet stream   a winding ribbon of strong wind about 5–10 miles (8–16 km) above the surface. Jet streams are typically thousands of miles long, hundreds of miles wide, and several miles deep

key   *see* SAMARA

krummholz   stunted, gnarled, small trees that grow on mountainsides between the upper limit for forest and the TREE LINE

K-species   species adapted to a stable environment; they produce few offspring and devote much care to their young, and most of the young survive

lapse rate   the rate at which the air temperature decreases (lapses) with increasing altitude. In unsaturated air, the dry ADIABATIC lapse rate is 5.38°F per thousand feet (9.8°C per km); in saturated air the saturated adiabatic lapse rate varies, but averages 2.75°F per thousand feet (5°C per km)

latent heat   the heat energy that is absorbed or released when a substance changes phase between solid and liquid, liquid and gas, and solid and gas. For water at 32°F (0°C) the latent heat of melting and freezing is 80 cal. per gram (334 J/gram); of vaporization and condensation 600 cal. per gram (2,501 J/gram); and for SUBLIMATION and DEPOSITION 680 cal. per gram (2,835 J/gram)

Laurentide ice sheet   the ice sheet that covered northeastern North America during the most recent GLACIAL

lichen   a composite organism comprising a fungus and an ALGA or cyanobacterium

lifting condensation level   the altitude at which the air is at the DEW-POINT TEMPERATURE and water vapor begins to condense to form cloud; the lifting condensation level marks the cloud base

lignification   the process by which LIGNIN accumulates in the cells of woody plants after the cells die

lignin   a hard substance that forms in the cells of woody plants, binding other cell components together and remaining in position after the cells have died

lumber   felled trees that have been stripped of their branches and cut into logs of a length that can be transported conveniently

macronutrient   a nutrient substance that living organisms need in relatively large amounts

mantle   that part of the Earth's interior lying between the outer edge of the inner core and the underside of the crust

meiosis   a form of cell division that occurs in sexually reproducing organisms, in which the cell divides twice, producing four HAPLOID daughter cells

meristem   plant tissue composed of cells that are capable of dividing indefinitely

mesophyll   the tissue lying just below the surface of a leaf, where PHOTOSYNTHESIS takes place

micronutrient   a nutrient substance that living organisms need in relatively small amounts

mitochondria (sing. mitochondrion)   a body (ORGANELLE) present in large numbers in every fungal, plant, and animal cell, that is responsible for releasing energy by the process of RESPIRATION

mitochondrion *see* MITOCHONDRIA

mitosis cell division in which the cell divides to produce two identical daughter cells, both of which are DIPLOID

mycelium the mass of hyphae that make up the main part of a fungus; *see also* HYPHA

mycorrhiza a close physical association between a fungus and the roots of a plant from which both organisms benefit

nectary a plant gland that secretes nectar

niche the function an organism performs in its environment

nitrification the oxidation by bacteria of ammonia to nitrite and/or of nitrite to nitrate

nitrogen fixation any chemical reaction incorporating gaseous nitrogen into a compound that can be utilized by plants

occluded front *see* OCCLUSION

occlusion (occluded front) the stage in the life cycle of a frontal weather system at which advancing cold air has pushed beneath warmer air and begun to lift the warm air clear of the surface

organelle a structure that has a specialized function within a cell

orographic lifting the movement of air as it rises to cross a mountain or mountain range

ovary the female reproductive organ of a flower

ovule the structure in ANGIOSPERMS and GYMNOSPERMS that develops into the seed following FERTILIZATION

paleoclimatology the study of ancient climates

Pangaea the SUPERCONTINENT that came into existence about 260 million years ago and began to break apart about 220 million years ago

Panthalassa the world ocean that surrounded PANGAEA

pappus a tuft of hairs or bristles that forms a "parachute" allowing plant seeds to be carried long distances by the wind

parenchyma plant tissue composed of unspecialized cells

peat partly decomposed plant material forming a distinct SOIL HORIZON; peat of suitable quality is dried and burned as fuel

pedicel the stalk attaching a flower to the plant

pedology the scientific study of soils

peduncle the stalk attaching an INFLORESCENCE to the plant

perianth the CALYX and COROLLA of a flower

permafrost permanently frozen ground. To become permafrost the ground must remain frozen throughout a minimum of two winters and the summer between

permeability the ability of a material to allow water to flow through it

petal a modified leaf, often brightly colored; the petals surround and partly enclose the reproductive organs of a flower

petiole the stalk that attaches a leaf to the stem of a plant

phellem *see* CORK

phellogen (cork cambium) a layer of tissue beneath the outer bark of a tree comprising cells that divide to produce new cork and new bark

phloem tissue through which the products of photosynthesis and hormones are transported from the leaves to all parts of a vascular plant

phosphorylation a chemical reaction in which phosphate (PO_4) is added

photosynthesis the sequence of chemical reactions in which green plants and cyanobacteria use sunlight as a source of energy for the manufacture (synthesis) of sugars from hydrogen and carbon, obtained from water and carbon dioxide respectively. The reactions can be summarized as:

$$6CO_2 + 6H_2O + light \rightarrow C_6H_{12}O_6 + 6O_2 \uparrow.$$

The upward arrow indicates that oxygen is released into the air; $C_6H_{12}O_6$ is glucose, a simple sugar.

photosynthetic pigment a chemical substance that absorbs visible light, thereby making energy available for PHOTOSYNTHESIS. Chlorophylls *a* and *b* are the most important photosynthetic pigments; carotenoids are accessory pigments that transfer energy to chlorophyll *a*

pith ray structures radiating from the center to the exterior of a tree trunk or branch that store starch

plane of the ecliptic the imaginary disk with the Sun at its center and the Earth's orbital path around the Sun as its circumference

plant association a type of vegetation comprising certain species that are always present and other species that are often present

plantation a forest consisting of trees that have been planted to provide a crop of timber that will be harvested

plate *see* PLATE TECTONICS

plate tectonics the theory holding that the Earth's crust comprises a number of rigid sections, or plates, that move in relation to each other

plumule   the part of a plant EMBRYO that will grow into a shoot

plywood   a product made from thin sheets of wood that are glued together in layers, with the grain in each layer running at right angles to the grain in the layers on either side

polar cell   part of the general circulation of the atmosphere in which air subsides over the North and South Poles, moves away from the poles at low level, rises in about latitude 60°, and flows back toward the poles at high altitude

pollard   to cut off the top of a tree about six feet (1.8 m) above ground level. This produces a crop of poles that emerge too high for browsing animals to reach

pollen   the grains containing male sex cells that are produced in the ANTHERS of flowers

pore space   the total interconnected space between the mineral particles in a soil

porosity   the percentage of the total volume of a material that consists of spaces between particles

pressure gradient   a change in air pressure across a horizontal distance

pressure potential   *see* TURGOR PRESSURE

prevailing wind   the direction from which the wind most frequently blows in a particular location

primary growth   plant growth occurring at the tips of the stem and branches causing the plant to grow taller and its branches longer

pyroclimax (fire climax)   a CLIMAX that develops where fire occurs at fairly regular intervals; it is dominated by plants that survive fire or benefit from it

radicle   the part of a plant EMBRYO that will grow into a root

radiocarbon   carbon-14 (^{14}C), a radioactive isotope produced in the atmosphere by cosmic-ray bombardment of nitrogen-14. ^{14}C has a half-life of 5,730 ± 30 years, allowing it to be used to date material from organisms that absorbed it and stored it in their tissues while they were living

rain shadow   the drier climate on the lee (downwind) side of a mountain range caused by the loss of moisture as air approaching the mountains is forced to rise, resulting in the condensation and precipitation of its water vapor on the windward slopes. Compression raises the temperature of the subsiding air, further reducing its RELATIVE HUMIDITY

receptacle   the part of a PEDICEL from which all parts of the flower arise

refugia   *see* REFUGIUM

refugium (pl. refugia) an isolated area in which plants and animals survive major climatic changes taking place elsewhere

relict an organism that has survived while related species became extinct

respiration the sequence of chemical reactions in which carbon in sugar is oxidized with the release of energy; the opposite of PHOTOSYNTHESIS. The reactions can be summarized as:

$$C_6H_{12}O_6 + 6O_2 \rightarrow 6CO_2 + 6H_2O + energy.$$

$C_6H_{12}O_6$ is glucose, a simple sugar

rhizoid one of the hairlike structures through which simple plants such as mosses and liverworts absorb water and nutrients

ridge a protrusion of high air pressure into a region of low air pressure

ringbarking (girdling) making a cut all the way around the trunk of a tree that is deep enough to penetrate the bark and sever the VASCULAR TISSUE, thereby killing the tree by preventing the transport of water and nutrients

root plate the roots of a tree, together with the soil attached to them, that are exposed as a flat, circular, platelike structure when a tree is blown down by wind

roundwood wood of all kinds that is taken from a forest commercially

r-species a species that is adapted to an unstable environment. It produces many offspring and devotes little attention to them. Most of the offspring die, but enough survive to continue the species and, should conditions improve, many more will survive and the population will increase

samara a winged fruit in which the wings carry one or two seeds (those with two seeds are called schizocarpic samaras)

sapwood the active, living part of the trunk or branch of a woody plant, lying immediately beneath the bark

saturated adiabatic lapse rate *see* LAPSE RATE

scarification breaking up the soil and BRASH and scattering the brash in preparation for planting the next tree crop in a plantation

schizocarpic samara *see* SAMARA

seafloor spreading the theory that the ocean floor is created at ridges where MANTLE material rises to the surface and the crustal rocks move away from the ridges on either side, causing the ocean basin to widen as the seafloor spreads

secondary growth the thickening of the stems and branches of a woody plant by laying down successive layers of new cells around the central HEARTWOOD

seed the body, formed from a fertilized ovule, from which a young plant emerges

seed bank the seeds that lie dormant in the soil, or a facility in which plant seeds are stored

sepal modified leaves attached to the RECEPTACLE that enclose the flower bud and surround the PETALS of a flower after it opens

serotiny the retention of seeds by a plant until conditions favorable for their germination trigger their release

shelter belt trees grown along a strip of land at right angles to the PREVAILING WIND that shelter crops grown downwind

shrub a perennial woody plant less than 33 feet (10 m) tall with several main stems arising at or close to ground level, but with no clearly identifiable trunk

sieve element one of the long, slender, tapering cells, terminating in a perforated region called a sieve plate, that join end to end in a sieve tube, forming part of the PHLOEM tissue

silviculture management of a forest for the benefit of the plants and animals living in it, regardless of whether or not all or part of the forest is being exploited commercially

skidder a device that grips one end of the trunk of a felled tree and drags it out of the forest

snedding removing the branches from felled trees

soil horizon a horizontal layer in a SOIL PROFILE that differs in its mineral or organic composition from the layers above and below it, and from which it can be clearly distinguished visually

soil pores *see* PORE SPACE

soil profile a vertical section cut through soil from the surface to the underlying rock

solstice one of the two dates each year when the noonday Sun is directly overhead at one or other of the Tropics and the difference in length between the hours of daylight and darkness is at its most extreme. The solstices occur on June 21–22 and December 22–23

specific heat capacity the amount of heat that must be applied to a substance in order to raise its temperature by one degree. It is measured in calories per gram per degree Celsius (cal/g/°C) or in the scientific units of joules per gram per kelvin (J/g/K; 1K = 1°C = 1.8°F)

spore   a reproductive unit, usually consisting of a single cell, that can develop into a new organism without fusing with another cell

sporophyte   the reproductive stage in the life cycle of a plant. In GYMNOSPERMS and ANGIOSPERMS this is the dominant stage, comprising the visible plant. In mosses, liverworts, and hornworts the sporophyte is small and inconspicuous

stadial   a prolonged period of cold weather that is shorter and milder than a GLACIAL

stamen   the male reproductive organ of a flower, comprising the FILAMENT and ANTHER

stigma   part of the female reproductive structure in a flower; it has a sticky surface that holds POLLEN grains

stomata (sing. stoma)   small openings, or pores, on the surface of a plant leaf through which the plant cells exchange gases with the outside air. Stomata can be opened or closed by the expansion or contraction of two guard cells surrounding each stoma

stratosphere   the region of the atmosphere that extends from the TROPOPAUSE to an altitude of about 31 miles (50 km)

style   the part of the female reproductive structure in a flower that connects the STIGMA to the OVARY

suberin   a waxy substance in the walls of CORK cells that make cork waterproof

succession   a sequence of changes in the composition of a plant and animal community occupying a site that continues until a stable equilibrium, the CLIMAX, is attained

supercontinent   a landmass formed by the merging of previously separate continents as a result of CONTINENTAL DRIFT. PANGAEA was a supercontinent comprising all the present-day continents

swidden farming   a farming method in which farmers clear forest from an area of land and grow crops there for several seasons before abandoning the site and moving to another, allowing the forest to regenerate

taiga   the conifer forest forming a belt across northern America and Eurasia

taproot   a plant root that is large and descends vertically

temperate rain forest   forest that occurs in temperate regions where the annual rainfall is typically 60–120 inches (1,500–3,000 mm)

temperate zone   the region of the Earth lying between the Tropics (23.5°N and S) and the Arctic and Antarctic Circles (66.5°N and S)

tepal SEPALS and PETALS when these are so similar in appearance as to be indistinguishable

thermal wind a wind generated by a difference in air temperature. JET STREAMS are thermal winds

thylakoid membrane one of the membranes inside a CHLOROPLAST that hold the PHOTOSYNTHETIC PIGMENTS

timber wood that has been cut into large pieces for use mainly in construction

timberline *see* TREE LINE

tinder fungus (hoof fungus, touchwood) a parasitic fungus that attacks trees, especially beech and birch, hollowing them out and eventually killing them

touchwood *see* TINDER FUNGUS

tracheid a long, cylindrical cell with a tapering, perforated end. Tracheids join end to end to form the XYLEM tissue in GYMNOSPERMS

trade winds the winds that blow toward the equator in equatorial regions, from the northeast in the Northern Hemisphere and from the southeast in the Southern Hemisphere

transpiration the evaporation of water through leaf STOMATA when these are open for the exchange of gases

tree a perennial, woody plant that is more than 33 feet (10 m) tall and has one or more than one clearly identifiable trunk

tree line (timberline, forest limit) the elevation or latitude beyond which the climate is too severe for trees to grow

trophic pertaining to food or feeding

tropopause the boundary separating the TROPOSPHERE from the STRATOSPHERE. It occurs at a height of about 10 miles (16 km) over the equator, seven miles (11 km) in middle latitudes, and five miles (8 km) over the North and South Poles

troposphere the layer of the atmosphere that extends from the surface to the TROPOPAUSE; it is the region where all weather phenomena occur

trough a protrusion of low air pressure into a region of high air pressure

tundra a treeless plain in the arctic or Antarctic, where the vegetation is dominated by grasses, sedges. rushes, and wood rushes, together with dwarf shrubs, LICHENS, and mosses

turgor rigidity of plant tissues due to water held under pressure in the cells

turgor pressure (pressure potential) the pressure under which water is held inside plant tissues

understory   the trees that are shorter than the trees forming the forest CANOPY

vascular bundle   a strand of PHLOEM and XYLEM tissue; groups of vascular bundles form a continuous system extending throughout the plant

vascular cambium   a layer just beneath the outer bark of a woody plant where dividing cells give rise to new PHLOEM and XYLEM tissue

vascular plant   a plant possessing PHLOEM and XYLEM tissue through which water and nutrients are transported

veneer   a thin layer of high-quality wood that is glued to the surface of an inferior wood to improve its appearance

vessel element   one of the cells forming the XYLEM tissue in ANGIOSPERMS

volatile   describes substances that vaporize at low temperatures

water table   the upper margin of the GROUNDWATER; soil is fully saturated below the water table but unsaturated above it

xylem   plant tissue through which water entering at the roots is transported to all parts of the plant

Younger Dryas   a period of cold, dry weather lasting from about 11,000 to 10,000 years ago and affecting all of northern Europe, but not North America

zygote   the fertilized ovum (egg) of a plant or animal at the stage where it is DIPLOID, but before it has begun to divide

BIBLIOGRAPHY AND FURTHER READING

Allaby, Michael. *A Change in the Weather*. New York: Facts On File, 2004.

———. *Fog, Smog, and Poisoned Rain*. New York: Facts On File, 2003.

———. *Temperate Forests*. New York: Facts On File, 1999.

Ashman, M. R., and G. Pun. *Essential Soil Science*. Maiden, Md.: Blackwell Science, 2002.

Brewer, Richard. *The Science of Ecology*. 2nd ed. Fort Worth, Tex.: Saunders College Publishing. 1988.

Burroughs, William James. *Climate Change: A Multidisciplinary Approach*. Cambridge: Cambridge University Press, 2001.

Foth, H. D. *Fundamentals of Soil Science*. 8th ed. New York: John Wiley, 1991.

Heywood, V. H., consultant editor. *Flowering Plants of the World*. Updated edition. New York: Oxford University Press, 1993.

Peterken, George F. *Natural Woodland*. Cambridge: Cambridge University Press, 1996.

Rackham, Oliver. *Trees and Woodland in the British Landscape*. 2nd ed. London: Weidenfeld and Nicolson, 2001.

Roberts, Neil. *The Holocene: An Environmental History*. New York: Basil Blackwell, 1989.

Tansley, A. G. *Practical Plant Ecology*. London: George Allen and Unwin Ltd., 1923.

———. *Introduction to Plant Ecology*. London: George Allen and Unwin Ltd., 1946.

Williams, Joseph H., and William E. Friedman. "Identification of Diploid Endosperm in an Early Angiosperm Lineage." *Nature* 415 (January 31, 2002): 522–526.

The World Commission on Environment and Development. *Our Common Future*. Oxford: Oxford University Press, 1987.

Web sites

Arroyo, Mary T. Kahn, and Adriana E. Hoffmann. "Temperate Rain Forest of Chile." Available online. URL: www.nmnh.si.edu/botany/projects/cpd/sa/sa45.htm. Accessed May 8, 2003.

Cranshaw, W. S., and D. Leatherman. "Insect and Mite Galls." Colorado State University Cooperative Extension. Available online. URL: www.ext.colostate.edu/pubs/insect/05557.html. Accessed October 5, 2004.

Forschungsstelle für Paläeobotanik. "A History of Palaeozoic Forests: Part 1, Early Land Plants." Available online. URL: www. uni-muenster.de/GeoPalaeontologie/Palaeo/Palbot/ewald0.htm. Westfälische Wilhelms-Universität Münster, January 2002. Accessed December 1, 2003.

Gates, Matthew. "*Hemidactylium scutatum:* Four-Toed Salamander." Michigan State University. Available online. URL: animaldiversity. ummz.umich.edu/accounts/hemidactylium/h._scutatum$ narrative.html. Last updated October 17, 2002.

National Park Service. "Discover Olympic: The Rain Forest." Available online. URL: www.nps.gov/olym/edurain.htm. Accessed May 8, 2003.

———. "The General Sherman Tree." Available online. URL: www.nps.gov/seki/shrm_pic.htm. Accessed May 8, 2003.

Swiecki, Tedmund J., and Elizabeth Bernhardt. "A Delicate Balance: Impacts of Diseases and Insects on the Health of California Oaks." Available online. URL: phytosphere.com/ publications/Oakdiseaseinsect.htm. Updated December 20, 2002. Accessed October 1, 2004.

Synge, Hugh. "The Biodiversity Convention Explained." Plant Talk, March 1995. Available online. URL: www.plant-talk.org/ Pages/cbd11.html. Accessed December 19, 2003.

United Nations. "World Charter for Nature." 48th Plenary Meeting of the General Assembly. October 28, 1982. Available online. URL: www.un.org/documents/ga/res/37/a37r007.htm. Accessed December 19, 2003.

United Nations Educational, Scientific and Cultural Organization. "Belovezhskaya Pushcha/Bialowieza Forest." Available online. URL: whc.unesco.org/sites/627.htm. Updated November 6, 2003.

United Nations Environment Programme. "About the Convention on Biological Diversity (Biodiversity)." Available online. URL: www.unep.org/unep/secretar/biodiv/home.htm. Last updated November 24, 1998.

———. "Air Pollution and Air Quality." *GEO: Global Environment Outlook 3.* Available online. URL: www.unep.org/geo/geo3/ english/366.htm. Accessed October 6, 2004.

U.S. Geological Survey. "Major Tectonic Plates of the World." Eastern Publications Group Web Team. Available online. URL: geology.er. usgs.gov/eastern/plates.html. Last updated June 27, 2001.

Viau, Elizabeth Anne. "Temperate Rain Forests." Available online. URL: www.world-builders.org/lessons/less/biomes/rainforest/ temp_rain/temprain.html. Accessed May 8, 2003.

Wayne's Word. "The Magnolia Family (Magnoliaceae): A Primitive Family of Flowering Plants." Available online. URL: waynesword. palomar.edu/trmar98c.htm. Accessed May 15, 2003.

Note: *Italic* page numbers refer to illustrations.